The Psychology
of Moviegoing

The Psychology of Moviegoing

Choosing, Viewing and Being Influenced by Films

ASHTON D. TRICE *and* HUNTER W. GREER

McFarland & Company, Inc., Publishers
Jefferson, North Carolina

ALSO OF INTEREST

Ashton D. Trice *and* Samuel A. Holland, *Heroes, Antiheroes and Dolts: Portrayals of Masculinity in American Popular Films, 1921–1999* (McFarland, 2001)

ISBN (print) 978-1-4766-7724-8 ∞
ISBN (ebook) 978-1-4766-3610-8

LIBRARY OF CONGRESS AND BRITISH LIBRARY
CATALOGUING DATA ARE AVAILABLE

© 2019 Ashton D. Trice and Hunter W. Greer. All rights reserved

No part of this book may be reproduced or transmitted in any form or by any means, electronic or mechanical, including photocopying or recording, or by any information storage and retrieval system, without permission in writing from the publisher.

Front cover: Anthony Hopkins as Dr. Hannibal Lecter in the 1991 film *Silence of the Lambs* (Orion Pictures/Photofest)

Printed in the United States of America

*McFarland & Company, Inc., Publishers
Box 611, Jefferson, North Carolina 28640
www.mcfarlandpub.com*

Table of Contents

Preface 1

Part I: Choosing a Movie — 3

1. Personality and Movie Choice 5
2. Emotion and Mood 30
3. The Social Context of Choosing and Viewing Movies 46

Part II: Experiencing the Movie — 67

4. Sensation and Perception 69
5. Learning from the Screen 96
6. Cognitive Psychology and Understanding Movies 112

Part III: After the Movie — 131

7. Selling Watches, Changing Hearts and Minds 133
8. Depictions of the Mentally Ill, Therapists and Therapy 162

Epilogue 188
References 195
Index 205

Preface

This book is about two things I enjoy, psychology and the movies. It is primarily about how they interact, and how and why they sometimes do not.

Over the past decade and a half, I have occasionally offered an advanced undergraduate course in the Psychology of Film, but the right textbook didn't exist. There are a few specialized books on narrow aspects of the psychology of movies, and several excellent texts on the broader topic of the psychology of media. But I believe that, in many important ways, movies are different from TV, radio and Facebook, and I wanted something general as far as psychology was concerned, but specific to film. I think that, for psychology, it is ideal if some senior-level courses go back to the beginning, the introductory course, and use a similar organization to review this specialized subject.

So this book covers many of the same topics as an introductory psychology text—personality, cognition, learning, etc., but the order is different. General psychology goes from the inside out: brain to sense organs to whole organism to social interaction. Here we have put the chapters into the sequence of events that occur around movies: Choosing a Movie (personality, emotions and social context), Experiencing the Movie (perception, learning and cognition) and After the Movie (social influence and how movies affect our views of mental health, the profession of psychologist, and the process of therapy).

While I wrote this book with such a course in mind, I did not think of it primarily as a textbook. First, with the exception of key terms listed at the end of the chapters, the book has few of the trappings of a textbook. I thought about this as a book to read rather than one to study—and one to engage readers other than psychology undergraduates. I also envisioned it triggering recollections about the movies readers have seen and liked (or disliked).

Each chapter focuses on a particular film. For example, the first chapter, which examines personality factors involved in selecting movies, focuses on *Casablanca*. Today *Casablanca* is thought of and marketed as a "classic" or a "World War II movie," but at the time it was a "romance" or a "suspense" movie. There are some people who like classics and some who avoid them. Some people like romances; some people avoid suspense. In picking the films to cover, I have selected ones that were popular, won awards, and were made before 1997—this last stipulation means that all of the movies were made before the students in my class were born. As I show these movies in the current version of the class, I wanted to increase the probability that the students will be experiencing the movies we see in the class for the first time. The questions that might be on a reader's mind: "Why is this movie so broadly popular?" or "What kind of person would like a movie like this?" If you need to have your memory refreshed or get an idea of how these movies look and feel, I recommend the following clips:

> *Casablanca.* Play it, Sam! For old time's sake. (YouTube) (4:07)
> *Life Is Beautiful.* The school speech. (YouTube) (4:36)
> *Psycho.* Nobody ever stops here. (Turner Classic Movies) (3:55)
> *Rear Window.* Miss Lonelyheart and Miss Torso. (YouTube) (3:20)
> *Jaws.* Chrissie's last swim. (YouTube) (3:06)
> *8½.* The first three minutes. (YouTube) (3:00)
> *The Best Years of Our Lives.* Homecoming (Critical Commons). (4:07)

The final reason for writing this book was to undertake an effort in positive psychology. When I began to study psychology in the mid-1970s, psychology was not as much about pathology as it is now. Humor, exercise, reading, leisure, children's developing perception of the world, were all valued topics—and we were making progress into understanding them. But then a new generation of psychologists thought of psychology as a shadow of psychiatry, where depression and anxiety, intervention and prevention, "best practices" and licensure became far more important than understanding the complexities of a common human behavior. The abruptness of this change was a mistake—from which we are slowly recovering—because it turns out that those positive things we used to study in psychology, art and humor and leisure and movies, are as much the keys to mental health as counseling and therapy (Brown & Bobkowski, 2011). I want in this book to look at one tool in crafting a life well lived, cinema, and show to some extent how it contributes to well being and having a satisfying and meaningful life (Jaffe, 2007).

Mr. Greer, a former student and a mental health counselor, worked closely with me on the last two drafts of this book and his perspective has been invaluable. He grew up with a different set of movies than I did and he is more comfortable with new technology for viewing movies. Without his presence and input, this would never have become a book, but would have remained a perpetual work in progress.

Part I

Choosing a Movie

In these first three chapters, we will consider psychological factors that influence why we choose to watch some movies and avoid others. In the first chapter, we will be concerned with the stable characteristics of the individual viewer, which are referred to as personality traits. Is there a trait that predisposes some people to seek out black-and-white classics like *Casablanca*, while viewers without that trait will avoid them? What is it about some people that leads them to watch many movies a week, while others rarely if ever watch one? Why do some people have a narrow range of movies they like, while others enjoy a wide range of films? Why do some people like graphically violent and sexually explicit films, while other seek to ban them?

In the second chapter, we will examine the evidence that indicates that our mood also influences our choice of movies and that we use movies and other media to alter or maintain our mood. But movies are more than quick fixes to being in sour moods, which brings us to the perplexing question (to psychologists, at least) of why we like *sad* movies. In the final chapter in the section, we will examine the social context of watching a movie. Some people see watching a movie primarily as a social occasion, while others enjoy watching films by themselves as entertainment or as works of art. We watch different kinds of movies depending on whether we are with family, friends, romantic partners or alone, and how these relationships influence us varies with age and experience. For example, early in a friendship or a romantic relationship, we may pretend interest in a kind of movie in order to impress or fit in; later in the relationship, such pretense becomes hard to maintain.

It is surprising there is not more information on this topic—influencing movie choice is a big business. In 2014, the worldwide motion picture industry sold over $34 billion in tickets. In the U.S., it was over $10 billion. Neither of these figures include revenue from cable, DVD sales and streaming. Still, the average movie loses more than $17 million (Elberese & Bharat, 2007), which suggests that despite the huge market for movies, filmmakers don't know their audiences very well.

Not only are movies big business, but we spend a good deal of our time engaged with movies. In an activity diary study, Finn (1997) found that college students watch movies about an hour a week during the school year, which suggests they watch an average of 30 movies per academic year and additional ones in the summer and holidays. In the U.S., about 11 percent of the population goes to see a movie in the theater at least once a month, and this segment accounts for more than half of the tickets sold. While college students are the most likely group to be in this segment, attendance at movies in theaters is increasing among middle-aged and older adults. Only about 30 percent of the population doesn't go to movies at all (MPAA, 2016).

Of course, we don't always see movies in a theater. In fact, when we consider movie-watching in all its forms, we see many more movies than the data from the MPAA would suggest. Research indicates that adolescents watch an average of more than 100 movies a year, thus spending as much time watching movies as they do reading. But in this section, most of the research still focuses on viewing movies in theaters. There is little research on movie-watching on TV screens, and none that looks at watching movies on laptops and phones. Not one study has been published to date on choosing movies from kiosks or online. Perhaps this is because psychologists who study movies are most likely movie fans, and movie fans still prefer the big screen, the darkened room and the smell of popcorn.

1

Personality and Movie Choice

For what was just one of the 21 movies released by Warner Brothers in 1943, *Casablanca* did excellent business and quickly developed a reputation as a good film. As with many of the films released that year (Harmetz, 1992), *Casablanca* has as its background the wars in Europe and the Pacific. In fact, the two days of the main plot of the film are the day before and the day of the attack on Pearl Harbor in 1941. It won Oscars for Best Director, Best Screenplay and Best Picture. But unlike most studio films from that era, it did not disappear into obscurity after a few weeks of release. By the mid-1950s it was showing up regularly on television and being shown in independent "art house" movie theaters, most notably the Brattle in Cambridge, Massachusetts, where it has played during Harvard's exam week since 1955. The film was rated #2 in the American Film Institute's *100 years ... 100 Movies* (1998). It has been said that *Casablanca* may not be the best American film, but it is the best-*loved* American film (Ebert, 1996).

Choosing a Movie: Then and Now

To a psychologist, one of the most intriguing film-related questions is "How do we decide to see a movie?" There are at least four issues here:

1. What brings about an individual's preferences for certain types of movies and a wariness about other types? Psychologists have generally turned to personality theory for answers to this question, and this is the central topic in this chapter.

2. What happens to make people go outside their comfort zone and try a new kind of movie? People do go there. Sometime they find it unpleasant but other times they discover a new, favorite type of movie. Often it is

Rick (Humphrey Bogart) listens to Sam (Dooley Wilson) entertaining the regulars at Rick's Café in the opening sequence of *Casablanca* (Warner Bros, 1942).

the social context that gets us out of a comfort zone, someone or a group with whom we would like to spend time. This will be the topic of the third chapter.

3. In the real world, when do individuals actually make the decision to see a movie? Is it when they see a trailer months before the movie's release? Is it when they see an actor on a talk show showing a clip from the movie? Is it when they learn it is playing in a local theater or finally available on Netflix? Or is it when a friend agrees, after some negotiation, what movie to see and when? This complexity matters, because so much media research on decision-making is based on individually consumed, easily accessed activities like turning on CNN or listening to a song.

4. On what do we base our decision to see one movie over another? There are a lot of suspects here: favorite actors or directors, genres, word of mouth, print and online reviews. This issue comes up in several places in this section of the book.

When *Casablanca* was released, choosing a movie was a simple decision. Movies were only shown in theaters. The studios controlled what movies were made and where and when they were released. If you lived, as most Americans did at that time, in an area that had only one or two movie theaters, your decisions were whether to see what was playing or not and with whom to go. Today most college students can choose from among thousands of streaming titles, and they can watch them at home on a flat screen, anywhere on their laptops, and even on their phones. Many still choose to watch what is showing at the local theater.

In 1943, going to the movies was a common activity, particularly among American adolescents and young adults—the average American went to the movies twice a week, usually once during the week with friends at a neighborhood theater, and once on the weekend, often with a romantic partner or the whole family, perhaps to a downtown movie palace. Movies were made to appeal to each of those groups. The movies shown on weeknights were often B pictures, made on smaller budgets. They were often shown in double features with newsreels and cartoons between them. These films usually targeted either mostly male audiences (Westerns, sports movies, etc.) or mostly female audiences. During World War II, a popular film genre, "weepies," showed women struggling and suffering while their husbands and sweethearts were off fighting the war (Trice & Holland, 2001). The movies watched by dating couples and families were bigger-budgeted A pictures with well-known stars. They consisted mostly of comedies, musicals and dramas.

But that decision-making process has changed. Here is an example of how two students who had been dating for about six months and were big movie fans a few years ago decided on a movie by texting:

She: Wanna go to a movie tonight?
He: What?
She: Comedy. Something funny.
He: There's only one listed: *The Hundred Foot Journey*.
She : Never heard of it.
He : Helen Mirren's in it. You like her.
She : Yes I do but no.
He : How about we rent something?
She : What?
He : *The Interview*.
She : Gross. Not that kind of funny. Actually funny.
He : *Despicable Me 2*?
She : Not animated.
He : Joss Whedon's *Much Ado*.
She : What's that?
He : Shakespeare.
She : Lighter.
He : It's in Hollywood.
She : What's in Hollywood?
He : *Much Ado About Nothing*.

She : Some other time
He : *Inglorius Basterds.*
She . Boys flick.
He : You name one.
She : *Bridesmaids.*
He : *The Interview* for chicks. What about *Grand Budapest Hotel*?
She : ?
He : You'll like it. Everybody's in it.
She : Like who?
He : Adrian Brody. Jude Law. Bill Murray. Willem Dafoe.
She : You're kidding.
He : Ralph Fiennes. Owen Wilson.
She : What time?
He : Let's do 8:15.
She : Pick me up at 7:45.

This exchange shows that one way people today make decisions about their thousands of options is by using movie categories or genres (Austin & Gordon, 1987). Not only do people use them in everyday social decisions as in this example, we navigate kiosks, like Redbox, and large databases like Amazon and Netflix with them. The woman in this example uses this technique effectively. People show consistent preferences for specific genres of movies, such as romantic comedies, horror or Westerns. Here, the woman first limited the search to comedies and then further indicated disinterest in gross-out comedies, animated movies and Shakespeare. The man employed a less useful strategy by suggesting specific films, but together they reached a decision in less than six minutes.

Psychologists have suggested that these preferences for genres are not fortuitous but are related to underlying personal characteristics. One characteristic would be gender. Both the man and the woman in the exchange, for example, indicated in the exchange their belief in "chick" and "guy" flicks. Because of the viewing patterns in the 1930s and 1940s, films were specifically made to appeal to mostly female or mostly male audiences. Today with rising production costs and a shrinking market, most films are made with the goal of capturing as wide an audience as possible. But for reasons sometimes beyond the intentions of the filmmakers, some films get the reputation of appealing only to one sex or the other. Psychologists interested in movies have been more likely to investigate the relationships between personality traits and preferences for movie genres than gender.

Do Men Like "Chick Flicks"?

It is generally assumed that there are movies that are made for just men or just women, and that those made for men will not appeal at all to women and vice versa. There is surprisingly little research on the topic. It is perhaps easy to assume that most heterosexual men will not like *Magic Mike XXL* (2015), but what about movies like *Titanic* (1997) and *The Notebook* (2004)?

Harris *et al.* (2004) asked several hundred college students: "Think of a date that you went on as a teen or young adult in which you watched what might be termed a romantic movie, either in a theater or on video. Think about that movie and the experience of watching it and how it made you feel at the time and afterwards." Although this research was published in 2004, most participants remembered movies that had been released around 1998 and 1999. Most were remembering watching a movie in a theater. The most often mentioned movies were *Titanic* (1997), *Runaway Bride* (1999), *Notting Hill* (1999), *Shakespeare in Love* (1999) and *Ever After* (1998). The woman had most often chosen the movie.

The women in the study rated the movies very positively ($M = 6.0$ out of 7) and their dates similarly estimated the women had liked the movie very much ($M = 6.1$). Contrary to expectations, the men also reported enjoying the movie ($M = 4.8$) and their dates estimated that they had ($M = 4.9$). Yet both the men and women indicated that they thought that "most men" would not have enjoyed the movie. Indeed, more men (15 percent) than women (four percent) remembered being bored, but still 85 percent of men *were not* bored. This research suggests that while women enjoy "women's movies" somewhat more than men, men do enjoy them. What is yet to be researched is whether women (or maybe some women or some women in some situations) enjoy "guy movies."

Personality

In 1937, Gordon Allport famously opened his classic textbook on personality by examining 50 different definitions of what personality is. The situation has not gotten much clearer in the intervening eight decades: How to define personality remains controversial in psychology, but we will define personality as *characteristics that are stable over time and across situations that influence attitudes, beliefs and behavior*. Personality characteristics can be compared across individuals. Everyone can be thought of as more or less gregarious or usually open to experience or not. Other characteristics which influence attitudes, beliefs and behavior are specific to individuals or groups and are often called **identity**. Not everyone, for example, has a degree of "Irishness" or could be rated on their enthusiasm for aviation. Irish identity and enthusiasm for aviation may help define an individual and influence his or her behavior and beliefs, but it is not considered part of personality.

There are several ways in which personality theories differ:
Some describe differences in normal personality function, while others

are exclusively concerned with psychopathology. A few, like the theory of Hans Eysenck, described below, combine an interest in both the normal and abnormal personality.

Some personality theories concentrate on qualities that are thought to be biological in nature, such as **extroversion**, *the tendency to seek out the company of others and to experience some discomfort when alone*, while other theories concentrate on personality factors that are mostly developed through experience, such as **empathy**, *the ability to understand other people's perspectives and experience their emotional reactions*. Empathy is stable over long periods in development, but as experience can modify it, a person can become more or less empathic.

Another way that theories of personality differ is in their model. For example, Freud's theory is said to be **dynamic**. He posited that the personality had three components, the id, the ego and the superego, which are dynamically vying for control. Most contemporary personality theories are **trait-based**. Traits are characteristics, such as empathy and extroversion, which can be measured along a continuum from one extreme (extroversion) to another (introversion). Individuals can be located along the continuum. Trait theories can be limited to a single trait or to a comprehensive list of traits believed to map the entire personality.

Most often personality traits in research on movies are measured by self-report questionnaires. The scores on several items will be added together to make a scale. For example, a participant might have reached a score of ten on the extroversion scale by answering "2" to all of the five questions in Table 1.1.

Typically, in research into personality and movies, participants complete a questionnaire measuring the traits in question and then the scores on the traits are compared to a measure of interest in, liking for, or experience with certain kinds of movies. A correlation coefficient is computed showing the degree the personality measure is related to the measure of the movie. Correlation coefficients with values of 0.00 indicate no relationship between the measures. The highest possible correlation is 1.00, which indicates that the two variables are identical. Most correlations lie between these two extremes. The higher the correlation, the stronger is the relationship.

Table 1.1

Sample items from a measure of Extroversion

Score:	0	1	2
1. I like parties	Never	Sometimes	Always
2. I like meeting new people	Never	Sometimes	Always
3. I eat alone in a restaurant	Never	Sometimes	Always
4. I prefer reading to talking on the phone	Never	Sometimes	Always
5. I enjoy being in a crowd	Never	Sometimes	Always

Empathy

Empathy is the ability to take another person's perspective and to understand and share his or her feelings, even when those feeling are quite different from one's own. While there are different conceptualizations of empathy, the one most often used in media research was developed by Davis (1996). He conceived of empathy as being divided into four components:

1. **Perspective-taking**: the ability to understand a situation from another person's point of view
2. **Empathic concern**: sensitivity to the plight of others and compassion for them; this compassion arises from the ability to experience, to some degree, how they are feeling
3. **Emotional distress**: a feeling of discomfort in response to the emotional problems of others
4. **Fantasy empathy**: the ability to become engaged in fictional situations like movies; particularly to have an understanding of the emotions the characters are experiencing

Components 1 and 4 are said to be cognitive, that is, they deal with our ability to *understand* another's dilemma, while components 2 and 3 are emotional, that is, our ability to *experience* what another person is feeling.

How fantasy empathy relates to movie-watching is straightforward. People who are high in fantasy empathy follow the emotional storyline of a film and identify with and care about the characters more than those who are low in this trait. People who are high in this trait feel "transported" when they watch movies, that is, they feel fully engrossed in the movie (Hall & Bracken, 2011). This factor predicts interest in watching movies frequently and is associated with positive interest in all genres of movies. People who are low in fantasy empathy tend to shun fictional narratives in favor of social activities and media entertainment such as sports and news. Cheetham, Hanggi and Jancke (2014) found that those who were high in this dimension had distinctive brain structures, most notably in areas such as the left hippocampus and the left, dorsal medial prefrontal cortex, areas previously associated with the ability to form imagery.

Kim and Richardson (2003) found that the ability to empathize with movie characters spilled over from interest in the characters and influenced audience members interest in visiting the location in which the film was set. These researchers showed a group the movie *Before Sunset* (1995) in which an American student meets a French woman on a train and they spend the next day exploring Vienna and falling in love. Those who were high in fantasy empathy developed higher interests in visiting Vienna after the experience, while those who were low in fantasy empathy did not.

Individuals who are high in *perspective-taking* choose movies about the emotional lives of complex characters because they are good at reading others' takes on situations. Those who are not good at perspective-taking find movies about subtle or ambiguous emotions difficult to follow. They choose to watch movies where the characters are defined by their static roles: Westerns, action-adventure movies, comic-book fantasies and slapstick comedies. Those who are good at perspective-taking also like films where it is important to imagine or guess what is going on inside a character's mind. For example, early in *Casablanca,* the audience is puzzled by the sudden changes in the main character, Rick, an American who owns a popular bar in Casablanca. When Victor Laszlo, a famous Nazi-fighter, and his wife Ilsa arrive, Rick shucks off his reclusiveness and becomes gregarious and generous. He breaks some of his own rules, like never drinking with customers. In the second half of the movie, after Rick's behavior change is understood, audience members who are high in perspective-taking may look for clues as to what Ilsa will do at the end of the movie.

Davis, Hull, Young and Warren (1987) examined the influence of perspective-taking on college students' reactions to a series of segments from two highly emotional movies, *Who's Afraid of Virginia Woolf* (1966) and *Brian's Song* (1971). The segments, edited to last 15 minutes, provided one of the main plotlines in each of the films. *Who's Afraid of Virginia Woolf* is about the destructive relationship between a college professor and his wife, played out in an alcohol-fueled get-together after a faculty party. The segment ends with the professor apparently on the verge of shooting his wife. *Brian's Song* is about football player Brian Piccolo, who forms a (then) unlikely friendship with another player, and is subsequently stricken with cancer. These segments end with a highly charged scene in Brian's hospital room.

This study also provided some different viewing instruction to different students, but with regard to perspective-taking, in every case—for both movies and across all three viewing instructions, those who were high in perspective-taking enjoyed the movie more. In reports of their mood, they were significantly friendlier, happier and more tranquil than those who were low in perspective-taking. While neither movie was friendly, tranquil or happy, the viewers' responses indicated that they had been able to understand the emotional content of the movies and had enjoyed the experience.

Individuals who are high in *empathic concern* have been shown to like emotionally charged movies, at least some of the time, particularly sad movies (Oliver, 1993), but to dislike movies involving graphic violence (Tamborini, Stiff & Heidel, 1990). Empathic concern allows the audience member to feel the same way as the characters in the film. In the study described above by Davis, Hull, Young and Warren (1987), those who were high in empathic concern felt more depressed, angrier, and more anxious after the film segments than those who were low in empathic concern. These moods reflected the moods of the main characters in the films. Appropriately, they were angrier after watching *Who's Afraid of Virginia Woolf* and sadder after watching *Brian's song*. As it is quite possible to be high in both empathic concern and perspective-taking, it may seem a contradiction that it is possible to be happy, and at the same time sad or angry, but it is. Very broadly, empathic movie watchers both feel the pain of the characters and enjoy the process of doing so.

The fun of a movie like *Casablanca* is to experience the thoughts and feelings of characters who are facing situations that we will likely never confront. If one identifies with Rick, one gets to experience jaded indifference, jealousy, anger, the return of a lost love, and heroism. If one identifies with Ilsa, one can vicariously experience pride, love, recklessness and confusion. There are times when one wants to feel these emotions vicariously, even if they are sad or angry ones, but there are few times when one wants to experience what it is like to be the victim of gruesome violence.

It is easy to understand why audiences in 1943 liked *Casablanca*. Like Rick, they had ultimately been unable to maintain self-interested neutrality in the face of the Axis powers, and embraced the conscientious resolve of joining the fight. There is a highly dramatic scene in the second half of the movie in which the musicians in the bar begin to play "La Marseillaise" and the head of the Nazis tries to shut them down. Victor Laszlo, with Rick's approval, urges them on, until everyone is standing and vigorously singing the French national anthem. We may want to stand up with them and sing along.

Finally, high *emotional distress* has been shown to lead potential audience members to avoid movies with likely unpleasant aspects to them, such as explicit violence. Individuals who are high in emotional distress react strongly to distress in others. In real-life high-stress situations, those with high emotional distress will help out unless there is a way to leave the situation, perhaps to get help. Even then, their response is less about aiding the victim than it is about relieving their own distress. So, while being high in the other components of empathy makes it *more likely* that one will seek out and enjoy serious movies about the emotional lives of others, being high in emotional distress may make one avoid many kinds of serious films. It is not hard to imagine that some potential audience members in 1943 did not want to see *Casablanca*. The themes of fidelity to marriage and Nazi occupation were too real and immediate to be comfortable.

There is controversy in interpreting the direction of the relationship between low empathy and interest in portrayals of graphic violence. We know that people who are low in empathic concern may be willing to watch and enjoy graphically violent movies. But does having a low degree of empathy make watching movies involving graphic violence appealing? Or does watching a lot of graphic violence lower one's level of empathy? There are psychologists who will take both sides of that argument. But an alternative, more developmental explanation exists: that low levels of empathy, particularly when coupled with other traits such as sensation-seeking, lead an individual to watch graphic violence and that watching of a lot of media violence leads to further lower empathy. So the question may not be "Which direction is right?" because the answer may be that they both are.

Sensation-Seeking

While empathy is a personality characteristic that influences our interactions with others and appears to be mostly learned, sensation-seeking seems more determined by biology. Zuckerman (1979) defined sensation-seeking as individuals' needs for varied, novel and exciting experiences and their willingness to take risks for the sake of having these experiences. Sensation-seeking, like empathy, has four components that potentially influence movie choice differently.

Thrill and adventure-seeking refers to the need for excitement among sensation-seekers; they enjoy being "jagged up" and will pursue activities that will result in that sensation. Zuckerman believes that this component is genetic as it can be detected early in life and tends to be very stable over the lifespan. Those who are high in thrill- and adventure-seeking like movies that are fast-paced, involve unexpected changes in the direction of the plot, and are full of action. Those who are low in thrill- and adventure-seeking find the physiological responses to excitement unpleasant and choose calmer entertainment.

Disinhibition refers to the risk-taking associated with sensation-seeking. Sensation seekers are less restrained by social conventions and fears about safety than others; their behavior may seem spontaneous or even "wild." They appear to be drawn to the taboo and perverse. People who are high in disinhibition have been found to enjoy explicit sex and violence, particularly unusual forms of them. Among adolescents, those with high disinhibition are drawn to movies and videos that are prohibited: They will choose an R- or X-rated movie over a G-rated one even if the content is not particularly interesting to them.

Experience-seeking refers to the pursuit of the novel among sensation seekers. They want to do things that they have never done before; they want to watch movies set in unusual locales and to be about people who are dissimilar to people they know.

Boredom susceptibility is the need for varied stimulation among sensation seekers. This is the component of sensation-seeking that pushes individuals to constantly change TV channels or to fast-forward through long scenes in a movie. They experience boredom more than others, complain that everything is boring, and restlessly move from one experience to another. They have no tolerance for seeing a movie they have seen before.

Research has most often focused on whether overall sensation-seeking indicates interest in or experience with the genres of movies of most concern. High sensation seekers attend graphic horror, violent action and X-rated films more frequently than those who are low in sensation-seeking (Zuckerman & Litle, 1986). This preference has been found in both men and women, adolescents and adults, and in the U.S. and other countries (Aluja-Fabregat, 2000; Harris *et al.*, 2000; Johnston, 1995). Trice (2010) found that these effects could be found in seven-year olds. He had children choose whether to watch a movie about a "scary shark" or a "cute bunny." Those who were high in sensation-seeking were more likely to choose the shark movie. Two videos were used for each animal, one scary that emphasized predation, and one not scary that emphasized maternal nurturance. Children high in sensation-seeking who saw the scary videos rated them more positively than those who were shown the less scary videos. For example, children high in sensation-seeking who picked the shark video and saw the version about maternal behavior in sharks rated the video lower than those who watched sharks chasing baby seals. This study demonstrates that sensation-seekers not only seek out exciting entertainment, they prefer it to less exciting fare when they view it.

Why sensation-seekers may not like less exciting fare was examined in a functional magnetic resonance imaging (fMRI) study by Straube *et al.* (2010). Participants were shown minute-long clips from four frightening movies, *The Shining* (1980), *The Silence of the Lambs* (1991), *The Others* (2001) and *Aliens* (1986). One clip showed a suspenseful, uncertain threat, while the other clips from the same movies showed an unfrightening scene. The scenes were selected through a careful process of finding clips that were deemed very frightening, but which would not cause subjects to move their heads abruptly, as that would have rendered their fMRI readings invalid. All participants showed high activity in the dorsal medial prefrontal cortex during the frightening scenes. What distinguished the sensation seekers from those low in sensation-seeking was a general lack of arousal during the non-frightening scenes. It appeared that sensation seekers have a very high threshold for stimulation: They need exciting stimulation if they are to become engaged at all. This suggests that susceptibility to boredom is the major factor.

One study that did examine the subscales of sensation-seeking was done by Tamborini, Stiff and Zillman (1987). This study employed a fairly complicated methodology and was designed primarily to address a question of whether there were significant difference in individuals who like horror movies between those who prefer male victims and those who prefer female victims. The study involved college students enrolled in an introductory mass communications class.

In the first part of the study, participants filled out questionnaires measuring the personality traits of sensation-seeking, androgyny and Machiavellianism. By 1987, sensation-seeking had been linked to liking of the horror genre in several studies. Androgyny, which is having both traditional male (e.g., competitiveness and aggression) and female characteristics (compassion and care-giving) was included because these was a possibility that women who liked horror and men who did not might be high in androgyny, as it was assumed that liking horror movies was a traditional masculine propensity. The androgyny hypotheses did not pan out. Machiavellianism, the willingness to use deceit and/or power to attain one's goals, was another personality variable that seemed a plausible determinant of interest in horror.

In the next part of the study, participants were given a list of 317 films and asked to rank them on a nine-point scale (-4 to +4) if they had seen them, as to how much they had enjoyed them. The films were aggregated into six categories: light entertainment (comedies and musicals), dramas, violent dramas, horror, graphic horror, and pornography. This procedure produced *exposure* scores for each of the genres, the number of films in each category seen, and an *enjoyment* score, which was the average rating for films in the genre. These two measures were used to predict the dependent variable. Then participants were asked to rank order 13 film descriptions. A typical description went like this:

> *Deep Dropping Red.* Terrifying suspense horror film with buckets of blood.
> A deranged phone fanatic follows up his conversations with beautiful women by deadly personal appearances. A sense of eeriness prevails as the killer is seen prowling restless through dark houses spying on his victims. Chilling silence fills the scene as the killer surprises his victims with a hatchet and uses it to decapitate and dismember their bodies. (Graphic Scenes of Violence).

Six of the films contained graphic violence. In these descriptions, the sex of the victim was varied for different participants. Six of the films did not contain graphic violence and no gender was assigned to these victims. The ranking of these films was used to determine a *preference* for graphic horror (how many films with graphic horror appeared at the top of the list) and a preference for male or female victims (which gender of victims was rated higher than the other). These measures were the study's dependent variables.

Preference for graphic horror rankings of the vignettes were related to three of the four sensation-seeking scales, disinhibition ($r = .29$), boredom susceptibility ($r = .18$) and experience-seeking ($r = .17$), but not significantly for thrill and adventure-seeking.

To fully account for preference for graphic horror scores, the enjoyment and exposure scores from the ratings of the 317 movies and the other personality variables were entered into a regression equation. In addition to the significant correlations with sensation-seeking subscales, preference for graphic horror also correlated positively with the deceit subscale from the Machiavellian measure, exposure to horror, enjoyment of violent drama, and enjoyment of pornography. It correlated negatively with exposure to light entertainment.

In the regression analysis, among the male participants, those preferring male victims were high in boredom susceptibility, while those who preferred female victims were both high in boredom susceptibility and high in enjoyment of pornography.

Kids, Gore and Personality

Since the 1980s, there has been a particular interest among psychologists and media scholars in the horror genre. This was partially due to its rise in popularity with a number of film franchises including *Nightmare on Elm Street, Halloween, Scream, Scary Movie* and *Saw*, which were aimed at teenagers and which contained graphic portrayals of violence toward young women. This popularity occurred at a time when the perception was that teenagers were becoming more violent. Gangs were re-emerging as a national concern. There were mass shootings at high schools. Occasionally teens recreated particularly gruesome scenes from their favorite films. Freddie, Leatherface and Michael Myers became favorite Halloween costumes, indicating that even children may want to be like them.

What was seen as a contributing factor was the advent of the VHS tape. Horror films usually received R ratings for violence and sexuality, which meant that they could not be viewed by children under the age of 16 without the presence of an adult in a theater, but they could be rented or purchased and then viewed, and viewed repeatedly, by anyone. Early viewing of frightening and violent material has been shown to have emotional consequences for children, among which is a morbid and continuing fascination with this kind of media (Hoekstra, Harris & Helmick, 1999).

Some media theorists concluded that early exposure to graphic portrayals of violence has led to a generation of children who accept violence as the norm, based on the finding that repeated exposure to violence makes one have lower and lower reactions to it—that is, lower and lower emotional distress. But research also points out that most children and adolescents distinguish between real violence and pretend violence (Blumberg, Bierwirth, 2008; Peters & Blumberg, 2002), and that exposure to real violence in the home, neighborhood and school is the biggest reason children become unresponsive to aggression, not the violence of video games, television and movies.

Johnston (1995) also found evidence that the concerns about a "generation of violence-addicted children" may be overwrought. She examined adolescents who watched "slasher" movies and found that there were actually four sub-groups.

Some participants who had low empathy and high sensation-seeking just seemed to enjoy watching acts of violence; she termed them *gore watchers*. These children did not watch slasher movies when they were in particular moods: They enjoyed watching brutality all the time. These children were of the greatest concern. They often identified with the killer and liked films where the killer gets away after a lot of random carnage. Getting away with carnage is a prerequisite for having a slasher franchise. These children said that slasher movies were funny and that the best ones show torture, revenge and sex. Most of them were boys.

Other children who occasionally watched slasher movies actually had high levels of empathy, but also high sensation-seeking. They liked all sorts of exciting media. These she called *thrill watchers*. These viewers most often watched exciting movies when they were sad, frustrated or angry. Most often these children identified with a spectator in the movie. Like the gore watchers, they thought slasher movies were interesting and funny, but they reported watching mostly horror-comedies, like the *Scream* series.

Some children watched slasher movies as a way of testing themselves. They wanted to see if they were "tough enough." While these children were low in empathy, they were not high in sensation-seeking. They did not become regular users of violent media. These children most often identified with the victim of the movie and regarded the movies as frightening.

A small group of these young adolescents were identified as *problem watchers*. Low in empathy, these children also reported high levels of substance use and reported that their moods were worse after watching slasher movies. They were considered problem watchers because they watched slasher movies when they were lonely and experiencing difficulties in certain aspects of their lives. They too identified with the victims.

It is also of some interest to return to the original assumptions: Are today's children and adolescents more violent than those of previous generations and is the violence they observe particularly graphic and primarily directed toward women? The answer to these questions is no. Despite beliefs, we live in a relatively non-violent period and adolescents are less violent than those of previous generations (Smith, 2015). Sapolsky and Molitor (1996) found that most of the victims in the horror movies of the mid–1980s and 1990s were men, although women were in the majority during the early 1980s. And it is clear that violence has been part of narrative for many generations. The Iliad and the Bible have gruesome scenes in them. Hamlet kills three people on stage and several more off-stage. *Moby Dick*'s Ishmael is the only survivor of a killer white whale.

Movie-Watching and Academic Achievement

Other concerns that have been expressed about adolescents have to do with the effect of movie-watching on school performance. The first concern has to do with how much they watch, particularly which activities their movie-watching displaces. A second concern has to do with *what* they watch. There are whole laundry lists of concerns here. Do they see smoking, alcohol and illegal drug use? Do they see violence and other antisocial behavior? Do they watch explicit or otherwise inappropriate sexual content? While all of these issues are concerning in and of themselves, they could also have a negative impact on school behavior.

Surveys from a decade ago indicated that American adolescents engaged with media about seven hours per day. This included about three hours of TV-watching on weekdays and four hours on weekends (e.g., Bucksch *et al.* 2016). TV-watching includes watching movies on TV. In the last decade, overall media use has increased, largely because of a change from an hour and a half of computer use a day to two and a half hours per day. TV-watching decreased about half an hour a day during this same period, but the number of movies adolescents are seeing in theaters has risen slightly, and some watch movies on tablets and phones. All in all, movie-watching consumes about 45 minutes a day which translates into between 120 and 150 movies a year.

Amount of movie viewing

The amount of time spent watching movies has not been studied by itself, but a number of studies have found that the amount of "screen time" is associated with such things as poor school performance and obesity (Wanner *et al.*, 2016). Those who watch a lot of TV fail to complete homework, don't do recreational reading, don't participate in extracurricular activities, and have lower scores on standardized achievement tests.

These patterns often begin early in life. Anderson, Huston, Linebarger and Wright (2001) re-contacted adolescents they had studied as pre-schoolers and found that their earlier TV use predicted their current achievement. For example, the more educational TV that the participants had watched as four- and five-year-olds, the higher their grades, the more they read, and the less they engaged in aggressive behavior. Girls who were exposed to violent programming as children had lower grades as teenagers.

These authors specifically addressed the question of which was more important: total hours of TV watched or specifically what was watched. They came down heavily on the side of content rather than amount. They conclude: "The medium is *not* the message. The message is" (Anderson *et al.*, 2001, p. viii). As clever as this is, it is not at all surprising that time spent watching

TV at age five did not have a great impact on behavior a dozen years later, but that the content did. And yet these authors found that high users of TV in preschool tended to be high users later.

R-rated movies

Sharif and Sargent (2006) studied several thousand high school students and found that amount of TV screen time was significantly related to poor academic performance. For example, 50 percent of those who did not watch TV at all were rated as having excellent school performance, while of those who watched four or more hours a day on weekdays, only 24 percent had excellent performance. Weekend screen time did not seem to have an effect on grades. The strongest predictor in their study, however, was not amount of time spent watching TV but parental control of R-rated movies. Less than 0.5 percent of those whose parents did not allow any access to R-rated movies were receiving failing grades, while among those whose parents had no restrictions, 13 percent had failing grades. In this study, seven percent were receiving failing grades, and 32 percent of the teens had no restrictions on what they watched.

Sharif, Wills and Sargent (2010) studied over 6500 adolescents in a national sample of media use. In contrast to most studies in this area, this one used a **prospective methodology**. That is, instead of looking at all the variables at the same time, the measures that were thought to predict poor school performance were looked at two years before measuring school performance—and school performance at the end of the study was measured both by its absolute value (e.g., GPA at Time 2) and in change (GPA at Time 2, minus GPA at Time 1).

They asked the participants in this study whether they had seen a sample of 50 popular movies and coded the percentage of the movies they had seen which were R-rated. Thirteen percent of the movies seen by those who had excellent school performance were R-rated; 16 percent of those movies seen by those with good school performance were R-rated, while 22 percent of the movies seen by those with average or below performance were R-rated. Boys had higher rates of R-rated movie viewing than girls (20 percent vs. 14 percent) and younger participants had lower rates of R-rated movie-viewing than older participants; for example, 11 percent of the movies viewed by ten-year-olds were R-rated, while 24 percent of those viewed by 14-year-olds were R-rated. These authors also found that children who watched a lot of R-rated films had more school behavior problems than those who watched fewer R-rated movies.

The reason for including these studies in the chapter on personality is the role of sensation-seeking in many of them. Sharif, Wills and Sargent

(2010) explained their results by positing that watching a lot of R-rated movies caused many adolescents to increase in sensation-seeking, and as sensation-seeking increased, the children's levels of school problems, both social and academic, increased. The prospective nature of the study allows for us to see that. While not all children who watched R-rated movies had increases in sensation-seeking, it was those adolescents who watched R-rated movies *and* had increases in sensation-seeking who, two years later, had poorer school outcomes.

But isn't sensation-seeking supposed to be a biology-based personality trait? If that is the case, how can watching a few, or even quite a few, R-rated movies increase one's level of sensation-seeking? Zuckerman *et al.* (1972) found that while there is a very constant effect of sensation-seeking over time on risky behavior, which suggests a biological origin, experience effects the specifics. One might be very high on sensation-seeking, but if her first experience with rollercoasters was unpleasant, she might avoid them in the future and fail to endorse the item on the measure of sensation-seeking that asks about liking of roller coasters.

In this study, sensation-seeking was measured by only four items:

I like to do scary things.
I like to do dangerous things.
I often think there is nothing to do.
I like to listen to loud music.

It is possible to imagine situations in which experience might modify one's response to these questions. Perhaps you broke your arm doing a dangerous thing a week ago or perhaps you have a brother who annoys you by playing music just beyond your ability to tolerate it. These events would make you less likely to endorse questions 2 and 4. Watching R-rated films, likewise, is both dangerous and scary (sometimes). If a teenager had had a lot of experience watching fairly violent, fairly sexual movies with a lot of swearing, drinking, drug use, etc., he could report higher levels of sensation-seeking, which might indicate that his experience has pushed him to be willing to try more and more extreme activities in order to feel an edge.

Multi-tasking. Multi-tasking is the notion that we can do two high-engagement activities at the same time (Junco & Cotton, 2012). We *can* do two things at the same time, as long as one of them is routine. An experienced driver can listen to the radio and drive a familiar route at the same time. Most people, however, when they were learning to drive, could not drive an unfamiliar route and listen intently to the radio. Likewise, you cannot watch the news on TV and study new material at the same time. Research consistently finds that what we do is alternate between the two tasks. So if you are watching the news and studying for an hour, part of that hour you were watching the news and part of that hour you were studying (Salamé & Baddeley, 1989). And you were neither watching the news nor studying very well. Those who use media while studying (even college students who say they use background music to filter out dormitory noise) remember less and read more slowly than those who do not use media. So one of the concerns about media use and academic achievement is whether adolescents try to multitask. And one of the best indicators of multitasking is having a TV in your bedroom.

Having a TV in the bedroom has been found to be related both to adolescent and family characteristics but also significantly predicted school outcomes (Sharif et al., 2010). For example, among children from families where the parents had high school educations or less, 71 percent of the adolescents had TVs in their bedrooms, while among adolescents with parents with college degrees, only 44 percent had TVs. Seventy-four percent of children from single parent homes had TVs in their bedrooms while only 55 percent of those who lived with both parents had TVs. More than 70 percent of the adolescents living in poverty had TVs in their bedrooms, while among those whose families made more than $75,000, less than half had TVs. Why does this matter? Because 54 percent of those with excellent school performance had TVs in their bedrooms, while 68 percent of those who were performing average or below in school had TVs in their rooms.

Eysenck's Theory

Hans Eysenck's theory of personality (Eysenck & Eysenck, 1985) consists of three traits that are believed to cover the most important aspects of the total personality. They are believed to have a physiological and genetic basis and thus should be very stable over time. These traits are:

Introversion vs. extroversion
Neuroticism vs. stability
Psychoticism vs. socialization

Individuals who score high on extroversion tend to be sociable, risk-taking, active and impulsive; individuals who score high on neuroticism are anxious, depressed, tense and moody; those who score high on psychoticism are aggressive, egocentric and manipulative, and lack empathy.

Introversion-extroversion

Hall (2005) found that extroverts preferred viewing movies at home. They see movies as events around which social occasions are built and, therefore, enjoy the home environment more than the theater, which constrains interaction. They prefer movies that require only modest attention, particularly light comedies (Weaver, 1991), because the main event is not the movie but the social gathering: Extroverts like to talk while engaging in media. Introverts, in contrast, like going to a movie theater *because* of its constrained nature: Usually one goes to the movie theater in pairs and while there is unstructured social interaction prior to the movie, there is little during the movie, and afterwards the social interaction consists of talking about the movie.

Extraverts are more willing than introverts to go along with the group, and therefore, when researchers ask about *experience* with different genres, extraverts have had a wider range of experience with different genres than introverts. In the research cited above, women who are extraverted have had more actual exposure to violent movies than women who are introverted, but they are not more likely to enjoy them. And men who are extraverted have viewed more pornography than men who are introverted, but are not necessarily fans.

Neuroticism

Gunter (1985) found that those who scored high on neuroticism found graphic violence to be very disturbing and Weaver (1991) found that those who were high in neuroticism avoided action-adventure movies. In other words, neurotics avoid genres of movies that they anticipate will cause them distress. One of the defining characteristics of neurotics is both anticipating distress across many different situations and avoiding anything that might cause distress, so it is not unexpected that they would avoid movies that have the potential for upsetting them and that they find movie selection itself a potentially distressing situation.

Weibel, Wissmath and Stricker (2011) conducted a study of neuroticism and the enjoyment of films. They showed a funny, a sad and a scary movie clip to a mixed age group (50 percent college students) and measured both their enjoyment ratings and their feeling of "being there" in the scene, which they referred to as *spatial presence*. In all three clips, those who scored high on neuroticism felt more present than those low in neuroticism. This feeling of presence may have led to lower enjoyment ratings of the two negative clips, sad and scary, and higher enjoyment of the funny clip.

Psychoticism

Those who scored high on psychoticism avoid comedies (Hall, 2005). Weaver (1991) also found those high on psychoticism showed little interest in comedies, while showing a high interest in horror movies. Weaver, Brosius and Mundorf (1993) found that those who were high in psychoticism showed high interest in horror, but little interest in tragedy. This study used short blurbs about imaginary movies. One category was described as sex-comedies and a typical blurb was:

> Five college kids party throughout their Florida vacation. On their last night they are having a pool party at their hotel. Swimsuits and bikinis drop and the pool fills with naked bodies. Everyone has a great time.

This study employed an American and a German sample. Those high in psychoticism in the American sample showed a keen interest in the sex comedies, but those in the German sample who were high in psychoticism rated their interest very low. The authors interpreted these findings in terms of high psychoticism individual's interest in the forbidden rather than a straightforward interest in portrayals of sex. They note that at the time, nudity and sexuality were novel in American movies, while they had been a staple of German cinema for decades. This finding cautions us that the results of these studies must be interpreted as related to culture and time.

Gunter (1985) found that those high in psychoticism found graphic horror humorous and Zuckerman and Litle (1986) found watching pornography was positively correlated with psychoticism in men.

We should be cautious about these findings because we are talking about "psychoticism" in a sample of normal individuals: Those college students who score at the highest level in psychoticism may, compared to individuals with certain mental illnesses, be relatively normal. They may merely be *somewhat* more aggressive and egocentric than their fellow students.

Big Five Theory of Personality

Although media researchers are most likely to use Eysenck's theory for research into the relation between personality and film preferences, in most situations psychologists use what is called Big Five Theory. The five Big traits arose over time and from a variety of perspectives, based on the most consistent findings from the entire field of personality research (McCrae & Costa, 1987). Two of the traits are the same as in Eysenck's theory, while the others come from other research traditions:

Openness to Experience: Those high on this construct exhibit curiosity, appreciation for art, and self-awareness, and are ready for emotional experiences.

Conscientiousness: People high on this construct have good self-discipline, show attention to details, and value planning and order.

Extroversion: These individuals have a wide range of interests, high energy, and enjoy engagement in the external-social world.
Agreeableness: People high in this trait show a concern with getting along with others through optimism, kindness and trustworthiness.
Neuroticism: These individuals have a lack of tolerance for stress, and exhibit conspicuous reactivity to negative situations.

To date, only three published studies on movies have been based on the Big Five perspective. In the first, Berenbaum and Williams (1995) had a small group of students watch film clips, two of which were deemed positive (stand-up comedy and a cartoon) and two negative, the alien exploding from the crew member's chest in *Alien* (1979) and a scene with a cave full of spiders. Participants reported their reactions to the film clips and were also videotaped. Their recorded facial expressions during the clips were rated by a panel of trained students. This study also included the variable of caffeine. Among the students who did not receive caffeine, those who were high in Extroversion reacted less to the negative film clips, while those who were high on neuroticism reacted less to the positive film clips.

Finn (1997) looked at time spent watching movies, watching TV, attending sports, partying, etc., among a large sample of college students and compared their reports to a Big Five measure. Throughout the year, students kept daily activity diaries. There was a small positive correlation between movie attendance and openness to experience ($r = .12$). Television viewing was negatively correlated with extroversion, openness to experience, and agreeableness, while partying and attending sporting events were positively associated with extroversion.

Krcmar and Kean (2005) looked at overall movie-viewing and the amount of violent material watched and enjoyed by a group of college students and older adults. This study also looked at TV use. The authors found that older adults who were high on openness to experience viewed more violent media than those low on openness. Extraverts watched more movies than introverts. Those who were high in agreeableness tended to dislike violent movies. Individuals high in neuroticism were more likely to watch violent movies than those who were low on neuroticism, but they did not enjoy watching them. Conscientiousness produced no significant predictions of general or violent media use.

Conclusions

What should we conclude from the research on the relationship between personality and movie choice?

Sensation-seekers look for excitement in movies. They tend to like extreme comedies, action films, graphic horror and pornography. They shy away from movies that they consider boring—subtle movies about relationships and movies that unfold at a leisurely pace. They do not like to watch movies they have seen before.

Persons with high levels of empathy like movies about relationships and movies about genuine emotions—not just getting an adrenaline rush. These people tend to avoid movies in which people are harshly treated because they "experience their pain." Individuals low in empathy are not particularly troubled by depictions of graphic violence, and when low empathy is coupled with high sensation-seeking it may lead an unhealthy interest in violence.

People high in neuroticism tend to like a narrow range of movies and they choose content they expect to be pleasant and familiar.

There is little evidence that introversion influences *what* people watch, although it may substantially influence *how* they watch. Introverts enjoy the restricted social experience of going to the theater to watch a movie and they do not mind watching movies alone. Extroverts see movies as a vehicle for social interaction. They like to watch movies at home with friends so that they can talk and be gregarious. That social activity may preclude serious movies.

There are some important caveats about these conclusions:

The correlations that have been found are very small. The significant correlations described above range in strength from .06 to a high of .38. This means that at best, when the correlation reaches .38, personality predicts about 14 percent of movie choice. (We calculate the "percentage of common variance" by squaring the correlation coefficient. In this case, if $r = 0.38$, then $r^2 = .14$ or 14 percent.) But it is more often less than that. Personality does play a role in movie selection, but a small one. Even when the correlation suggests that 14 percent of a movie choice may be due to a personality factor, 86 percent of that choice is due to other things.

Most of the studies in this area have utilized college students. While college students are the demographic that consumes the largest number of movies, it is a limitation of the research. Research described in later chapters indicates that older adults use movies differently and watch different films from those who are college-aged. Moreover, those in their twenties still have time to develop their preferences. Most college students just have not had time to discover silent movies, or the films of Kurosawa, or the joys of watching horrible science fiction movies from the 1950s. Most of the students in our class have never even seen *Casablanca*.

There are several different ways of asking and answering these questions, and how you ask the question matters. One way of asking about movies is to see whether there are correlations between a personality characteristic and a preference for a genre of film. That preference may be assessed by asking "How much do you enjoy watching romantic comedies?" or it might be "How often do you watch romantic comedies?" Sometimes the differences between these two question might not be much, but other times it is. Maybe you have a girlfriend who loves romantic comedies. You may love your girlfriend and therefore watch a lot of romantic comedies, but you don't like them at all. Moreover, when we use genres, they may not mean the same thing to all people. One might legitimately ask, "What constitutes the line between *horror* and *graphic horror*?" And it may not be the case that we all think in the same way about films. In a class where we recently asked about favorite genres, the first favorite genre identified was "zombie movies."

Other times, researchers have had people rank order or rate blurbs about imaginary films. I might generally like romantic comedies, but not like this one because of its setting:

> Love blooms in a sharecropper's cabin between the daughter of an angry, injured WWII veteran and an itinerant ventriloquist who has been injured in a hit and run accident. The implausibility of the situation provokes hilarity.

Still other research uses ratings of actual movies, where one's ratings might be influenced by aspects of the movie from the style of photography to the actors playing the roles. It is not surprising that there is some inconsistency in the findings in this chapter.

Finally, the ways we watch movies now and in the foreseeable future have not been studied. Devices and streaming services may change viewership patterns and choice decisions as much as the advent of movies on TV in the 1950s and the videotape in the 1970s.

* * *

The end of *Casablanca* poses some challenges for contemporary young audiences, which also speaks to why the correlations between personality and genre may be so small. Redbox classifies *Casablanca* as a *classic*, but it could just as easily be called a romance. Good movies are complex and multifaceted, and people will find different things to like and dislike in them. Genre is a convenient research variable, but it tells us very little about a movie.

Casablanca may not be what an audience member today thinks of as a romance, because, among other things, Rick and Victor are neither young nor conform to today's definition of handsome, and Rick and Ilsa do not fly away to Lisbon at the end because there are inconvenient things going on around them like black marketeering, political corruption and the swelling tide of Nazism—not to mention the fact that Ilsa is already married. In the second most famous speech in the film, the "hill of beans" speech, Rick tells Ilsa that given the fact that the world is going to hell in a handbasket, the lives of three little people do not amount to a hill of beans. He has made the decision that will increase the likelihood that they all will survive. He also

The four major characters in *Casablanca*, Captain Louis Renault (Claude Rains), Victor Laszlo (Paul Henreid), Rick Blane (Humphrey Bogart) and Ilsa Lund (Ingrid Bergman) listen to the news that the Gestapo is on the way (Warner Bros, 1942).

acts in a way that reinforces the importance of marriage. He does not give up everything for love. But, he says, seeing her again and understanding why she left him in the railroad station has given him back Paris.

Key Psychological Terms

Empathy: The emotional and cognitive ability to understand and to feel what others are experiencing.
Disinhibition: A shucking-off of the normal restraints on behavior.
Extroversion: A characteristic where one likes active socializing and avoids solitary and reflective experiences.
Introversion: A willingness to be alone, along with a strong disinterest in large public events.

Neuroticism: A strong desire to have things done in a way which will cause as little upset and discomfort to oneself as possible.
Personality: Generally persistent behaviors, attitudes and beliefs which are manifested in many different settings.
Perspective-taking: The cognitive ability of take another person's point of view.
Psychoticism: A trait which is associated with highly unusual and disturbing thinking and behavior.

Key Cinema Term

Genre: A conventional film category, such as sci-fi, suspense, romantic comedy or musical.

2

Emotion and Mood

We wonder if you receive many messages like this:

There's a really sad movie on at the Cineplex about a man and his young son in a World War II concentration camp. Are you in? By the way, it's really a comedy and it's in Italian.

It may seem ridiculous that anyone would want to see this movie, but in 1997, Roberto Benigni's romantic comedy-drama *La vita è bella* (*Life Is Beautiful*) was a surprise hit in the United States, doing $60 million in business in a year filled with worthy competition. It won Academy Awards for Best Foreign Language Film, Best Musical Soundtrack and Best Actor for Benigni, who also wrote and directed. It *is*, in part, about a man and his son in a concentration camp, but it is also a movie whose title is not ironic. Despite what eventually happens, most people leave the film feeling uplifted, even if they still have tears in their eyes.

Why people ever choose to see sad movies seems to be a problem for psychologists and media scholars. But people do. When we have surveyed undergraduate classes about favorite movies over the past several years, *The Notebook* (2004) has turned up in first place each time, a distinction such tearjerkers as *Gone with the Wind* (1939) and *Love Story* (1970) once held. *Hamlet* was the most popular play in the 17th century, and it is not exactly a barrel of laughs. According to some psychological and media theories, we should always choose happy movies. Indeed, comedies have been and remain the most popular genre, but people like to examine a lot of different moods and emotions when they go to the movies.

So, having found out in the previous chapter that some personality factors, particularly empathy and sensation-seeking, play a role in movie selection and avoidance, we will consider in this chapter the role of emotions and mood in picking a movie. We will also examine how movies change our moods. We will particularly explore the issue of why we decide to watch sad movies, and along the way, address the issue of whether watching movies, at least some of them, may be good for our emotional well-being.

What Are Emotions and Moods?

If we asked average people what an **emotion** is, we would get a variety of answers. Some would say an emotion is a sudden feeling. Some who have taken a psychology course might include that an emotion has an observable manifestation. Others may say an emotion is a response to a certain situation. Some may even say that emotions exist to protect us by raising our cortisol levels or our heart rate in preparation for action, but others may say that emotions hurt us. Some examples of emotions readily come to mind such as joy, sorrow, amusement and anger, but there are many more than these. Certain things that we may never consider are emotions, such as disgust, desire and shame.

The way psychologists conceive of emotions can be summarized by the phrase "all of the above." They are usually sudden; they involve a situation, a feeling, physiological responses, behavioral manifestations; and often, although not always, they result in an overall action. Some emotions are good for us; others are not, at least in large doses. Table 2.1 shows a timeline of these interrelations:

Table 2.1.

This schematic shows that the situation first brings about a physiological response that may be accompanied by behavioral manifestations. (For example, seeing a frightening animal brings about a flood of hormones which then leads to muscular tension.) After these things occur, we become aware of the feeling and we label it "fear." All of these things may culminate in an action (running away or attacking) or they may lead to a kind of inaction (staying perfectly still and hoping the animal passes by).

A more relevant example might be that you are walking down the street and encounter someone you met a few days before. Certain bio-chemicals flood your brain (physiological response); you find yourself smiling and your palms are sweating (behavioral manifestations). You become aware of the situation and your feeling and you determine that what you are experiencing is *attraction*. You walk in her direction and end up asking her to see a romantic comedy playing at a nearby theater with you (action).

Mood, on the other hand, is persistent, not sudden. If the woman you have just invited to see a movie declines, you may become sullen or sad or embarrassed for the rest of the day. On the other hand, if she agrees and you have a pleasant time, you may experience a happy, elated or hopeful mood, even after the movie is over and she has gone her own way.

Our emotions evolved over a long period and they do not necessarily serve us well in today's world. For example, if you get back an essay in an English class with the grade of D- or receive a below average performance evaluation at work, this will likely lead to a feeling of anger, assuming that you worked hard. Anger provokes aggression, but it is probably good that most of us do not pick up a blunt object and traumatize our professors or supervisors to the head. But because this anger is not released by aggression, the emotional system is out of balance. Millennia ago, when you got angry, you aggressed toward the object of your anger, and then went on about your business. Today that anger turns into an enduring negative mood. We also have plenty of time to nurse our moods. Perhaps our less sophisticated ancestors, when faced with a romantic turn-down, just continued on hunting and gathering. Now we brood. We text our friends about it. They text back. Someone we barely know posts a sympathetic response on our Facebook page, thus validating our feelings. All of this prolongs the feelings of rejection and anger. What was formerly a brief emotional burst has become a protracted mood.

Two Ways of Thinking About Emotions and Mood

The usual way of thinking about emotions and moods is to assume that there are quite a few of them and that they are all different. This is what we were describing above. Fear is different from anger and anger is different from disgust. We might admit that some emotions are just more or less intense versions of other emotions, for example, *rage* may be intense anger, while *pique* might be just a little bit of anger. Most of the time we do not give much consideration to *how* fear is different from anger, but we assume that it is. This is the approach that Darwin (1872) took in his major contribution to psychology, *The expression of the emotions in man and animals*. He discussed several dozen emotions and posited that the way that they are expressed is very close to universal: We can clearly read emotional expression in individuals from different cultures. He believed that certain situations give rise to specific emotions and that the emotions lead to a very specific behavioral manifestation and other people, regardless whether they know you or not, can read your emotions by the behavioral manifestations. A smile is the result of joy or happiness anywhere in the world.

But several other early theorists had very different interpretations of the sequence of events in an emotional episode. Fundamentally, they said that the emotion *is* the behavior. The physiological response is mostly just arousal and we know that we are afraid, or hostile, or in love by what we do. Darwin thought that we saw a bear and became afraid, and that the fear led us to run away. These other theorists, including American psychologist William James and Danish physician Carl Lange, proposed that we see a bear and become aroused: *If* we run away, we say that we are afraid. The same arousal might lead us to grab a spear and charge the bear, in which case we would say that we were hostile or brave.

Why this distinction matters is that it influences how psychologists measure emotions and moods in their research on movies. For example, in a study of how movies might affect our moods and our political opinions—in this case attitudes toward capital punishment—Till and Vitouch (2012) had participants watch one of two movies in their original or edited form. They measured their mood and their views on capital punishment before and after watching the films. After the film, they also had participants rate how much they had identified with the main character, the one who is executed.

The two films were *Dancer in the Dark* (2000) and *The Chamber* (1996). The first film focuses on a woman struggling with a disease that will make both her and her son blind. When her friend, a police officer, steals money from her to pay off his debts, she confronts him and shoots him in self-defense. She is hanged at the end of the movie. In *The Chamber*, a young lawyer appeals the death sentence of his grandfather, a member of the Ku Klux Klan who unintentionally killed a lawyer and his two small sons in a bombing. At the end, the grandfather dies in the gas chamber. The edited versions of these films were the same as the originals, except that they did not show the executions.

Mood was measured using a "mood adjective checklist." Such a checklist follows the James-Lange Theory of emotion in that it primarily measures dimension (high vs. low arousal) rather than specific moods. Most often mood adjective checklists have two dimensions, "Aroused" to "Not Aroused" and "Positive" to "Negative," as shown in Table 2.2. Associated with each dimension are adjectives. High arousal might be indicated by words such as "excited," "jittery" and "aroused," while positive items might be the adjectives "happy," "pleasant" and "content." Participants rate each adjective for how well it describes them at the present moment on a Likert scale, where higher scores indicate being like the adjective, and low score feeling the opposite of the emotion. They sum all the items that are on one dimension and then they can locate themselves in the grid.

Table 2.2.
Schematic of Moods

High Arousal

	High Arousal	
Negative	angry frightened distraught	happy fond brave
	bored melancholy annoyed	peaceful content calm

(Negative — Positive; Low Arousal)

All four versions of the films resulted in audience members feeling less positive and sadder after the films than before, while only the unedited versions of both films resulted in significant changes in views toward capital punishment. Those who saw either film, without the execution scene, became less sympathetic toward capital punishment, but it should be noted that all of the groups were somewhat against capital punishment to begin with. The finding that the movies *without* the execution scenes were more effective in reducing support for capital punishment came as a surprise to the authors, because broadcasts of actual executions has been found to dramatically decrease viewers support for capital punishment (Howells, Flanagan & Hagan, 1995). But the authors note that quite often what works for documentary films or news, does not translate very well to fictional films.

What relates this research to the previous chapter is the finding that those who identified with the main character both became sadder and became less in favor of the death penalty. That is, those who had high levels of empathy were the most impacted by the film. Those with high empathy felt the emotions of the main character who had to face their execution, which made them sadder. And like the finding that audience members who identified with the young couple in *Before Sunset* also wanted to go to Vienna, those who identified with the person who was executed also thought less positively of capital punishment.

In other research, psychologists may measure many specific moods. For example, in the study by Strizhakova and Krcmar (2007) discussed below, video rental store customers ranked their mood on nine different emotions. This approach would be more like that utilized by Darwin.

Mood Induction

Psychologists use clips of movies routinely to induce moods in research participants (Gross & Levenson, 1995). Emotionally charged scenes from movies lasting no more than five or six minutes can reliably change a participant's mood (Del Palacio-Gonzalez et al., 2014). Remember that in research, volunteers come to participate in a research study with no expectation of what they will be seeing and that they do not, like real audiences at movies, decide to see something that would make them happy or sad, fearful or angry. But a few minutes later, they are. So the moods they report must be related to the clips they watch.

Why would psychologists want to do this? Moods influence the way we think and behave, and psychologists are interested in how this takes place. For example, psychologists have studied the influence of mood on altruism. A procedure that is fairly often used in laboratory demonstrations would have students watch a movie clip and then fill out a questionnaire about their mood. This would show that the clip influenced their mood in the way it was predicted and it is called a **manipulation check**. The participants would then leave the laboratory, only to find that another student has just dropped all of her books or they are asked to donate to a charity or solicited to sign a petition. Normally those who watched the happy movie clip would help more often, donate more money, and be more willing to sign a petition than those who watched the sad or the frightening clip.

Does the same thing apply to actual movies? Underwood et al. (1977) observed moviegoers who had just attended a sad double feature or a neutral double feature, to see who were more likely to donate to Muscular Dystrophy. They found that those who had attended the neutral movies were three times more likely to donate than those who had attended the sad movies. The findings were interpreted in light of previous research that suggested that altruism was related to being in a happy mood (Underwood et al., 1972; 1974).

We repeated as many of the original conditions of the Underwood et al. (1977) study as we could at showings of three movies at the theater on our campus. The movies we looked at were *Chef, Harry Potter and the Goblet of Fire* and *E.T.*

To determine whether these movies were *happy, sad or neutral*, we asked ten individuals going into the first showing of each movie to rate it as Sad (-1), Happy (+1) or Neutral (0). Six of the ten raters found *Chef* happy and four rated it as neutral for an average rating of +0.6; eight out of ten found *E.T.* sad and two found it to be neutral for an average rating of -0.8, and four found *Harry Potter* to be happy, four found it sad and two found it neutral for an average of +0.0. Thus, using the same method and criterion that Underwood did, *Chef* was found to be a happy movie, *Harry Potter* a neutral movie and *E.T.* a sad movie. After subsequent showings of each movie, we surveyed 33 individuals about their mood (Happy, Neutral, Sad) and observed whether they made a donation to charity.

Ten (30 percent) of those who had seen *Chef* made a contribution; eight (24 percent) of those who had seen *Harry Potter and the Goblet of Fire* made a contribution; while nine (27 percent) of those who had seen *E.T.* made a contribution. The differences were too small to confirm the hypothesis that the highest rate of donation would be among those who had attended the happy movie, and unlike the study by Underwood, more of those who attended the sad movie made contributions than those who attended the neutral movie.

The question arises, however, about the actual movies. *Harry Potter and the Goblet of Fire* might get a average rating of neutral, but there are sad and scary things that happen in it and some people found it happy and others found it sad. That's a different situation than a movie where everyone agrees that the movie is neutral. And while *Chef* is a comedy, it isn't a laugh-a-minute riot. Doesn't the exact nature of mood depend on the specific movie?

We think it does. And because of that, we wanted to measure the mood that the participants are in, not just relate their altruism to whether the movie was rated as happy, sad or neutral by others. First, we measured the mood of the participants using a mood adjective checklist. Then we divided their happy-sad mood ratings into thirds: The highest third was "happy"; the middle third was "neutral"; the lowest third was considered to be in a sad mood. Then we compared moods to the movies our participants had seen. Table 2.3 shows the results:

Table 2.3
Movie Rating × Audience Mood Contingency Table

Movie:	*Happy*	*Neutral*	*Sad*
Audience:			
Happy	18	14	1
Neutral	5	17	11
Sad	10	2	21

If you look down the diagonal line from the upper left corner to the lower right corner, you will see that more than half of the ratings (57 percent) were as predicted (e.g., people who had just seen a happy movie were in a happy mood), but 43 percent were *not* as predicted. This alignment was statistically different from chance (we would expect 33 percent to be in the diagonal if it were a chance relationship), but it allows a lot of errors to be made if one assumes that a person who sees a certain kind of movie is in a certain mood. Almost a third of the people who saw the sad movie indicated that they were happy, for example. So we cannot predict that a whole movie will produce a specific mood as reliably as a short clip in a laboratory study can.

Finally, we wanted to see whether the mood that a participant was in was a better predictor of whether they made a contribution or not. In this case, 11 people in a sad mood made contributions; six who were in a neutral mood made a contribution; while ten in a happy mood made a contribution. So neither mood nor the kind of movie that the participants had attended substantially predicted their altruism.

Things that work well in laboratories, often do not work so well in "real life." While normally people in happy moods give more than people in sad moods, there are some times when that is not the case. If you are sad about real people or real situations, then being sad means you will give more than if you are happy (Thompson, Cowan & Rosenhan, 1980). That is why appeals for donations to feed the hungry that feature big-eyed street children and requests for money for animal shelters that feature abused dogs and cats are very effective. Our research may have been complicated by the fact that we focused on a charity for the homeless, and *E.T.* is a movie about an alien wanting to be home.

We will return to this study in the next chapter and see that there may be something as important as mood in predicting altruism after a movie.

* * *

Behaviors other than helping have been shown to be influence by the mood induced by a movie. Forgas and Moylan (1987) interviewed individuals either coming out of or going into movies that were classified as happy (e.g., *Back to the Future*), sad (e.g., *The Killing Fields*) or aggressive (e.g., *Rambo*). They asked them a number of questions like those asked in political polls. There were no differences among groups *before* going to the different movies, but afterwards, those who had seen the happy films were more positive in their evaluations of political leaders; thought that nuclear war and other catastrophes were less likely to happen; were less positive toward tougher penalties for heroin trafficking and drunk driving; and said they had higher quality of life than those who had seen the aggressive or the sad film. There were no differences between those who had seen sad and those who had seen the aggressive films. These were small differences, but certainly large enough to be concerned about polls that are taken outside of movie theaters. While movies are sometimes made to change our attitudes or beliefs (which will be the main topic in Chapter 7), that is not what is happening here, because the topics of these movies were not related to the poll questions: Why would a movie about going back into the past to watch your parents meet, influence your opinions about the death penalty? This indicates that the moods created by movies can widely influence our behavior.

So it is plausible that our moviegoing influences our mood and therefore some of the choices we make afterwards. But now we want to consider how our mood influences our moviegoing choices. You could imagine that if you returned to your apartment late at night and your building was nearly empty but there were unusual sounds coming from outside, you might be more interested in watching a romantic comedy than a slasher film. On the other hand, if you just broke up with a long-term boyfriend or girlfriend, you might decide against a romantic comedy in favor of an energizing, angry action film. But do ordinary fluctuations in mood influence what we watch? There is some research on media use and mood that suggests that there might be, and there is a single study of a nearly bygone institution, the video rental store, that shows how mood can have an influence on movie choice.

Mood Management Theory

Media theorists (e.g., Knoblock-Westerwick, 2006; Zillmann, 1988) have proposed that media are a useful tool in regulating moods. In its earliest theoretical account, called Mood Management Theory, the focus was exclusively on the happy-sad continuum of mood. The theory proposed that media are used to prolong a good mood and can be used to change a bad one.

A few examples of typical studies: Knobloch (2003) manipulated the mood of participants to be either happy or sad and then told them that they had to wait before the "real" experiment would begin. They were placed in a room where they could choose what music they would listen to. Top 30 songs had been rated along the two continua we discussed previously, high-low arousal and happy-sad.

The first choice or two conformed with the predictions from Mood Management Theory: Almost everyone chose to listen to upbeat music—but then, the participants began making more and more choices that did not conform to expectations. The participants, whether they had been manipulated into sad or happy moods, sometimes chose to listen to sad songs.

Kubey and Czikszentmihalyi (1990), in support of this theory, found that in their large sample of adult workers, heavy nights of TV viewing were preceded by late afternoons with negative affect, although affect earlier in the day did *not* predict TV usage. Participants reported that on heavy-use nights they had wanted to do "something different," although the study does not report the kinds of TV programming they watched.

Mood Management Theory seems to suggest that we would always use happy media, at least when media is used to manage moods. One problem with the theory, then, is the fact that people do not always select comic movies or other happy media. In fact, why would sad songs or movies even exist, if people would always select upbeat media? Especially when individuals are in unhappy moods, they turn to sad music (Knobloch & Zillmann, 2002), and when they are bored they turn to TV, but not always humorous TV (Greenwood & Long, 2009).

A further problem with this theory, with regards to movie selection, is that unlike going to your playlist or scrolling through your video guide, going to the movies has not been, until very recently, something that was capable of providing immediate gratification. You had to plan to go to the movies: you assessed your options; found someone to go with; you negotiated a final choice with that person; decided what to do before and afterward; and the actual movie may be attended hours or even days later. And the movie you had in mind at the start may not be what you ended up seeing.

To understand movie choice, we should be interested in all of these stages of the decision-making process. The first stage is the point at which a person becomes aware that a particular movie exists and makes a tentative judgment of whether they would like to see the movie. Often this is when a person sees a movie trailer—a form of promotion unique to movies because they target a person at a time when they have already shown interest in attending movies. They are shown in theaters before the feature film and they frequently are found on DVDs before the main film and on film websites. Faber and O'Guinn (1984) found that trailers were the most significant influence on movie selection, but it must be remembered that this study was conducted at a time when most movies were either seen in a theater or rented from a video store.

In a one-of-a-kind study in this area, Boksem and Smidts (2011) found that ratings of trailers and ratings of how much a viewer would be willing to pay to see the movie correlated strongly with each other, indicating that if we like the trailer, we may be simultaneously forming an intention to see the movie. This study also found that beta and gamma oscillations using electroencephalography (EEG) measured while viewing the trailers predicted both ratings of the trailers and the amounts viewers were willing to pay. So, our liking of a trailer and forming an intention to see the movie is related to brain activity. Moreover, the average amount of EEG activity across all of their participants was a good predictor of the film's eventual box office gross.

Develin, Chambers and Callison (2011) looked at how mood influenced college students' views of trailers and their intention to see the movies. Their moods were manipulated by having them watch a late-night talk show comedy routine (positive mood) or a TV program about children dying from cancer (negative mood). They were then asked to view two trailers, either both comedies or both serious films. Their findings differed for men and women. Men like trailers that were different from their current moods: that is, the men who were in a negative mood rated the trailers for comedies higher than the men who were in a positive mood. Likewise, men who were in positive moods indicated a preference for serious movies and gave a higher indication of intention to rent them than men in negative moods. Women had a preference for films that were congruent with their moods. Women in positive moods rated comedies higher than women in positive moods rated serious movies. Women in negative moods rated serious movies higher than women in negative moods rated comedies. It can be noted that many studies based on Mood Management Theory find different results for their male and female participants.

Movies are not three-minute shots of adrenaline like pop songs or 22-minute installments of hilarity like TV sitcoms. They are most often about two hours in length and contain material that touches on many moods. Oliver (1993) offered a solution that a sad film that ends happily may function as a happy film, but *Life Is Beautiful, Gone with the Wind, Love Story* and *The Notebook* are all films that begin happily and end sadly. Guido does not go to the concentration camp until halfway through *Life Is Beautiful*, after he has fallen in love, moved, romanced Dora, married her and had a child. Without this tender, quirky, romantic and funny backstory, the end of the movie would be incapable of breaking your heart. But the end does break your heart.

Moreover, even when more immediate media choices have been studied, only limited support for the hedonistic hypotheses of Mood Management Theory has been found. Lee, Andrade and Palmer (2013) determined that people in sad moods sometimes turned to happy music and sometimes to sad music. They found some support for the idea that we turn to sad music in situations when we would turn to sympathetic friends—usually when we are sad because of problems with interpersonal relationships. What we want is for someone to listen and reflect the legitimacy of our sad mood. We are more likely to listen to happy music when we would turn to upbeat friends who would distract us—usually when the reasons for our upset are not interpersonal, such as doing poorly on a test.

Sometimes watching humorous movies does have positive consequences. For example, Gelkopf, Gonen, Kurs, Melamed and Bleich (2006) showed humorous movies to a group of institutionalized schizophrenics daily for three months and assessed the changes in their functioning, compared to a control group that viewed neutral movies. Those who had seen the humorous movies were less angry, depressed and anxious than controls after intervention, although no differences were found in their positive behaviors or in their progress in therapy.

Strizhakova and Krcmar (2007) wanted to know whether mood predicted rentals at a movie rental store. They surveyed 264 individuals. A third of the participants came to rent a specific movie, and 82 percent planned on watching the movie with someone else.

Being happy did not predict what genre of movie the participants selected, but those who were sad were more likely to select crime dramas and serious drama and *less* likely to select comedies. This finding was not expected. Nor was it expected that those who reported being nervous had an increased likelihood of selecting horror movies. (Were they nervous because they had already decided to watch a scary movie?) Comedies were picked by those who were calm, while being avoided by those who reported being either energetic or bored. The most enigmatic finding of this study was that people who were in unpleasant moods were more likely to select documentaries than others.

Emotional Regulation

One of the stereotypes of psychological counseling, which is sometimes exploited for comedic effect in movies, as in *Analyze This* (1999), discussed in Chapter 8, is that the counselor is repeatedly asking, "How does that make you feel?" This kind of questioning is an aspect of Rogerian counseling, and its purpose is to find out whether the client is feeling the "right" emotion and in the appropriate strength. A person who is angry, rather than sad, at the loss of a family member or someone who blames himself for something that he had no part in, needs assistance regulating his emotional life.

Even if a person is having the "right" emotional response, a person can become overwhelmed by it, and one aspect of cognitive-behavioral therapy is to help clients find means of controlling their emotions. For example, depression is very common among low-income single mothers. In some ways, it is the "right" emotion for these women to have, at least on occasion. But it has been found that those who escape from developing chronic, debilitating depression often report that they have means of changing their negative mood (phoning friends, reading, watching TV, doing crossword puzzles, going to the movies) while those who succumb to depression report few, if any means of doing so (Silverstein *et al.*, 2010). Instead they spend a great deal of time **ruminating**, which is defined as "perseverating on past events and being unable to inhibit recurrent, distressing thoughts about the self." An example of this would be going over and over in your mind that you should have spent time studying for the test you failed instead of spending all evening on Facebook, and while ruminating over this, you are also not studying for your next test.

Emotional regulation refers to those things one does to keep from being mired in negative, persistent unproductive moods, things like reading, going to the movies, and phoning friends (Gross, 2014). While there are some similarities to mood management, it is more comprehensive and it refers to a set of skills that can be useful not only in isolated mood states (such as when you have just been in a traffic back-up) but in more structural, long-term situations (such as recovering from a break-up of a long-term relationship). There are a number of specific emotional regulation techniques that psychologists have studied:

Situation selection: getting out of one situation that is associated with negative emotion and into another which can be associated with more positive emotion; for example, getting out of your apartment to visit a friend who is usually cheerful;

Situation modification: changing some aspect of the situation that causes negative emotions; for example, cleaning up the apartment so that it not only looks nicer but your roommates will stop complaining about your mess;

Reappraisal: thinking about and elaborating on emotional information to bring about a change in perspective; for example, coming to understand that your low grade on a test was not because the test was unfair, but because the material required a level of detailed knowledge that you rarely have had in other classes;

Distraction: disengaging with current emotions by deliberately focusing attention elsewhere; for example, watching a reality show on TV.

Not all forms of these strategies are necessarily productive:

Situation selection: leaving a crying toddler to go to have a drink at the bar across the road;

Situation modification: stocking the refrigerator with a case of beer;

Reappraisal: deciding that the professor was so unfair in designing the test you failed that it makes no sense for you to study for that class any more;

Distraction: well, watching a reality show on TV.

Movies could be part of any of these strategies.

Situation selection: leaving the stresses of home at home and going downtown with your cheerful friend to see a movie;

Situation modification: instead of continuing an argument with your girlfriend, you decide to go to a Redbox and rent a movie of her choice and watch it together;

Reappraisal: after watching the first half of *Life Is Beautiful*, you decide that the unattainable beauty in your statistics class may not be completely unattainable; you wonder where you can get a green horse;

Distraction: you decide that you need to take a break from studying for exam; you decide to watch *The Notebook* again and have a good cry.

In the psychological literature, there is a tendency to view Situation

Modification and Reappraisal as worthier than Distraction or Situation Selection. But research by Sheppes et al. (2011) suggests that it isn't that simple. These researchers showed participants high intensity and low intensity visual images and looked at the emotional regulation strategies they utilized to minimize their impact. An example of a high intensity image was a photograph of a woman who had been beaten, while the low intensity image was of a woman crying. They found that most participants used distraction when confronted with high intensity images, and used reappraisal when confronted with low intensity images. This suggests that some situations are so serious that a useful reappraisal or an appropriate situation modification may not be immediately possible and may not be possible even over a longer period of time without professional help.

Conclusion

We return to our original question, "Why do we sometimes like sad movies?" We do not have all the answers, but we think that there are several things to consider:

Unlike sad pop songs, which are sad from the beginning to the end of their three-minute length, sad movies are not unrelenting misery. They have their high points. If we didn't care about Guido, the tragedy of *Life Is Beautiful* would be far less compelling. But he has been funny and romantic; he has defied convention in winning Dora's affections and mocked the local government officials and Fascists. He has been brave and has shielded his son from the horrors of a concentration camp. And so there is something uplifting at the same time as genuinely sad and genuinely memorable about the last time over the loudspeaker Guido wishes Dora, "*Buon giorno, principess*," and declares his love for her through highly specific memories of their life together. There have been some unrelentingly sad movies, but they have not been very popular.

A sad film can help us reappraise. However bad we may think our life has become, we are not living in a death camp. And in *Life Is Beautiful*, we are given an exemplar of reappraisal. Not only does he change the camp into a game for his son, he changes the meaning of his own incarceration by seeing his main task that of keeping his son safe and happy, rather than merely surviving at any cost.

Boredom is an emotion that can be changed in many ways. We can seek out amusement, but what we really need is stimulation. We can seek fear (suspense movies) or disgust (graphic horror) or just raw excitement (comic-book action movies). Movies that are filled with romance and tragedy will also do the trick.

An emotion that we have encountered in the psychological literature only once is *aesthetic pleasure*. Tarvainen, Westman and Oittinen (2015) had adults look at clips from 14 movies. All of the clips were complete scenes. Participants rated each clip for its aesthetic features (loud, smooth, tiresome, understandable, etc.), the mood created in each scene, and its beauty and pleasantness. Interest in the clip was strongly related to its rhythm, which was primarily a brisk pace that could be regular or irregular. Beauty and pleasantness were primarily related to the scene being bright. This study indicates that an aesthetic experience is related to wanting to see a movie and, likewise, enjoyment of a movie can be related to aesthetic variables. This is certainly an area that deserves additional attention.

Seeking out an aesthetic experience would not come as a surprise to students of art, literature or music, but apparently it is to psychology and communications professors. Works of art can be enjoyed, whether they are happy or sad or terrifying or thought-provoking, simply because they are beautiful. One does not watch *King Lear* or listen to Beethoven's Ninth Symphony or attend a performance of *La Traviata* merely to get over a sulk. In his work on tragedy, *The Poetics*, Aristotle proposed that we get pleasure out of watching the depiction of realistic human behavior. When that depiction involves an individual who is morally "higher" than average and when a reversal of fortune or a revelation changes her circumstances, we have tragedy. In tragedy, we experience intense fear and pity which leads, Aristotle believed, to **catharsis**. At the end of a work of art, we let go of the built-up emotions, which then allows us to face the challenges of real life with an enriched understanding of the human condition. Freud modified the concept of catharsis in two significant, but not helpful, ways: First, he focused it on the self rather than others: in psychoanalysis, one tries to recreate emotionally intense past events in the patient's life which are seen as the root of present problems. Freud believed that by reliving them in the therapy room, catharsis would occur. Second, Freud posited that such a catharsis would permanently undo the effect of those events. Research has thoroughly discredited this idea.

Key Psychological Terms

Catharsis: A release of pent-up emotions; Aristotle proposed catharsis made us view our situation more humanely; Freud proposed it cured mental illness.

Emotional Regulation: The ability to change aspects of our emotional life through techniques such as situation selection and reappraisal.

Manipulation check: A feature of a research study which assesses whether the independent variable was presented at a level that it could plausibly affect the dependent variable.

Mood: A persistent emotional state.

Mood induction: A research procedure where an activity, not uncommonly watching a movie clip, produces a sudden change in mood.

Reappraisal: An emotional regulation technique that allows a person to reinterpret his or her situation.

Rumination: Repetitive unproductive thinking about one's situation often associated with depression.

Key Cinema Terms

Mood Management Theory: A media theory that suggests we use media, including movies, to maintain a good mood or to create one.

3

The Social Context of Choosing and Viewing Movies

In 1960 in cities across the United States, long lines of fans formed outside of theaters waiting to see the newest Alfred Hitchcock thriller, *Psycho*. The lines were due not only to the popularity of the movie but to a policy that Hitchcock had announced: The theater would be emptied at the end of each showing and only then would the audience for the next showing be seated. No one was to be allowed into the auditorium after the feature began. So, to be sure you got to see the movie, you had to show up early and buy a ticket. And so that you could not overhear part of the ending of the film, you were not allowed to wait in the lobby. This was not a publicity stunt, Hitch assured the evening news: *Psycho* was a film that needed to be seen from beginning to end. And because people were going to be so very frightened, in the larger cities there were ambulances waiting near the lines of excited fans, *just in case*. And on occasion, they were needed. Part of the fun of going to see *Psycho* was waiting in line with others who wanted to see it, speculating what would happen, wondering whether the ambulances would be speeding off with panicked audience members, watching the faces of those leaving the earlier showing, looking for signs of what to expect.

Until very recently, movie-watching was almost always a planned social event, and those you went with affected both what movie you saw and how you experienced it. In the previous two chapters, we reviewed studies that related movie choice to personality and mood. We were struck with how little these factors contributed to what movies people choose. But if you are going to see a movie in a theater, your choice is restricted by what is playing, and if you are going with someone else, your preferences will be compromised by the moods and personalities of those who will be going with you. It is therefore not startling that the relation between one person's personality or mood and what he ends up seeing is small. In this chapter, we will be looking at research on group choice, particularly choices made by couples, and research on how others influence the experience of going to the movies.

Social Decisions

How couples and groups make decisions about what movies to watch has not been studied in much detail. This is surprising, given the economic significance of movies. We know that in romantic couples, the woman more often picks the movie than the man (e.g., Bonds-Raacke, 2005). But what does that mean? Is it entirely up to the woman? Or does the man have a veto? In such studies, large numbers will say that the choice is usually a mutual one. How does that happen? Do they take turns? Are they so much on the same page that they almost always agree and when they do not, they arm wrestle for the choice? Here is a narrative on such a choice which shows how complicated this question is:

> I asked my wife if she'd like to go and see a movie three nights ago. I could tell by her face that she wasn't into it, but she said, "Well, it depends on the movie. Nothing too light and nothing too dark." So, I got online and I found a movie that I thought she would like. I didn't really care. I just wanted to get out of the house for a bit, maybe have dinner. But she wasn't interested. She looked at everything that was playing all around and said, "No, I don't see anything." I knew we could never agree on renting a movie, so I dropped the whole thing, but a few minutes later she came into the study and said, "While I was online, I noticed that *Lincoln* is opening this week. I could see that." So, we went to see Lincoln last night. She likes Daniel Day-Lewis. I like Lincoln.

The Bottom Line Approach

One way of studying decision-making is to skip over process altogether and look at the outcome. This is the way business has historically looked at movies: It does not matter if the decision is made in a five-step process or a 20-step one, the bottom line is the bottom line. This approach is done by gathering national data on how popular movies are and comparing that information to aspects of them that seem to be affecting that popularity. This is not a psychological approach to the question, which would involve individuals or individuals in small groups, but it is one that can help us understand what information the majority of people use when they choose to go to movies. In this kind of analysis, movies are classified by certain qualities they have (e.g., genre, color vs. black-and-white) and these are compared to their incomes.

For example, Desai and Basuroy (2005) looked at two periods, 1991–1993 and 2000, and examined the effect of "genre familiarity," "star power" and critics' reviews on the revenues produced by films. In their analysis, *genre familiarity* referred to whether the movies could be classified as comedies or dramas, which were considered *familiar* genres, because these are the most popular forms of movies. Foreign films, science fiction and horror movies were classified as *unfamiliar* genres. The authors also determined whether the casts featured "big names" or "relative unknowns," based on the salaries of the actors. They also collected a variety of major newspaper reviews and averaged the ratings that the critics gave the films. Most critics will give stars in their reviews: Very bad films may get one star or maybe even a half a star, while great films will get four or five stars. They then developed a formula that accounted for the amount of money each movie made.

For comedies and dramas, neither star power nor critical reviews seemed to matter, but for the unfamiliar genres, star power and critical reviews were important. It was further noted that for movies in the unfamiliar category, if there was no star power, then critical reviews did not seem to matter either. What this indicates is that for comedies and dramas, the studios are wasting their money hiring expensive actors. If the movies are based on a best-seller or a story that people think they would like to see, they can use relatively unknown actors, and they really should not care what the critics say. A case in point would be *The Passion of the Christ* (2004), which had no major stars and got negative reviews from mainstream newspaper critics. People went to see this movie in record numbers. The *Harry Potter* movies, on the other hand, were helped initially by having well-known actors in small roles, because a children's fantasy might not be expected to attract a huge number of adults.

This kind of analysis has its limitations. The *Harry Potter* movies were from an unfamiliar genre, but they were based on the most popular books in the last several decades, and while *The Passion of the Christ* had few known actors in it, it was produced by Mel Gibson, who has star power. Both of these movies got a lot of press attention for various reasons. One reason that people often give for going to the movies—to be able to talk about movies that are being discussed—was not considered in this study. Nor were directors. Nor were special effects. Nor were the advertising campaigns.

In the case of the unknown actors in unfamiliar genres, where reviews seem not to matter, one of the issues might be who the reviewers are. In this case, the data were reviews in major newspapers. But for science fiction films and other specialized genres, many audience members rely on sources for information other than major newspapers. *The Passion of the Christ* was helped by reviews in conservative evangelical publications. Cult science fiction films get a lot of buzz on the Internet today, but that would not have been possible in the period from 1991 to 1993. Limited though this study is, it does tell us that people sometimes choose movies on the basis of the kind of movie it is, the actors, and reviews. Returning to the couple in the vignette above, one chose on the basis of the actors and the other one the theme of the movie.

The Desai and Basuroy (2005) study is limited by the variables the authors chose to look at. They chose the variables that they did because research in earlier decades indicated that star power and newspaper reviews were important variables. They seem to be less important in the 1990s, which is an interesting finding.

* * *

It has long been assumed that one of the main reasons that people are interested in watching a movie has to do with the actors in it. Hitchcock played with his audience in *Psycho* by having the star of the movie, Janet Leigh, killed off just short of midway through, in the famous "shower scene."

Norman Bates (Anthony Perkins) has a pleasant conversation with Marion Crane (Janet Leigh) in *Psycho* **(Universal Studios, 1960).**

Stars of movies don't die in the middle. Up until the shower scene, the movie is a suspense film. Leigh's character, Marion Crane, works for an insufferable boss and is having an affair with a divorced man who lives quite a distance away, in the back of a hardware store. She sees an opportunity to steal money from her boss and heads out of town, only to find herself wracked with guilt. She stops for the night at the Bates Motel, intent on returning home the next day and returning the money. But first she has a little light dinner with the motel's owner, Norman Bates.

Psycho played with viewer expectations in many ways. For many years, movies had been challenging TV with big screens, big casts, long movies and sweeping, epic stories with sweeping epic symphonic musical scores. *Psycho* was shot in black-and-white. The score was entirely for strings. The screen size was not wide, but more like a TV. And the whole genre of the movie changes at midway, from a suspense movie to a horror movie.

The reviewers of *Psycho* in 1960 were not kind. They thought it was violent. They thought it was sleazy. They thought it offended the moviegoer's sensibility. The *Time* reviewer summarized it by saying, "[W]hat is offered instead is merely gruesome. The trail leads to a saggy, swamp-view motel and to one of the messiest, most nauseating murders ever filmed." There was even a toilet flushing. How could a sensation-seeker resist?

* * *

An early study referenced by Desai and Basuroy (2005) was by Litman (1983), who tried to predict revenues on the basis of 1) production costs, 2) genre, 3) critics' ratings, 4) the involvement of a major distributor, 5) Christmas release, and 6) the presence of actors who had been Oscar-nominated or who had received an Oscar. He examined movies in the early 1970s and found that having a major distributor, a Christmas release and high critical ratings were the best predictors of revenue.

Zufryden (1996) looked at a different set of variables—generally those things that distributors do—and found that they, too, predicted box office revenues: amount of advertising dollars spent prior to release, genre, and the number of theaters in which the film opens. Zufryden was taking into account that most movies do most of their business during the first days of their release. He made the assumption that in order to go to a movie, a person first has to be aware of the movie; second, has to decide that he or she wants to see the movie; and third, has an opportunity to see the movie. Since many movies are in major release for only one or two weeks, they can make money only if people know about them in advance (advertising prior to release) and they are shown somewhere near where the people live (opening in many theaters). Genre plays into this analysis because the studios have different expectations about different kinds of movies. Teen comedies have relatively short life cycles, unless they hit big for the first week. Serious dramas are released for longer periods and may profit more from word-of-mouth.

What about critics? Eliashberg and Shugan (1997) examined movies from 1990 to 1993 and looked at how critical reviews correlated with box office receipts early in the release of the movies and later in the release. What they found was that critical reviews only predicted revenues in the later part of a film's release. These authors interpreted their data by suggesting that critics are better at *predicting* box office than *influencing* it: If people went to movies on the basis of reviews, then good reviews should lead to high revenues during the first week.

Wallace, Seigerman and Holbrook (1993) collected reviews on almost 2000 films released between 1956 and 1988 and found that critical reviews predicted box office revenues, but the relationship was U-shaped. Below are two tables. In Table 3.1, we show a traditional positive correlation between reviews and revenues for 20 films. In general, the higher the ratings, the higher the revenue. In this graph, there were two films that got one star, and both of these films made less than $10,000,000. There were five films that got five stars: one made between 30 and 50 million dollars, while four made more than 50 million.

Table 3.1.
The relation between number of "stars" in a critical review and the box office receipts of 20 films showing a positive correlation.

Revenue					
> 50M				1	4
30–50M			2	3	1
10–30M		2	3	1	
< 10M	2	1			
Ratings (stars)	1	2	3	4	5

Table 3.2 show a U-shaped relationship. Here some of the films that got the worst reviews did rather well, while those that got two or three stars did poorly. Those films that got four or five stars also did well. There are always a few films released each year that do very well (e.g., the mega-blockbuster *Titanic*) despite universally terrible reviews. Is it possible that a bad review can make people want to go see a movie?

In a series of laboratory studies, Wyatt and Badger (1984; 1987; 1990) found that the actual ratings of reviews were not as important as the information they convey. If a review is just bad and tells us nothing about the film, we probably will not want to see it, but if the review is bad or mixed, and along the way the reviewer tells us interesting things about the film that pique our curiosity, we might go and see it anyway. Particularly, according to these authors, if it has an actor in it we like. The initial reviews of *Titanic* are instructive. Reviewers thought it made little sense and had been obscenely expensive to make—one reviewer claimed that it cost more than the combined GDPs of the world's 15 smallest countries. But in their grousing about the movie, they mentioned the effectiveness of the special effects. And that Leonardo DiCaprio was the star. Initially, mostly teenage girls who liked Leo went to the movie, but over time, it gained a huge general audience. Fewer and fewer people are getting their information today from critics at big newspapers, and the study of the effect of reviews from the blogosphere has just begun, with confusing results (e.g., Yeap *et al.*, 2012).

Table 3.2.
The relation between number of "stars" in a critical reviews and the box office receipts of 20 films showing a U-shaped relationship.

Revenue	1	2	3	4	5
> 50M	2			1	4
30–50M	2			2	1
10–30M	1	1	2	1	
< 10M		3			
Ratings (stars)	1	2	3	4	5

Studies That Consider Individual Moviegoers

A more psychological approach to studying how people make movie choices was taken by Moller and Karppinen (1983). They approached individuals attending one of four movies (an action-adventure movie, a comedy, a social drama and a pornographic film) in a city in Finland and asked them to fill out a questionnaire which had 15 items describing their motives for going to the movies (e.g., to relax, for excitement, to learn about themselves, to learn about history) and 14 items about the characteristics of movies they usually choose (director, color vs. black-and-white, Finnish vs. foreign). They first examined the whole group of respondents by a statistical technique called Factor Analysis and then used the results of that analysis to see whether they could predict which movies the people had attended.

In brief, Factor Analysis is a method of data simplification that looks at a group of questions to determine which ones are correlated with each other. When a group of questions correlate highly with each other and do not correlate with other questions, they are said to form a factor. The responses to the individual items can be added together and used as a scale. Let's say a researcher asked only six questions about why one goes to the movies. The questions were these:

1. I go to movies to relax.
2. I go to movies to encounter different types of people than those I encounter every day.
3. I go to learn about current events.
4. I like to be amused.
5. I like to look at beautiful actresses or handsome actors
6. I go to movies to unwind from a tough day at work.

The researchers may find that questions 1, 4, and 6 are correlated with each other. And they are not correlated with the other three questions. This would be a factor. These questions can be added together to form a scale that looks at something like "relaxation." The researcher then looks at the remaining questions and finds that questions 2 and 3 correlate with each other, but not with question 5. Questions 2 and 3 can be added together to form a factor that indicates "learning about things." The researcher now has three factors. The first factor has to do with relaxing, unwinding and being amused. The second factor has to do with learning about new things. The third, which consists of only a single item, has to do with looking at beautiful actors and actresses. Instead of having six variables, we now have three. This makes the interpretation of the data simpler.

The 15 motive questions in Moller and Karppinen's study formed four factors. The first consisted of items that measured intellectual curiosity, which included items such as understanding history and understanding one's self. The second had to do with relaxation. The third was labeled "social relationships," which was concerned with whether the movie was popular and being talked about, and the fourth included items such as whether the film had won awards or was in color, which the authors labeled aesthetics.

People who went to the action-adventure movies were found to be high on relaxation, low on aesthetics and intellectual curiosity, while people who attended the social drama were low on relaxation and high on aesthetics and intellectual curiosity. People who went to the comedy were rated high on social relationships and low on intellectual curiosity. Those going to the sex film did not follow a definite pattern; in fact, very few of these customers would fill out questionnaires.

The situation for the movie attributes was similar. There were three factors that came from the Factor Analysis. The first consisted of a combination of items that indicated that some people chose films on the basis of popularity, whether it was in color, and if it didn't have an "arty" director. Not surprisingly, this factor was negatively correlated with the aesthetic factor in the motivation items. People who scored high on this factor chose the comedy or the action-adventure movie. People who liked directors, black-and-white films, and went to films that were not necessarily popular, tended to go to the social drama, and were better educated than other moviegoers. The second factor had to do with whether the film had received a lot of attention in the media and among friends. This correlated with the social relationship motivational factor and predicted who went to the comedy and the action-adventure movie. The final factor had to do with actors and directors. This factor was not particularly useful in predicting which movies the audience members attended, although it negatively correlated with high movie attendance. People who make judgments about what movies to attend on the basis of favorite actors and directors attend fewer movies than those who are less selective in terms of actors and directors.

Tesser, Millar and Wu (1988) did a similar study except that they used college students in a classroom setting. Here three factors emerged: interest in entertainment; interest in self-improvement; and interest in escape. Those who had high entertainment motivations went to movies when they had nothing else to do; at the instigation of friends; and generally went to movies that they had learned about through the media. Those who were high in self-improvement were not influenced by friends, but went to movies to learn about others and to experience strong emotions, and to have resources to talk with others about. Those who had high escape motivations were interested in watching movies to improve bad moods. This last finding provides some support for Mood Management Theory, but it only applied to a segment of those studied.

Gazley, Clark and Sinha (2011) studied a sample of young adults in New Zealand to find out what factors influenced their intentions to see a movie in a theater during its first weeks of release. Comedies and dramas were preferred over other genres. There was a preference for movies based on true stories over fictional stories, and they preferred Hollywood movies to those from New Zealand. They learned about movies more from friends than from critics.

Likewise, Patil and Kumar (1987) studied reasons for going to the movies and movie choices among people in India. These authors examined age, sex and urban vs. rural differences. There were few differences in reasons for going to the movies among the groups. Three-fourths said they went for enjoyment, while about 15 percent indicated they went to learn and 15 percent said they went just to kill time. Of the three types of movies examined, rural women enjoyed romantic movies more than rural men, while rural men preferred epic and historical movies more than women. Few rural men or women were interested in realistic movies. There were no gender differences in the preferences of urban men and women, but overall, urban respondents liked epic and romantic movies equally, while those from rural communities vastly preferred epic and historical movies to romantic ones. Teenagers and young adults preferred romantic movies; older adults preferred realistic movies, while epic and historical movies were preferred by middle-aged respondents.

If we piece together the information from these four studies, and the more bottom-line ones, done at different times, with very different methods, in different countries, we find some interesting parallels. Many people go to the movies to unwind. They like action movies. They like color movies. They don't care much about critical reviews. And while they may have favorite actors, they are not necessarily the most prominent ones. The movie is part of a social occasion with like-minded individuals.

Other people go to movies to learn about themselves and other times and places. They care about reviews, and they have favorite directors and they care about the quality of the films they see. These people tend to be better educated than the average moviegoer. They see a lot of movies, and they go with different people to different kinds of movies.

Still others seem to go to movies because they want to be current, to be able to talk about films with their friends. They want to see films that are being talked about. They want to see movies with the most conspicuous actors in them. And they tend to see comedies. These people have characteristics of extraverts. Their social motivation is being able to talk about current movies after seeing them.

We do not rely much on the direction of critical reviews, but we rely on deciding whether we would like to see a movie on information we have about the movie, which comes from advertising, trailers in theaters, what a critic tells us about a movie, and word of mouth.

Some people go to the movies as a form of escape, or we might want to say, to regulate their emotions.

There are cultural differences in the uses of movies. Some cultures view movies as mindless entertainment. Others view them as serious works of art, among other differences.

The usual ways we talk about people's motivations to go to see films don't seem useful in predicting watching pornography.

Since people have such different reasons for going to movies, some couples are going to have a very hard time deciding which movie to see. If one person wants to view mindless entertainment to relax and the other wants a highbrow aesthetic experience, they may never reach a consensus. This conflict could result in either not going to the movies or adopting a strategy such as alternating choices. Of course, if people have very similar reasons for movie choice, going to the movies may be an effortless and frequent activity for them.

Recommenders

If the Brave New World Techies are correct, it is a good thing we wasted little time studying how people decide which movie to watch because now there's an app for that. Recommenders begin with an individual profile and then adjust as you rate each of the movies you see subsequently. There are now super-apps that will blend individual recommendations to come out with a recommendation of a movie for a group (Hennig-Thurau, Marchand & Marx, 2012).

The upside of these apps is that we will not waste time before a date getting to know the other person's likes or dislikes, their interests or pathologies. We will never have to get out of our comfort zone to discover a new genre of film that might turn out to be our favorite. We can happily repeat our preferences from the time we filled out our profiles. And perhaps the biggest upside is that Hollywood producers and distributors will have immediate access to this information and can start churning out movies with no distinctiveness but which appeal to the largest audience.

The Social Development of Moviegoing

These previous studies do not tell us a great deal about our own moviegoing. We do not think of ourselves as being motivated by "star power" or only going to a movie to relax or to prepare for water cooler conversations at work. When we suggest a movie to friends, we know their preferences and we know our own. We have broad interests in movies. We learn about movies from a variety of media sources and we have colleagues at work and school who are avid moviegoers and they recommend movies to us. Deciding to go to a movie almost always is a social decision, except in watching movies for this book.

The following section describes research that shows how there is not a single way those we see movies with influence us: Much of it depends on age.

Teens Going to the Movies

A few studies give us glimpses into the strange world of adolescent movie viewing and dating. For example, in a study of male celebrity idolization by junior high girls, Engle and Kasser (2005) found that girls who engaged in social activities, which included going to the movies and dating, were more likely to idolize male celebrities. They also found that these girls were more likely to like and trust boys than those who did not idolize celebrities and that these girls were more likely to spend money on their idolization of these male celebrities, including going to see their movies repeatedly and buying DVDs of their movies.

But do junior high school girls idolize male celebrities because they have seen them in movies or do they go to see their movies because they idolize them? This research cannot tell us. It also does not tell us whether the junior high school girls who are dating become more interested in boys or whether junior high school girls who are interested in boys start dating early. Because of the way the questions were asked, we do not know whether these girls go to see films featuring their idolized male actors on dates or with groups of girlfriends. But the authors suggest that one universal reason to go to the movies is to see their idol in romantic encounters with young women. These romantic encounters become scripts, or *mental representation of activities*, which form these young women's ideas about what dating and romance should be. For example, what should happen on a first date? Should you kiss and hold hands? What do people talk about on dates? How do you know if the two of you are meant for each other?

Asking a very different kind of question, Hur, McGue and Iacome (1996) looked at male adolescents' overall leisure activities to determine which kinds of activities might have a genetic basis. They examined the leisure activities of 100 identical (monozygotic) twins and 90 fraternal (dizygotic) twins. Through statistical analyses, they were able to determine the effects of genetics, shared environments and non-shared environments. **Shared environments** are usually the family and the school, while **non-shared environments** are the things that an individual chooses for himself alone (such as being part of the drama club or running track). The authors found that some leisure activities are closely linked to genetics. These were activities that were highly similar in the monozygotic twins, but far less so in the dizygotic twins. These activities usually involved a skill. Drawing, athletics, music and hunting are examples. Dating, watching TV and going to the movies were not very much related to genetics. In fact, they were related to both shared and non-shared environments. These results suggest that developing an interest in going to the movies is both related to the habits of the family you grow up in (for twins, their shared environment) and the circle of friends and the activities you choose (for twins, their non-shared environments).

In the past, parents selected the movies that their children watched. Parents still play a significant role in early adolescent dating experiences and in their choice of films, at least some of them, but this role has not been studied in detail. Many parents closely monitor what movies and TV programs their children watch, activate restrictions on cable access, go with their children to see films in theaters, and enforce definite rules about dating, including the age of first date. Other parents do not. As we will see in Chapter 7, many young teenagers report seeing dozens of R-rated films and even X-rated films. They often give researchers very immature reactions to these films, suggesting that they have watched them without their parents. A good deal more research is necessary on early exposure to movies and other media, both in terms of how it affects us emotionally and how it helps shape us as future consumers of media.

College Students

College students are the largest consumers of movies in theaters, and more than half of the time college students go to the movies, they consider it a date. It would therefore be of interest to those who make and distribute movies to learn about how dating couples in college determine what they see on a date.

This is easier said than done. Ross and Davis (1996) found that there are ethnic and socioeconomic differences in dating. In their study, which examined only two campuses, African-Americans and students from lower income families held the expectation that whoever pays for the date, usually the man, according to their "script," determines the activities on a date, while whites and students from higher income families, who believed that it was okay for the woman to pay or for the couple to go Dutch, thought that the activities on a date should be negotiated, regardless of who paid.

We also believe at least two kinds of dating need to be considered: early dates in a relationship and dates by committed couples. Early in a relationship, going to the movies may serve as a **filter**. Your date's choice of a movie and his or her reaction to it may tell you something about whether the relationship is going to work out. Robert Udry (1971) described a series of such filters in determining a romantic relationship. The first filter is that there has to be some meeting. Since Udry's research was published more than 45 years ago, he didn't consider people meeting over the Internet. Several studies of Internet relationships, however, have found that a movie is one of the most common ways in which people who have met on the Internet first come together face to face (see Sharabi & Caughlin, 2017). The second filter is physical attractiveness. The remaining filters deal with such things as similarity in interests and activities, social backgrounds and beliefs. You may meet someone who you find physically attractive, but in trying to arrange the first movie date, you might discover that there is something you don't like: he likes violent horror films or French films from the 1960s. Your date may insist on seeing his or her kind of movie, without taking your ideas into consideration. These situations might suggest you will have a difficult time finding compatible things to do in the future. If you do find a movie that you want to see together, in discussing it afterwards, your date may express cultural or religious or political opinions that make you aware that you either share significant attitudes and beliefs or that you do not.

In contrast to first or early dates in a relationship, deciding on a movie later in a relationship is a very different process and serves a different purpose. It is not a filtering process. You know your partner's likes and dislikes, and rather than trying to learn about your partner, you are looking for something enjoyable to do together. As mentioned earlier, when asked who made the decision in studies of couples who have been dating for some time, participants generally say that the decision was a mutual one rather than saying that one or the other had made the decision. In a study that we conducted on this topic, we asked for a narrative of how a movie was decided on. A typical scenario for committed couples was:

> I saw that *Batman v Superman* had opened downtown. We both like Marvel, so I figured that this was one we wouldn't have any arguments over, so I called him at work and we decided to go that night.
>
> This might be compared to a scenario that was reported about a first date:
>
> We were talking after class one day and Greg asked me if I'd like to go to see a movie. We were both in education classes, so I thought that we'd have something in common, and I said, sure, give me a call, and I gave him my cell number. He called three times and each time he suggested a movie I didn't want to see. He likes the guys-with-guns kind of movies. The fourth time, he asked me to pick a movie. By then I knew what he liked, at least a little, and I thought I could tolerate *World War Z*. It was okay. He loved it. I doubt if we'll be going out any more.

One of the main findings from our study of giving to a charity after the movies, described in Chapter 2, was that it mattered less what movie the couples had been attending than what stage they were in their relationship. Men going to the movies with male friends or committed partners, women going with female friends, first or second dates, or committed partners made a donation to charity less than 20 percent of the time, regardless of what film they had seen, but men on a first or second date made a donation 74 percent of the time. Maybe they were trying to impress their dates.

Harris *et al.* (2004) conducted two studies of romantic movie-watching on dates among college students. The first study surveyed a large group of students individually, the second study surveyed a smaller group of couples who filled out questionnaires independently about the same date. The findings of the two approaches to collecting data found very similar results. Overall, about half of the students reported that the woman had chosen the movie; less than ten percent indicated that it had been the man's choice, and the remainder indicated that it had been a joint or group decision. About two-thirds of the couples went to the movie alone, with about 15 percent going with another couple and ten percent going with a group.

This study confirms and challenges some of our stereotypes about male and female viewership and our ideas about what are "women's films." Women cried more at the movie (over a third of women and only six percent of men), but about ten percent of both men and women said they felt like crying but held it in. Women also laughed more than men. About a fifth of the men wished they had watched another movie, but so did eight percent of the women. Both men and women, however, thought most men would not like the movie they had seen or movies like it. The authors also asked the participants which scene they would like to be in. Both men and women chose what was described as a romantic scene involving cuddling and kissing. While men guessed that their date would like to be in a romantic scene, more women thought that their date would choose a sex scene.

In 2014, we saw a newspaper cartoon strip that might be the prototype of future movie-dating. In it, the father says to his son, stretched out on the sofa with his phone and laptop, that he thought he was going to be hanging out with his girlfriend. The son replies that he is. They are both at their respective homes, texting, while streaming the same movie. When we first saw this cartoon in 2014, we thought it was funny. Now, we understand students who are in long-distance relationship do this routinely. As Jeremy comments in the last frame of the strip, "The malt shop closed a long time ago, Archie."

Married couples

Research has shown that decision-making among married couples is different from that of dating couples. Aash and Byers (1990) found that those early in a dating relationship and married couples engaged in fewer activities, including going to the movies, than couples who had been dating for a long time.

Matzkin (1999) interviewed older married couples at an expensive film festival in Philadelphia. The husbands and wives in this study were highly successful and highly educated, most over 40, few with children still living in the home. The study divided participants into two groups. One group saw movies at least weekly, while the others saw movies only once or twice a month. The frequent moviegoers were different from the occasional moviegoers. The frequent moviegoers had a wide range of interests in movies. They talked about the movies before they went and afterwards. They saw art films and "summer sillies." They did not like renting videos. They picked movies based on directors. They said there was pressure among their friends to see certain films. They reported little conflict in their discussions about what movies to see. They said they rarely saw films with other people, and when they did, the social requirements caused a lot of stress for the woman. One interviewee said that having friends along made it difficult even deciding where to sit in the theater. The wife generally had read reviews in newspapers and magazines, even though negative reviews did not keep them from seeing some films. These individuals tended to be politically liberal.

The occasional moviegoers (although it must be remembered that they had attended a movie festival that cost several hundred dollars) reported much more conflict in deciding what movies to attend and rarely talked about them afterwards. The husbands tended to want to see an action movie "to unwind" while the wives tended to want to see "something of substance." The wives also did not want to see slapstick comedies, while the husbands did not want to see gay-themed movies. Most were politically conservative, and they picked movies based on actors. The wives tended to be the one who suggested a compromise, and the women were also likely to see films occasionally with women friends.

Bonds-Raacke (2004) studied 26 married couples selecting a movie and a restaurant. In selecting the movie, she showed them clips for six movies that were about to be released. There were two dramas, two science fiction films, and two romantic comedies. One of each genre had major movie stars in it, while the other did not. The participants first selected their preference after seeing the clips, and then the couple made a decision on which one they wanted to see.

There were substantial differences in the ways the couples went about making the decision, and their ways of selecting the movie was not at all the same as the way they selected the restaurant. About a fourth of the couples, when making their individual choice, selected the same movie. Their decision-making processes were direct and short. A larger number were able to choose a genre, but differed over whether major stars were important. About a fourth of couples arrived at their choice differently from anyone else. So, basic agreement in the beginning simplifies the process of making a decision.

Older Singles Dating

With half of first marriages ending in divorce, and other marriages ending because of the deaths of spouses, there are large numbers of single people over the age of 60 in the U.S. McElhaney (1992) reviewed a number of studies and suggested that going to the movies is a common dating experience for older singles, along with visiting family, playing cards, going to dinner, and attending church functions. Older adults, however, report difficulty in finding movies they would like, as most of them want to avoid violence, overt sexuality and obscene language.

Cohort Effects

We need to be cautious about accepting the previous material as being entirely a function of age—for example, that in young adult dating couples, it is the woman who chooses the movie or that older people have difficulty finding movies that do not have too much sex and violence. These findings are just as likely to be the result of a **cohort effect**. A cohort effect has to do with the generation you were born in. So, in 2020, the attitudes and beliefs of those who will be 70 years old are both reflective of the fact that they are 70, but also because they spent their childhood during the 1950s, their adolescence in the 1960s, and their young adult years during the 1970s. Their socialization into the movies as children was mostly to go to theaters. Teens in the 1960s consumed vast quantities of network television. When this generation was in college and establishing careers as young adults in the 1970s, there were substantial changes in what could be shown and said on the screen. It is likely that this generation will still like to go to the theater to see movies, but also be comfortable with watching movies on TV. They might be more tolerant of profanity and nudity in films than previous generations of senior citizens, because they have known movies with nudity and profanity most of their lives. The next cohort, those who become 70 in 2030, may have been socialized to watching movies on screens that theaters will drift off to becoming things of the past.

"Snuggle Theory"

Zillmann and Weaver (1996) proposed that horror movies can serve a function in the development of sex-role behavior in adolescents and young adults. They suggested that young men learn to display protectiveness and bravery, while young women learn to display protective need and fearfulness. Although these behaviors rarely are needed in contemporary society, and when they are, both men and women should be brave and protective, horror movies give people opportunities to practice traditional sex-roles. Displaying these behaviors is seen to be pleasurable, and the members of the dating couple reinforce each other for doing so. These ideas have merited the irreverent nickname of **snuggle theory**.

The theory was based on research these authors had conducted a decade earlier (Zillmann *et al.*, 1986). In the main part of the study, the researchers showed a gruesome 15-minute sequence from *A Nightmare on Elm Street 3* to male and female participants who watched it in the presence of an opposite sex confederate. The confederates displayed one of three verbal and nonverbal reactions to the film:

1. *Mastery*, which consisted of being very relaxed during the clip and cheering the victims on to take up weapons and defend themselves;

2. *Indifference*, which consisted of the confederate being still and silent during the clip; and

3. *Distress*, during which the confederate fidgeted and verbalized with fear and disgust at the actions in the film.

Women found the movies more enjoyable when their male confederate exhibited mastery than when he showed distress. They also rated the confederate more attractive and indicated a higher interest in dating him when he showed mastery rather than indifference or distress. Conversely, men enjoyed the movie better and rated the female confederate more attractive when she showed distress.

While this is interesting and supports the theory (as it should, as the theory was based upon it), watching a 15-minute clip isn't watching a whole movie and sitting in a laboratory next to a stranger who is pretending to have a specific kind of reaction to the movie clip isn't a date. But studying real dates presents both logistical and ethical issues.

One alternative is to ask people to remember a real situation. Harris *et al*. (2000) asked a group of college students to recall going to see a frightening movie on a date. Ninety-seven percent could do so. They asked a number of questions about the context of the date, their reactions to the movie and their date's, and the long-term consequences of seeing the movie. They related this information to the usual suspects of personality measures: empathy, sensation-seeking and sex-role orientation, as well as their reactions after the movie.

Most of the movies seen were R-rated. Thirty-seven percent indicated that the movie had been *Scream* or *Scream 2*. About half of the dates had been in a theater and 96 percent of the dates had taken place in the evening or at night. Half of the men and a third of the women said that the date consisted of only themselves and their dates, but about 40 percent said that they attended with a group. Eighteen percent of the men said they had picked the movie, while 13 percent of the women indicated they had.

During the movie, men and women had very different reactions. Both men (53 percent) and women (67 percent) felt their hearts beating fast and about a fourth of each group indicated that they had tried not to show how scared they were. Fright reactions were more common among women. For example, 32 percent said they screamed, while only six percent of males recalled screaming. Men were more likely to be entertained (59 percent vs. 41 percent)

A large number of individuals reported longer term consequences of the movie. Forty-four percent of the men and 61 percent of the women reported feeling fearful or anxious; eight percent of the men and 19 percent

The final, lingering image in *Psycho*'s shower scene (Universal Pictures, 1960).

of the women indicated they had been afraid to sleep alone; and six percent of the men and four percent of the women reported insomnia.

* * *

Psycho is not a movie made to be watched alone. Not that it is so frightening that it will result in unrelenting terror, but that the half dozen jolts that occur in it are more fun when shared. Whether snuggling with a romantic partner or sharing moments with friends, the experience of *Psycho* is better with others.

Psycho is also a movie designed to be talked about afterwards. Why does Norman kill Marion? What provokes him to become his mother? Will Marion's sister and her boyfriend hit it off?

* * *

These three chapters have reviewed psychological research on how we select movies. There are individual processes, such as personality, sex, age and mood, as well as social factors—who you are going with, what movies people you know are talking about, and which movies are available. Personality, mood, age and social context have been examined mostly in isolation, and in isolation they account for little. In combination, they may be more powerful. You may not be predisposed toward sci-fi movies, but if someone you want to spend time with wants to see that kind of movie and you are a little bored, you may go. Likewise, while you normally see all of the Marvel movies, if during the week of the newest one's release at your local theater, you're under a lot of stress at school and your usual moviegoing partner is out of town, you may put it off.

We also note hints in the literature about viewing history that have not been studied. How were movies regarded in your family? Were they seen merely as escapist entertainment or were they regarded as serious works of art? Were you told that movies were bad for you? Did you watch movies with your whole family and if so, were those times of fun and intimacy or was everyone doing their own thing? Did you grow up with the Turner Classic Movies channel or the Sundance Channel? Did you grow up in a community where there was a theater that showed classic and independent films? Did you fall in with a group of Film Studies majors in college? Have you been in a serious relationship where you disagreed about movies and in discussions (arguments?) about them you clarified your values toward cinema and life. These are all issues that could be productively explored, not only helping to understand movie preference but how personality interacts with mood and the social world in a context that is not pathological and how developmental processes play out in one area of choice and interaction.

Much remains to be learned.

Key Psychological Terms

Factor Analysis: A data reduction statistical procedure that groups items in a scale together to form coherent subscales.
Filter: In a relationship, a filter is a psychological process that prevents or allows the relationship's progress.
Non-shared environments: Activities that siblings do by themselves and do not share with their brothers or sisters.
Scale: A group of items on a test or survey that are treated as a single score
Script: A mental representation of an action, such as how a date is supposed to occur.
Shared environments: Activities that siblings have in common.

Key Cinema Terms

Recommenders: Phone apps that make recommendations about movies, restaurants, etc.

Snuggle theory: The idea that some kinds of movies give modern audiences opportunities to act out traditional sex roles.

PART II

Experiencing the Movie

We have chosen a movie and we are now in the theater, or elsewhere, to experience it. We attend to the screen and to the soundtrack and assemble the bits of information we receive into a coherent narrative. We evaluate the characters; we anticipate what will happen next; we experience excitement or fright or sadness or disgust. We sometimes change our mind about what is happening or whether the characters are good or bad; honest or scheming; smart or insipid; brave or cowardly. We often leave the theater with a sense of having been on a meaningful adventure, of having learned something about human nature.

The first chapter in this section examines how the visual and auditory systems extract information from a film, while the following chapter uses principles of learning to examine how movies manipulate our emotions and give us new beliefs, attitudes and behavior, particularly through the combined use of visual images and music. This section's final chapter uses cognitive psychology to help us understand how we put together the various bits of sight and sound in a movie to come away with a coherent narrative.

Most of the research described in this section is not directly about movies, but it sheds light on how we process a movie. For example, in the 1970s there was a lot of funding available to study how children watched TV. While the way we watch a TV at home or in a laboratory is clearly different than how we behave in a darkened theater in front of a large screen, there are similarities and, more and more, we watch movies on TV and computer screens. There is also a good deal of information on how we search images, from photographs to digital displays, and this also tells us something about how we look at movies. Finally, there is a lot of research on how we put together information from text to get a whole story, but there is far less information about developing a coherent narrative from a movie, although, with some exceptions, there are many similarities in the processes.

A limitation of the research that *is* about movies is that psychologists have rarely studied whole movies: They tend to rely on short clips, sometimes edited, or at best whole scenes. Movies normally take two hours, but psychology experiments normally last an hour or less: so, it is impossible to include a whole movie. That's a shame: Watching *Psycho*'s "shower scene" out of context is a different experience than viewing it midway through the movie and then having the opportunity to see where the events take us.

4

Sensation and Perception

Rear Window (1954) is a film about watching; about paying attention and having lapses in attention; about forming a narrative from bits and pieces of observations. According to many critics, *Rear Window* is about going to the movies.

The movie is shot on just one set, a Greenwich Village apartment in which a photographer, "Jeff" Jeffries (James Stewart) is confined, after he was run over by a car in a race he was photographing. He has a broken leg and is in a wheelchair. He amuses himself by watching what is going on in the courtyard outside the rear window of the apartment. Inside his apartment, during three very hot days, he is visited by an insurance nurse, a policeman with whom he flew in World War II, and his girlfriend, played by Grace Kelly. Outside, he observes the comings and goings of his neighbors in nine apartments.

To the left are two apartments, one rented by newlyweds above the apartment of a middle-aged woman. Directly behind him are two buildings. One is two stories. On the ground floor is a middle-aged sculptor, who sometimes lounges in the courtyard. Above her is "Miss Torso," a dancer who entertains many male friends. On the roof of this little building, the two women who live on the fourth floor of the larger apartment building next-door sunbathe. On the third floor of the larger apartment building are an older couple who have a dog and who sleep on the fire escape at night. Below them live a salesman and his invalid wife, who are frequently arguing. The salesman also gardens in the courtyard. On the ground floor is a middle-aged woman who fantasizes about having a boyfriend. In the penthouse on the building to the right, a composer drinks too much. Additionally, pigeons flutter in and out, and between the small building at the back and the building to the left, is a passageway, where we see pedestrian and motor traffic, children skipping rope and people from the apartments coming and going. Sometimes in this film, we see all of these places at one time. At other times, the photographer takes his camera with a telephoto lens and looks at a small part of this overall

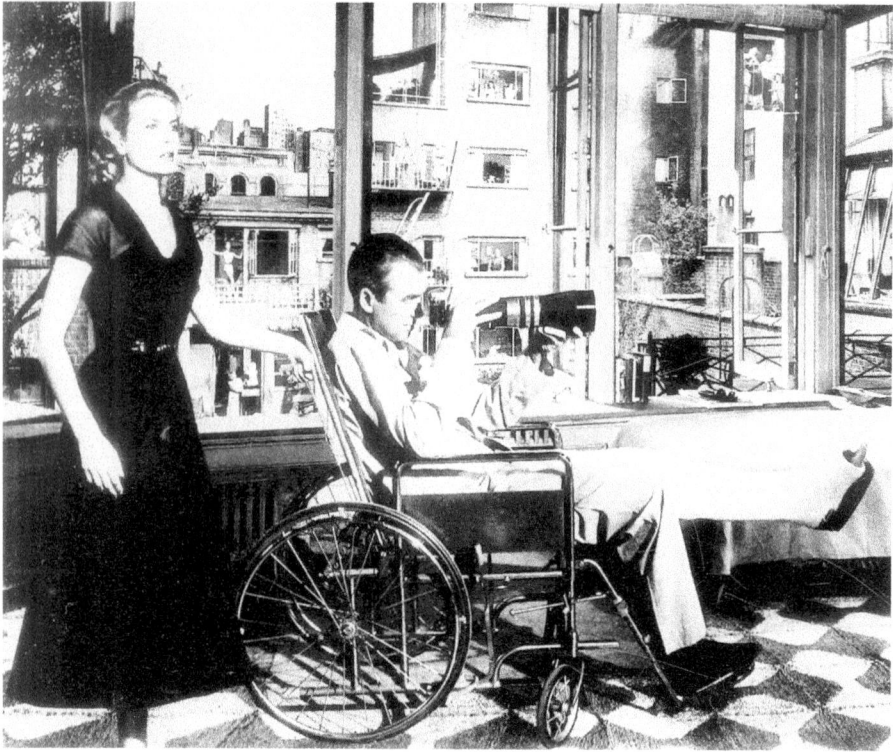

A publicity shot showing Lisa (Grace Kelly) and Jeff (James Stewart) in Jeff's Greenwich Village apartment overlooking its courtyard. *Rear Window* was entirely shot on this set (Universal Pictures, 1954).

picture. We move back and forth from extremely complex images to very simple ones. Maybe Jeff has seen evidence of a murder.

* * *

We have decided to see a movie, found people to go with us, and we have selected a movie. Now we go into a theater and watch the film, or we rent or stream it. Usually there is a lot to see and hear in a movie, and we take in *some* of this information. We do not take it all in, but normally we take in enough of it to make some sense of the storyline, to make judgments about the characters, and to come out of the movie experience either liking or not liking it, probably with our mood changed. In this chapter, we will discuss four issues: 1) how attentive are we to the movie; 2) where do we look for information when we are looking at the movie screen?; 3) how does movement figure into all of this?, and 4) how much information do we actually extract from the screen? We will also consider how different watching a movie is from our everyday experience of looking about our normal environment. But first we will consider a topic that has something "Urban Myth" about it: subliminal perception.

Selling Popcorn: A Very Short History of Subliminal Seduction

Films are projected at 36 frames per second. The reasons for this is that if there are fewer frames, there is a feeling of "flicker." Silent films were projected at fewer frames per second, and if you see one of them projected in a theater, you do see characters moving smoothly, but you are aware of the rapid flickering on and off of the images as they are projected on the screen.

The fact of the matter is, you can cut out one frame, replace it with something else, and you will not be aware of the inserted frame. You will see the action on the screen in an uninterrupted flow. The information from that one frame, however, will be projected onto the retina of your eyes and makes its way in some form to your brain. But not to the conscious area of the brain. The information contained in one added frame is said to be **under threshold**, that is, it *is under the minimum amount of exposure to make its way to conscious experience.* The technical term for this is **subliminal. Limen** is another term for threshold.

It is important to distinguish between images in films that are under threshold and those that are simply not noticed. If a filmmaker took out one frame of a movie and replaced it with another image, it is *impossible* to become consciously aware of what is in that one frame. No matter how hard you try, you cannot see it. Viewing it over and over will not help. Knowing what to look for will not help, either.

This is very different from something occurring in the film that you fail to notice. For example, music may be very quietly playing in the background as two actors talk. It is completely possible for you to hear that music if you chose to listen for it. But what the actors may be saying or doing is so much more engaging that most people are not conscious of the music. If you decide to listen to the background music, you may find yourself not really paying attention to what the characters are saying. There is a lot going on in a movie, and our consciousness is limited. In fact, research in the 1950s indicated that we can only hold about seven bits of information in our memory at one time (Miller, 1956). We often are amazed when we watch the credits after a movie at the number of songs that are listed. We don't remember hearing many of them because we were paying attention to something else. The same goes for visual images. If you are looking attentively at one part of the screen, you may not notice what is going on elsewhere.

In the 1950s, when American psychology was under the influence of many of Freud's ideas, psychologists were very interested in subliminal messages. Freud believed that the most powerful forces that influenced behavior were unconscious, and therefore it seemed reasonable that subliminal messages might be very powerful. There is reason to believe that in some movie trailers and popcorn ads, verbal prompts (BUY POPCORN or SEE *REAR WINDOW*) were placed subliminally, and it was hoped that they would make people want to buy popcorn or see the next movie. A few filmmakers have allegedly put individual graphic images of sex or violence into their films to arouse or frighten their audiences. People working for George W. Bush were accused of doing this in one of his negative ads against John Kerry in the 2004 presidential campaign. Some advertisers still believe that subliminal messages are an effective way of selling their products.

The good news is that subliminal selling doesn't work that well. While a subliminal message does get to the brain, its effect is very weak. And most psychologists believe that a single presentation of a message in words makes no difference at all (Cuperfain & Clarke, 1985). So moviemakers could insert BUY POPCORN or VOTE FOR GEORGE W. BUSH or KILL YOUR PARENTS with no effect. These messages would go to the left half of the brain where words are processed, but the left hemisphere doesn't seem to process subliminal messages very aggressively. Pictures, on the other hand, may make more of an impression, because these are largely processed in the right hemisphere, and there, subliminal messages have a larger effect, although not a very big one. But it would take multiple presentations for it to influence very many people's behavior, and images do not affect everyone the same way. Suppose that the image put in was an actor eating popcorn. Research indicates that this might make you a little more likely to think about buying popcorn *if you particularly liked that actor*. If you disliked that actor, you might be *less* likely to buy popcorn.

So why do we buy popcorn when we go to the movies? It's probably mostly due to the smell of the popcorn in the lobby. In the movie theater where we go most often, you buy your tickets about three feet away from the concession stand. You smell popcorn. You are standing there with your change in your hand. It's easy to say *yes* when the young woman behind the concession stand asks you if you want anything, particularly if she's attractive and you would like a short interaction with her. Most buying takes place prior to going into the auditorium, not after watching the trailers for the next movie.

Attention

In order to "see" a movie, the first thing one has to do is actually look at the screen. In truth, we know next to nothing about paying attention to movies in theaters, but most of us have had the unpleasant experience of sitting near someone who was not paying much attention. So we know that not everyone is looking at the screen all the time. It would be very difficult to study this behavior in a real theater situation. But there has been a good amount of research on attention regarding television viewing, and we will summarize this research. Certainly, this research is relevant to the situation when we watch a movie in our own home. But at the end of this section we will describe some cautions about the **ecological validity**, or the *ability to draw conclusions in a different context*, of these data when it comes to watching movies in theaters.

Watching TV

Anderson and Burns (1991) in a review of research up to that time conclude that attention to the TV screen is "highly variable." Some viewers look away from the screen hundreds of times per hour, while at times they watch the screen for long periods. Other viewers are more attentive, but there are things about the program they are watching that will make them turn their attention elsewhere. For both children and adults, most looks at the TV screen are short (less than one minute). But when total time of looking is examined, most of the time is accounted for by the relatively infrequent longer looks. Overall, viewers are not looking at the screen about a third of the time, although in actual TV viewing, participants look at commercials considerably less than the program, so they look at the program more than two-thirds of the time.

Listening to TV

Unlike visual attention, we are constantly exposed to the soundtrack of a TV program, unless we physically leave the room or "mute" the TV. Yet there is evidence that we pay attention to the sound at higher or lower levels. Children seem to pay more attention to the soundtrack when they are looking at the TV. We know this because when asked to recall sound information from TV programs, preschool children remember the information better when they were looking at the screen than when they were not. The same effect has been found for middle school children, although the differences in their recall for when they were looking and when they were not was smaller than for younger children (Field & Anderson, 1985). Yet young children seem to be paying attention at some level even when not visually attending to the screen, as specific auditory cues (such as children's voices and music) recapture their full visual attention immediately (Alwitt, Anderson, Lorch & Levin, 1980).

Environmental Distractions

Again, most of the studies in this area involve children. When there are other children present (Anderson, Lorch, Smith, Bradford & Levin, 1981), or when there are other distractions, such as toys (Pezdek & Stevens, 1984), children look less at the screen than when they are alone and in relatively quiet, uninteresting environments. If children are watching TV in a group and one stops paying attention to the screen, others will follow. This would imply that in a social situation, we are not only paying attention to the screen but, at least occasionally, checking to see what others are doing. Although there is no published research on the topic, it is reasonable to think that if you are on a date at the movies, you visually check in with your date occasionally. If your date is focused on the screen, this may refocus you on the movie, while if he or she is not paying attention to the movie, this may take your visual attention elsewhere. Your auditory attention will still be seeking cues about when you need to return to look at the film.

Individual Differences

Research on differences in looking at TV have examined sex, age and intelligence. Beyond these demographics, people seem to have an "attentional style." As mentioned above, some people look away from the screen frequently, while others look away less often but for longer periods. Regardless of other conditions, this attentional style appears to play a role in looking at and away from the screen. A friend of ours did a series of studies in the 1990s with a colleague where they needed to watch films intently, taking detailed notes. They began by working at the colleague's house, but he was always getting up and doing other things (making phone calls or going to the kitchen to get a drink of water). His notes were very incomplete. After a while, our friend decided that they should watch the movies at his house, but his colleague kept finding books on the bookshelves he wanted to look at or stopped the process by asking questions about anything that went through his head. Even when they went to watch a movie in the theater, the colleague was much less "on task" than our friend was. Over the last two decades in psychology, we have been interested in a phenomenon called attention-deficit/hyperactivity disorder (ADHD), where some individuals are disabled in their educational and social activities because of an "inattentive attentional style." These individuals seem incapable of sustained attention across many tasks. While our friend's colleague did not have ADHD, his ability to sustain attention was certainly less than desirable for the task. ADHD is probably an extreme form of attentional style, but the rest of us vary in our basic rate of attention. On the other end of the continuum, individuals with Obsessive/Compulsive Disorder and some forms of autism become so attentive to one thing that they cannot pay attention to anything else.

Sex. In a study of watching television in the home, Anderson, Lorch, Field, Collins and Nathan (1986) found that there were no differences in attention between boys and girls, but that adult men paid more attention to the screen than adult women. Alvarez, Huston, Wright and Kerkman (1988), however, found that male participants, at all ages, watch the screen more than female participants in a laboratory setting, but the differences were relatively small. There have been a number of other studies which have reached the same conclusion: Other things being equal, men and boys watch the screen more than women and girls. Researchers tend to find larger differences between the sexes, particularly for adults, when they look at "natural" TV watching at home. What appears to be happening is that when there are others around, female participants attend more to their social surroundings than males do, and that this social attention draws them away from the screen.

This finding might suggest that for men and women on a movie date, their definitions of the event are different. Women define going to the movies as a date, and spend some of their time attending to their companion and some of their time attending to the screen, while males may more often define the event as "watching a movie" and be more attentive to the screen. This is more or less a guess, but it seems to be supported by anecdotal responses on our surveys about movie dating. One male respondent wrote:

> If I'm going to see a movie I really want to see, I don't like to go on a date. I'd rather go with some of my guy friends or watch it by myself at home. On a date, my girlfriend keeps asking me questions. That doesn't bother me when I'm not all that interested in the movie, but it drives me crazy when it's a movie I've been look forward to seeing.

Age. Infants do not attend to a TV screen very often but attention increases dramatically until age five. Attention levels off during the school years and declines gradually into adulthood (Anderson *et al.*, 1986). This pattern as been found in both home and laboratory studies, looking at a wide variety of different kinds of material.

Intelligence. A number of studies (e.g., Anderson & Burns, 1991; Grieve & Williamson, 1977) have found that children with intellectual disabilities do not pay attention to the television screen as much as do average and above-average children, and above-average children pay somewhat more attention than their average intelligence counterparts. These studies have used educational programming as their focus.

Content

What we are looking at influences how intently we pay attention to it. There are some features of a television program that grab our attention: changes in scenes; the onset of certain kinds of music; loud noises; and, for children, the presence of child voices (Alwitt, Anderson, Lorch & Levin, 1980; Wakshlag, Reitz & Zillman, 1982). Other things seem to be conducive to our losing attention: long scenes where very little visually interesting happens, fadeouts that usually signal the end of a scene, and, for children, the presence of adult voices.

Among its many other functions, music may help us pay attention to certain aspects of movies. Boltz, Schulkind and Kantra (1991) conducted a study in which college students watched sequences from movies and TV programs and were later asked to recall as much as they could. Some of the sequences were positive, others negative. An example of a "positive" sequence is a brother and sister have just been reunited. He takes her upstairs to the attic and blindfolds her for a surprise. The surprise is a cabinet full of family memorabilia. A "negative" sequence would be a man breaks into a government computer and finds his name on a dangerous list. Music was provided either accompanying the action or before the action. Music provided before the action is called **foreshadowing**. Finally, the music was either congruent with the mood or incongruent. For example, as the blindfolding turned out to be before a pleasant surprise, if the music had been sad (made up of slow, minor keyed tunes played on low instruments), it would be considered incongruent, while if it had been upbeat and happy, it would be considered congruent. There was also a control condition where participants watched the sequences without music.

The findings regarding memory were complex. Music enhanced memory for the sequence, compared to the no-music controls, if **accompanying music** was congruent; while music enhanced memory for the sequence if **foreshadowing music** was incongruent. So, in the example of the blindfold, memory was enhanced if negative (incongruent) music was used in the beginning of the sequence, while it was also enhanced if happy (congruent) music accompanied the taking-off of the blindfold to see the memorabilia. The authors interpreted the findings to suggest that with the accompanying music, the music guided the audience's attention to the right information. The music suggests this is a happy scene, so the audience paid attention to details that confirmed it. In the case of foreshadowing, the authors suggested that the incongruent music set up certain expectations (something bad will happen in the attic) and when it does not, we remember the ending as a surprise. Research consistently shows that we pay more attention to things that violate our expectations than things that do not. For example, when someone is behaving normally, we generally encode what they are doing in large units (the secretary is typing), but when someone is violating what we expect, we pay attention to smaller details of her behavior (the secretary is putting on very red lipstick and blotting it with a paper tissue she got from her blue pocketbook).

Organizing Principles

In looking at this overview of TV-watching, mostly of research on children watching educational TV, there are four organizing principles:

Individuals have a characteristic attentional style. Across different kinds of viewing, this style will influence how attentive people are to the screen, although what the person is watching will modify to some degree their looking at the screen. This may be based on a biological difference, as in the case of persons with ADHD, or it may be something that is learned. If you watch children and parents together at movies, some parents ignore their children's inattention, while others will redirect their children's attention to the screen.

Two psychological constructs are helpful in understanding why we look away from the screen or not. At first glance, these two constructs seem to be contradictory, but they are complimentary. The first idea is **habituation**, the tendency to lose attention to any stimulus. The classic example is, as you are going to sleep, you hear the faucet dripping. It drips regularly. You think for a moment that you will never be able to fall asleep, and then you fall asleep, because you have habituated to the sound. Let's say that a filmmaker wants to show that a couple's relationship has reached a point where they have very little interest in each other. They are sitting next to each other on a train. The camera does not move. The characters do not talk. There is nothing going on around them. It is a long shot, where nothing happens. At some point, most of us will look away from the screen. Habituation has to do with the specific image on the screen. If the screen is full of movement, if the story is being told by a series of different camera shots, if there is interesting music in the background, if the characters are saying interesting things, we will not look away. We habituate only if what we are receiving is the same, constant sensory input. A corollary of habituation is **dishabituation.** This process takes place if something changes in the stimulus situation: Our attention is drawn back. If the dripping of the water becomes faster, we will start to attend to it again. In our scene of two people on a train, if one starts to talk or if one of them would take out a pistol and shoot himself in the head, we would look back. Dishabituation is the process that underscores why commercials are usually composed of quite a lot of different images. Each time the image changes, our attention is drawn back, despite our general tendency not to pay as much attention to commercials.

Of course, what grabs your attention does not have to be on the screen. If the couple behind you starts talking, your attention may be directed to their conversation, particularly if what is on the screen is not all that interesting or what they are talking about *is* interesting, or maybe just annoying. Or if your date squeezes your hand, or if someone's cell phone goes off. These things are not nearly as effective in getting your attention when the screen is full of interesting and changing images and sounds.

The other construct is **attentional inertia.** This idea is that the longer you watch something, the more likely you are to continue to watch it (Anderson & Burns, 1991). This seems to contradict the idea of habituation, but now we are talking not about a specific image, we are talking about "watching *Sesame Street*" or "watching *Rear Window*." As long as what is on the screen does not habituate us, we will continue to watch it. One textbook defines habituation as "becoming bored," but that isn't right. Boredom is an unpleasant state, and habituation is simply coming to a point in looking at a specific image on the screen that we feel we do not need to watch it any more. We understand that the couple has nothing to say to each other. We are active processors of information, and we look around for other information to process, whether it is to see that our date is having a good time or to notice the color of the wall in the theater. But if the couple on the screen is having a disclosing conversation, we do not habituate and we continue to watch because of attentional inertia. This accounts for the long bouts of attention that have been observed when most people are watching TV.

Jeff's behavior in *Rear Window* faithfully recreates these processes. He will look at one apartment until there is nothing more to see (habituation) and then look elsewhere. If something that has lost his interest becomes interesting again—say, there is commotion because the dog has been killed—this leads to dishabituation, but he keeps looking out his window at his neighbors (attentional inertia), even when he is warned by everyone who comes to visit him that spying on his neighbors can lead to no good.

The final construct, which helps us make sense of the age and intelligence data, might be called the "novelty/familiarity" factor or more formally **discrepancy.** The term refers to the amount of new or unfamiliar information compared to familiar information. Why don't infants look at *Sesame Street*? Well, they can't make any sense out of it: It's all new information to them. Why don't individuals with intellectual disability spend much time looking at the screen? They, too, have difficulty making sense of much that is on TV. Why do adults spend a lot of time looking away from TV? Because they can do so and still follow the story. Why do four-year-olds spend a great deal of their time attending to *Sesame Street*? Because there is enough that is familiar to them, that they can understand it, and there is enough that is novel that they need to watch carefully if they are going to make sense of it.

The novelty/familiarity factor can also refer to how much information in a written document or class lecture is new information and how much is familiar information. Texts or films or lectures which contain a great deal of new information are hard to decipher. We have to put more attention into this process, and in the case of live events, like a lecture or film, the new information may overwhelm our capacity to understand it. For a written text, we can either slow down our reading or close the book for a moment to catch up. If there is not much new information, we stop paying attention because the information we are getting is redundant, and we really are bored.

The example of a lecture may be useful. If you are not a chemistry major and you drop into a physical chemistry lecture, your attention would soon drift from what the professor was saying. Very little of it would make any sense because it was all new to you. If you went back as a sophomore to hear a lecture by your favorite freshman professor and the lecture had not changed at all, you, too, would quickly become inattentive. It is *all* familiar to you. But if you have done your assignment, and go to one of your current classes, there probably will be a good mix of familiar and novel information. It should keep your attention. Formally, **the moderate discrepancy hypothesis** says that we pay attention to movies, lectures, conversations and written passages when there is a moderate amount of new material and a good deal of that which is familiar.

We think the novelty/familiarity idea accounts for why so many people dislike watching foreign films in foreign languages. Not only do you have to pay attention to the subtitles, but the film itself is from another culture, and there are often images on the screen that do not make a lot of sense. In this case, the novelty/familiarity ratio is very high, and it requires intense watching, which, eventually, will cause us to become inattentive.

Children's TV-Watching Data

The studies that we have summarized probably tell us something about the basic processes in paying attention to movies, but there are many limitations due to the nature of the task and the physical and social environments in which the research was done. These studies suggest we look away often, but how often we do so in a theater is not clear. They suggest to us that there may also be sex, intelligence and age differences, but those differences may wash out to some degree when we factor in what we are looking at.

The nature of the task. Looking at a TV screen, even a big one, is different than looking at a movie screen. Although we change our eye fixations when looking at TV, it is not the same activity as looking around a big screen. To look at different parts of a big screen, you actually have to adjust your whole head, not just move your eyes. You cannot take in the whole of the image in the same way you can when watching a 32" screen from the recommended ten feet away. Also, the time element is different. Most of the studies cited above had children watching half-hour programs. Movies are generally two hours in length. There are no commercials.

The physical environment. The physical environment of a movie theater is designed to focus our attention on the screen. The seats are *moderately* comfortable, unlike TV-watching in our own home where we often try to become so comfortable that falling asleep is always a nagging problem. There are few physical distractions in a theater. The lights are dim. There are no toys to play with.

The social environment. There are many differences in watching a film in a theater and watching a TV, either in your own home or in a lab setting. In your home, you are either alone or with friends. In the lab, you are with a few other people, but they are probably strangers. In the theater, there are a lot of people, and there are social rules. You turn off your cell phone. You are not supposed to talk, and if you occasionally do, you should whisper.

Some of the studies that we summarized have used a physical and social setting very far removed from either watching TV in the comfort of your own family room or watching a movie in a theater. For example, Anderson *et al.* (1981) in their study of the effects of the presence of other children on three- and five-year-olds, had children watch a *Sesame Street* episode in a 7x12' viewing room. This is a very small room for three children who are strangers and a parent. In addition, there was a distraction, another screen that was showing slides of Disneyland, posters for movies, pictures of animals, etc. It is not surprising that the children failed to pay rapt attention to *Sesame Street*.

You have also had something to say about the movie you are watching when you go to the movies, so the stuff on the screen should be of interest to you. You are not looking at something selected by a researcher. And what you are watching is a professionally made narrative, not a simulation by a university professor.

Looking Within the Screen

We are now in the theater and we are sometimes looking at the screen and constantly hearing, at some level, the soundtrack. The next question we need to address is exactly what do we look at? In theory, we can look at anything we want, including looking away from the screen, but in practice, the film's director and cinematographer often help us to look at the "right" things. By "right," we mean the things that will help us understand the narrative.

An example: The scene in the 1981 thriller *Body Heat* where the audience sees the *femme fatale* for the first time. At a park concert, a symphonic band is playing to an audience of several hundred people. There is a lot of commotion—kids at play, people moving around, the conductor conducting the band. But the instant that Kathleen Turner gets up from her seat, we notice her, even though she is squarely inside all of this noise and movement. The reasons for this instantaneous recognition are:

Kathleen Turner is *near* the center of the screen. In general, we focus on that part of the screen when we are in a movie. Had her image been in the exact center of the screen, however, we may not have seen her as vividly, because in the center of the retina is a "blind spot" where there are no receptive cells.

She is wearing a white dress, while everyone else is dressed in bright colors. We attend to things that are different.

She walks directly toward the camera. The other activity on the screen is from side to side. Again, her movement sets her apart from everything else that is on the screen. And because her movement is toward us, if we do not see her in the first few milliseconds, her image is getting larger and larger as it comes towards us.

Again, as in the attention section, we have very little direct research on where we look in movie theaters. What we do have a great deal of information on is how we look at complex images, such as photographs and paintings. There is a substantial research literature on eye movements, both looking at images like photographs and paintings, as well as real-world situations. Some of the early studies (Gibson, 1947; Milton, 1952) examined where pilots looked as they flew aircraft. These studies indicated that there was much to consider: There were individual differences in pilots, some of which made them poor choices as pilots. The kinds of control panels, the types of maneuvers, and whether the maneuvers were done at night or during the day modified those individual differences. Similar research continues today on topics such as the differences in eye movements while driving between young adults and elderly drivers (Maltz & Shinar, 1999).

Research on eye movements and fixations requires a technology that would be cumbersome to use in a movie theater. For example, Mackworth and Mackworth (1958) describe an easily understood system in which a thin beam of light is directed toward the eye of a research subject. That light is reflected off the cornea, the outermost layer of the eye, indicating the direction that the eye is looking. That reflection is picked up by a television camera and magnified 100 times and then superimposed on the scene at which the research participant is looking, showing the pattern of fixations and movements between fixations. This basic technology has been enhanced by computers, and we can now very accurately examine where people are fixating their gaze. But the basic problem of intruding on watching a movie in a movie theater by shining a light in a participant's eyes remains a stumbling block. Also, the participant cannot move his head, or the reflections do not mean anything: so, in the Mackworth procedure, the participants rest their chins on a frame and bite onto a bite plate. Sometimes something akin to this is used in eye exams. As you might expect, this could disrupt your normal movie-viewing.

These practical studies, and studies of looking at pictures, whether still or moving, remind us that we have a visual system—both the biological structures of the eye, optic tract and visual parts of the brain, and the behavior that activates those structures—that evolved for very different purposes than driving cars, flying airplanes or watching movies. Vision developed to help us find food, select mates, nurture our young, avoid falling off cliffs, and getting eaten by predators. We are an animal that lives on the ground and moves around, at most, at a few miles an hour. Flying an airplane is not a natural event to our visual system. Nor is driving a car at 70 miles an hour. Nor is sitting still in a dark room and watching events unfold before us on a flat screen as a camera moves around an environment or quickly changes focus from one thing to another.

Sometimes we can take advantage of those biological functions. In the real world, sound often draws our visual attention toward something: We look at where the sound came from. Therefore, our vision is most sensitive to the center of the visual field which reflects lights on the central part of the retina, called the **fovea**. That may be why the director put Kathleen Turner near the center of the screen. We are attentive to color, because color signals, among other things, what can and cannot be eaten and what might eat you. But we only detect color in the center of the visual field. We are attentive to things that are different, because they may signal opportunities or dangers, so as Turner's appearance and movement signal that she is different from the several hundred people around her, we look at her to determine whether she is friend or foe. And we are particularly attentive to things that are coming at us. In the case of *Body Heat*, the main character should have run like hell.

Studies of Looking at Pictures

If you go into an art gallery and look at a painting or if you examine the stills from movies that are in this book, you may have the feeling that you are looking intently at the picture; that you are seeing the various elements in relation to each other. You feel you are getting a "picture" of the whole thing. But, in fact, you aren't.

You are looking at different parts of the picture. Your eyes fixate on one part of the picture, and then move very rapidly, so that you can fixate on another part of the picture. Our subjective experience of looking is not very accurate. When we look at a picture at an art gallery, we rarely have the sensation that we are zooming around from place to place in the picture, sometimes several times a second. The periods of time when our eyes are fixed on some area of a picture (or the real world) are called **fixations**, while the rapid movements are called **saccades**. Psychologists generally believe that the information that we get from looking comes only from the fixations. During the saccade, no clear information gets to the brain, only information about where the next fixation will occur and a "smear" of visual stimulation.

Our visual system is an impressive information extracting device. We have two eyes that work together, but they do not get exactly the same information, which you can check out by closing one eye and then the other. Our head moves around. We move through our environment. Our eyes glance from one thing to another. And yet our impression of the world is that it is real and continuous. This is a rather amazing thing. Because what that impression is made up of is, over the three minutes it takes to walk through the campus to our next class, assuming someone stole our smartphone, might be 100 or more images that come from individual fixations, all of which are different. Somewhere in our brain, this is all sorted out, and we can get from the Econ 201 classroom to the Psych 101 classroom without falling down, while noticing that it might be a good day to lie out in the sun, and observing that one of our friends has reconciled with her boyfriend.

What the eye detects is light, and specifically, in the real world, light that is reflected off surfaces. We see the light reflected off the psychology building, and we head toward it. We know how far away it is because something in the brain calibrates the change in the image with the speed we are walking.

This is what the visual system is designed to do. It is not designed to sit in a room and watch the light reflected off of surfaces that has been captured on film, either in a motion picture or a photograph. But the visual system also responds to this kind of light. And works of art, whether photographs, paintings or images in a motion picture, are not exactly the ambient environment that we walk through every day. The images are deliberately arranged by the artist to be understood easily (or not).

Look at the picture on the next page.

There are usually two different phases of looking (Buswell; 1935; Karpov, Luria & Yarbus, 1968). If you look at this image, there will be a very short time during which you are trying to discover what the content of this photograph is. You look all over the picture, very rapidly. In studies of picture-looking, typically viewers will make four or five fixations during the first

84 Part II: Experiencing the Movie

"Gathered for Burial at Antietam After the Battle of September 17, 1862," by photographer Matthew Brady.

second. You notice that it is a desolate landscape. You notice the two trees. You notice the cloudless sky. You see a long pile of objects in the left center of the picture. You see, in the distance, some sort of structure. Once you discover, however, that the pile of objects consists of human bodies, your gaze moves around that one area. You look at that area to discover why the humans are lying there, until, after a period of more focused looking, you determine that these are corpses. As you scrutinize this part of the picture, you notice that they are wearing uniforms; that the uniforms are old-fashioned; that they are all men, etc. This is Civil War photographer Matthew Brady's "Gathered for Burial at Antietam After the Battle of September 17, 1862."

These two phases have been given different names, but we may call them **recognition** and **scrutiny**. In the first phase, we look about the whole image widely to determine what it is we are looking at. Once we know what we are looking at, we then concentrate our looking at what we know to be the important part of the image. During the scrutiny phase, fixations are longer (maybe one or two per second) and the distance traveled during the saccades is usually much smaller. These periods are not absolute. During recognition, it is possible that you come up with a wrong idea. Then after some time in the scrutiny phase, when you discover that your idea is wrong, you may have to begin looking all over the image quickly again. Some images have more than one thing in them that is of interest. You may habituate to looking at one thing and look elsewhere, just to see if there are other interesting things in the image.

In significant ways, the "picture-looking" tasks that have been used in this research are quite different from the task of looking at a movie:

1. The objects that are looked at are still photographs, drawings or paintings. They are sometimes handed to the participants to examine; they are sometimes projected on a screen on the wall of a laboratory; or they are come up on a computer screen. But they are still. Images in movies are moving.

2. They are usually presented for a specific period of time, and usually the time is the same for all pictures, although in earlier studies, when people were asked to examine physical pictures in a set, they were sometimes allowed to look at the pictures for as long as they wanted. Images in a movie are projected for different lengths of time.

The pictures in these studies are rarely related to those that occur before or after them. Images in movies, on the other hand, bear a relationship to those that come before and after them.

In these studies, the participants were given a specific task. For example, Buswell (1935) asked people to look at pictures for as long or as short a time as they wanted *as if they were choosing one for themselves*. Sometimes people are asked to find something in the picture, such as a geometric design in a line drawing of a scene. We are not usually given a specific task when we go to the movies, although sometimes we are.

Before we move on to the issue of how movement within the images affects saccadic movement, we will consider three additional issues about still images, their relative complexity, their duration and the tasks that the viewers set themselves when coming into a theater.

Simple and More Complex Images

The image of the whole courtyard in *Rear Window* would be an example of a very complex image. We look from place to place, wondering what we should be looking at.

When "Jeff" takes out his camera to focus on one apartment, our eye movements slow down and we scrutinize what we are looking at.

86 Part II: Experiencing the Movie

Filmmakers use the relative complexity of their images in many ways. For example, a succession of complex images will keep viewers in the recognition mode for a long period of time—presumably their eyes are moving widely around the screen for cues as to what they are seeing. Simple images allow us to concentrate our scrutiny on some aspect of the image, usually

Lisa (Grace Kelly), below, considers exploring the scene of the suspected crime, Lars Thorwald's (Raymond Burr) apartment above (Universal Studios, 1954).

what a character is doing, often his or her face. A series of stunning close-ups introduces Grace Kelly when she awakens Jeff, who fell asleep watching his neighbors. Not only is she beautiful, we want to examine her face to determine her feelings for Jeff.

Image Duration

Movies give us a succession of images, and those images keep changing. Movies are also "moving pictures" in the sense that we move from one image to another. Some images are on the screen for a long time, others for mere moments. A short image, whether complex or not, may have us in the recognition mode for the whole time it is on the screen. A succession of very short shots will therefore have us in Recognition mode for a long time. Probably the most analyzed series of images in all cinema is the *Psycho* "shower scene" discussed in Chapter 3. More than 70 shots appear in about 45 seconds. Many of the shots are of objects (knife, shower curtain hooks, drain, parts of the victim's body) photographed close up, so they are hard to recognize in the half-second we get to look at them. The effect of this method of cutting is that when it is over, we are not completely sure of what we have seen. Which is exactly the point. We have seen something terrible take place. We know that the woman in the shower is dead, but there are many questions left unanswered.

This gruesome scene is immediately followed by a series of very lengthy shots of Norman Bates cleaning up the crime scene. We know what he is doing. We can scrutinize the mop, the shower curtain, the body. This scene is unsettling in its own way, because what we are asked to look at—and which we *do* understand—is unsettling. We are asked to scrutinize the results of a homicidal attack.

Filmmakers therefore have the choice of complex short shots, which leave us trying to understand what we are seeing; complex lengthy shots, in which we spend some time looking for what we are seeing and then looking around at the various elements, much like we do in the Matthew Brady photograph or in *Rear Window*'s first scenes when we see all the apartments in the courtyard simultaneously. Or short, simple shots, where we see something recognizable and then move on to something else; or long scenes of simple images, where our attention is on small features of what we are looking at. At the end of the *Psycho* shower scene, we have a lingering shot of the dead woman's face, her eyes unmoving. It is a very simple and very disturbing image. We get it. We feel it is time to move on. But that is all that is on the screen, and we are forced to regard the effects of the violence.

Passive and Active Watching

Two major reasons people give for going to the movies are to relax and to learn about new things. Relaxing and learning are really quite different tasks, comparable to the different task instructions in the picture-looking studies. Asking a participant to look at some pictures to see if there are any he or she might like is a relatively passive task, while looking for a specific object in a complex display is an active task.

If you want to go to the movies to unwind, you probably want a movie where the filmmaker does most of the work for you. The images that you see on the screen should be easily understood, and you should be in a kind of leisurely scrutiny mode most of the time. In a James Bond movie, most viewers go to relax and be passive. You look at the image: you have time to think, *Maybe I'd like to go there on my next vacation* or *I wonder how I'd look in that outfit?* or *I wonder how much that car costs?* The scenes in a Bond film are relatively long, and few of them are complex, except for the fact that there is often a lot of geographical and feminine beauty on display.

In more "serious" films, one has to be vigilant. In *Rear Window*, we are given the task of finding out whether a murder has taken place or not. One is constantly searching the images on the screen for something that might give us the answer. Those images are complex and there are many short shots. We are often in recognition mode. Today we may think, *Well, of course a crime has taken place*, but in 1941 Hitchcock made the film *Suspicion* in which nothing happens except that a wife believes that her husband is plotting to kill her. He isn't.

Filmmakers make specific genres of films and they adapt the images that we are to look at to those genres. If they are making an action-adventure movie, they know their audience wants to have a good time and not work too hard at understanding the film. The images are easy to recognize, and they give us interesting things to scrutinize, once we perceive the meaning of the image. Other film genres more actively engage our perceptual systems and our cognitive systems. The images are not as readily understood because they are more complex. The number of images we see adds to the complexity of a film. Active vs. passive watching figures into preferences for different genres of films. It may be useful to think of *genre* as a set of instructions for watching: You are supposed to try to figure out who the culprit is in a whodunit and watch until you find something horrible in a horror movie. You go to a tearjerker to find something to cry over.

Perceiving Movement

If movies were slide shows, then the research on picture-looking would be completely helpful. But movies are also "moving pictures" in the sense that there is movement within each image. Rarely in movies do we see a perfectly still picture.

To understand the perception of movement, we need to know a little more about the way the visual system is organized and works.

Visual information (light reflected off surfaces) comes into the eye and stimulates the retina. When light strikes a cell in the retina, and there are hundreds of millions of retinal cells, the cell fires, and that firing sets of a chain of reactions that may end up sending information to the visual cortex of the brain. In the center of the retina is the fovea, a mass of cone cells sensitive to color and detail. Around them are less packed rod cells that pick up light or no light information. For any 200 milliseconds, we can think of the retina as being like a digital camera and the brain as like the computer to which we just downloaded an image. Light comes in. A signal goes off. We have an image. The image is then sent down the optic tract toward the brain.

But the retina isn't a digital camera and the brain isn't a computer. First, unlike a digital camera, we only have detail and color in the central part of the image. But to make up for that, we keep making new fixations, and more information about other parts of the image comes in. Second, the cells that just fired, cannot fire again. The retina is not a physical system like a digital camera, it is a biological system. Once a cell has fired, there is a period of several seconds to several minutes when it cannot fire again. This is called the **refractory period.** But the eye fixates elsewhere in the image and sends another image down the optic tract. While we fixate at different parts of an image up to five times per second, our impression is of a continuous object. It is not like looking at the 600 slides your best friend took on her day trip to Amsterdam last summer. We do not see one image and then another and then another. Something in the central nervous system integrates all this information. Psychologists who specialize in this aspect of visual perception have theories about how this happens. For our purposes, it is just necessary to remember that a complex integration occurs, and this is a major way the visual system is different from a digital camera, even one attached to a computer.

Another way the visual system is different from a digital camera is that along the way from the retina to the visual cortex, the information that was retrieved by the retina from the light in the environment is modified. Some of these modifications are like enhancing computer programs we use to alter photographic images. We have cells in the optic tract, for example, that emphasize edges. This would be very much like making a blurry image from a bad photograph crisper. But in the visual system, this is automatic. Humans see edges very well, because of edge **feature detectors** in the visual system. Animals like turtles don't see edges very well, which is one reason they will walk off the edge of a table if left alone. Edge detectors help us find doors and places to sit and flat surfaces on which to put our lunch trays. They also allow us to make sense of line drawings which, among other things, allows us to understand animated films.

There are many feature detectors in the visual system that detect movement. It is believed that these are actually deep in the brain. And they are very specific. There are detectors that see movement to the left, and those that see movement to the right. There are detectors that see movement toward us, because this was a highly important thing to notice if we were to survive being attacked by a saber-toothed tiger or Kathleen Turner in *Body Heat*. There are detectors that help us see things that are moving in a different direction from everything else; and there are detectors that help us notice things that are moving faster than everything else.

It is probably safe to say that when we are looking at a complex visual array on a screen, we look at things that are moving more than at things that are still. Certain kinds of movement attract our attention more than others. And filmmakers, whether they have studied the psychology of visual perception or not, know this. We look at the seemingly bewildering amount of information on the screen in the battle scenes in a movie like *The Revenge of the Sith* (2005), where there are hundreds of objects moving in seemingly random patterns, and wonder how the viewer makes any sense out of them. But they are not moving in random patterns. The filmmakers know what kinds of movement attract our gaze and which ones do not, and they can create, for most viewers, a completely understandable narrative. Of course, other things, like dialogue, color, focus and music are also part of the equation.

There are even feature detectors that help us see human-like movement. In a series of experiments, Johansson (1973; 1975) placed pairs of reflective points at the six main joints of the human body (shoulders, elbows, wrists, hips, knees and ankles) and made movies of typical human movement like walking. All one can see in these movies are 12 lights moving in relationship to one another. People can reliably tell what is human movement from other kinds of movement in less than a second. Johansson's work has led directly to computer animation of human-like movement in films like *The Polar Express* (2004), in which an animated creature is morphed onto the moving joints of an actor.

Movement in the real world, of course, is a two-pronged process: Things move in the environment and we move through the environment. We see stationary things as we move, and they move relative to our retina, but we perceive them as stationary, again through a complex system. We perceive moving objects as we move, but our brain makes judgments about movement relative to our movement.

But we are sitting still in the movie theater. Sometimes the camera does something like moving through the environment for us. The camera can pan across a scene—which in some ways, is like our moving our head around to survey a situation. But in other ways it isn't. A pan is continuous, and when we "pan" the environment, we do so in a rapid series of saccades. The camera can also do a tracking shot, which is like our moving toward an object. But again, this is different from the fixations we make as we move through space. The camera can zoom in or out, which has some relation to moving toward or away from an object, but there are so many differences here that most of the time a zoom is perceived as being very artificial. Finally, the camera can give us a succession of shots (called **montage**, which will be discussed at length in Chapter 6). This can be something very different from our everyday experience. For example, in the *Psycho* shower scene, there seem to be images from four different people. Some of the shots seem to be from someone who is standing in the bathroom, observing the murder. We see the outside of the shower curtain and the shock on the victim's face when the curtain is opened. Some of the shots are from the vantage point of the murderer. Some are from the viewpoint of the victim. Then there are the shots from above. And finally, there seem to be images made by some mad photographer inside the shower with Janet Leigh, taking pictures of the faucet, drain and curtain hangers. Something in the brain tries to integrate all this information. But the result is unsettling and difficult to understand.

Continuity

If you watch of the credits to an older movie, you may discover that someone is listed as "Continuity." This person's job was to make sure that in a scene that may be composed of many different shots, that everything is the same from one shot to another. Since different shots may be made over several days or weeks or even months, it is quite possible that actors or sets would change. For example, the actor might be wearing a blue shirt for one take and a white one for another. Or an actor might have gotten a haircut. Or the items on the table might not be in the same place. Such problems in continuity should make movies look ridiculously inept or even confusing.

But research indicates that such problems do not make much difference. In fact, the study of such problems with continuity help elucidate how much of an event we see in a complex world. In a series of studies by Levin and Simons (1997), many changes were made between shots in a short film of two actors talking. There was an establishing shot of the two actors across a table, and then close-ups as the two actors talked. The color of the plates on the table changed from red to white. One actor had a colorful scarf that was absent in the next shot. The hand positions of the actors changed, etc. College students watched the film and were asked if they noticed any changes. Most noticed no changes, even though there were nine of them in the film that only lasted a couple of minutes. Then they were told that there would be such changes every time the camera changed, and they were specifically told it might involve body positions, objects on the table, clothing, etc. Still, most of the students failed to notice the changes. Later in this series of studies, the actors playing roles changed. Unless the students were specifically cued that the actors might change, most failed to notice. This phenomenon is referred to as **change blindness**. The authors concluded, "Our intuition that we richly represent the visual details of our environment is illusory" (Levin & Simons, 1997).

These were very short films with graduate students playing roles, and it does not mean that we pay so little attention in films that, say, halfway through *The Big Short* (2015), Ashton Kutcher could replace Ryan Gosling without anyone noticing. But it does suggest that we do not encode a wealth of information as we look at a movie or as we encode information in the real world. In a later article, these authors (Levin & Simons, 2000) give an example from a scene in the film *My Own Private Idaho* (1991). As the camera cuts between River Phoenix and Keanu Reeves talking, most viewers do not notice that in some shots Phoenix is leaning against a tree branch and in other shots there is no branch. In the John Waters film *Polyester* (1981), one of the secondary characters appears in some scenes with his eyebrows shaved off. This was done for a scene that was later cut from the movie. When test audiences failed to notice, no attempt was undertaken to reshoot the scenes to make the character's eyebrows the same from shot to shot. Perhaps the most famous continuity artist was Alma Reville, Alfred Hitchcock's wife and frequent collaborator.

How Difficult Is It to Perceive a Movie? Symbols and Icons

The relationship between the word *robin* and an actual robin is something that must be learned. You cannot say to a person who does not understand English *robin* and expect her to know what you are talking about. The word *robin* is a "symbol" for the actual class of things we call robins. **Symbols** must be learned. But **icons**, which are simplifications of the thing itself do not.

Film theorists often assume the same basic learning process in translating events and objects seen on the screen and reality. Why else would you need a course in film theory or a PhD in semiotics?

We're not so sure. And we'll give two reason for this.

First, we used the example of "robin" because one of us has a cat that, whenever there is a bird on TV, assumes his stalking behavior. If there is a picture of a bird in a tree making bird sounds, he will crouch; make "charming" noises; and start slowly creeping toward the screen. No one ever explained to him the relationship between the "symbol" of the robin on the screen and real-life robins. The image can be 18 inches tall or an inch tall. It can be seen straight on or from overhead. He is capable of this transformation of image-robin to real-robin.

Second, if you watch a Disney film with three-year-olds, they "get it." They understand that the moving drawings are characters and that they do things and that there is a story. They can understand that the blobs of computer-generated color are fish or lions. They don't have to take a class in film theory to understand that Nemo is a fish who wants to get home and his dad wants to find him.

It is, however, clear that we do perceive images differently with age and experience. Mackworth and Bruner (1970) found that children look around photographs, both in and out of focus, much differently than adults, and adults seem to be looking at the "right" parts of a photograph—that is, the parts that help understand what the image is—more than children. Perception is not just looking around an image for things that are biologically relevant. Our experiences shape what we attend to and the sense we make out of them. We don't know what a five-year-old would make of the photograph of the dead of Antietam, but it would certainly be different from someone who has seen a lot of Civil War photographs.

Our specific experience and state influence our ways of looking. Mogg, Bradley, Field and De Houwer (2003) found that when looking at pictures, smokers looked at smoking-related images longer than non-smokers, presumably because in the experimental setting they were experiencing some nicotine withdrawal. Men and women, gay and straight, look at erotic scenes differently. We probably look at the images on the screen differently, depending on whether we selected the film or were talked into viewing it. We will return to these issues in later chapters.

*　*　*

If you have ever been laid up with a broken leg in a small apartment during a sweltering summer, being taken care of by the most glamorous woman in the world, you may have a different perception of *Rear Window* than most of your fellow men and women. If you have ever believed that you have seen evidence of a crime and no one would listen to you, you will see one of Jeff's dilemmas differently than most viewers. If you are on a date and that date is pressuring you toward a more intimate commitment, you will see Jeff's other dilemma in a perspective that many others have seen before. For despite similarities in the way our sensory and perceptual mechanism modify our experience, our individual differences further modify them.

Key Psychology Terms

Attentional inertia: The tendency to continue to attend to the same stimulus over time.
Attentional style: Characteristic individual differences in attention.
Change blindness: Failure to note differences in subsequent shots (e.g., that a character has gotten a haircut or is wearing a different tie).
Dishabituation: After habituation has occurred, even very small changes in the stimulus will renew attention to it.
Ecological validity: Also called generalization. The ability for data collected in one situation or with one group to be useful to understand a different situation or group.
Feature detectors: A set of cells along the optic tract that modifies visual information, making some aspects of the information more intense.
Fixation: In visual perception, the part of visual search where the eye is steadily focused.
Flicker: When film is shown at less than 36 frames per second, there is a perceived flicker, even though movement is perceived as fluid and continuous. The point at which flicker goes away is called "flicker fusion" or Phi, and this discovery by sensory psychologists led to a collaboration between some psychology departments, most significantly Harvard's, and the movie industry.
Fovea: The center of the retina where focus and color vision occur.
Habituation: Ceasing to pay attention to a continuous or repetitive stimulus.
Limen: Another name for Threshold.
Recognition: Period in looking where the task is to discover what it is that we are looking at.
Refractory period: A period of time after firing when a neuron or retinal cell cannot fire again.
Saccade: The eye during this phase of visual search is moving.
Scrutiny: Period in looking when we examine the details of what we have identified.
Subliminal: Stimulation that is below the minimal amount necessary for conscious awareness.
Threshold: The minimum stimulation necessary for a stimulus to reach consciousness.

Cinema Terms

Continuity: A job on a movie crew that examines details so that everything (clothing, background, etc.) matches from shot to shot.

Foreshadowing: Material in a movie, often music, that happens immediately before a scene and sets up the scene.

Icon: A simplification of an object that represents the object without the need for learning.

Pan: A shot in which the camera moves horizontally.

Symbol: An object or event that stands for another object or event. Unlike an icon, a symbol must be learned.

Tracking shot: A shot in which the camera is moving toward an object.

5

Learning from the Screen

Our conditioning begins 15 seconds into the opening credits, even before the studio logo fades to black. There are unsettling ambient sounds, the sounds of being underwater. When the screen goes blank for a few moments, we are forced to listen— what we hear is something like running water and waves, and a distant, echoing sound. A submarine? A whale?

The first visual image of the film proper is what is called a moving perspective shot taken from the title character's point of view (**POV**). But this character is moving underwater as the names of the actors and the filmmakers appear over what he is seeing. Then the conditioning begins in earnest as two of the film's three principal musical motifs are introduced. Barely audibly, the bass strings introduce the first: a repeated, rising half-step. The half-step is dissonant and suggests no possible tonal world. It is disconcerting. Our reaction to it is reflexive. This interval, particularly alone, sets off alarms. And the use of the extreme bass register suggests something serious, certainly something large. Then over this motif we add the second, a rising, atonal figure in the horns. At first it is just three notes, but it becomes louder and more complex, almost a fanfare. We will come to associate these two musical motifs with the character whose point of view we have been sharing.

Then suddenly we are on land, by a bonfire on the beach, surrounded by college students. The music is familiar, tonal: a harmonica and guitar. As if we were one of the students, we move along the edge of the crowd until we stop to look at a handsome blond lad staring at an attractive blonde woman. The sheer amount of yellow hair each has reminds us this is the 1970s. The girl stares back and then takes off running down the beach.

* * *

Psychologists define **learning** as *a relatively permanent change in behavior caused by experience or practice*. It is "relatively permanent" because what can be learned can be unlearned, and we focus on *behavior* because that is what we can see. Often, we are really interested in what is going on in consciousness or memory, but behavior is what we can observe, so our knowledge of whether learning has occurred is based on observable behavior. Learning is differentiated from other changes in behavior that happen with age or trauma by specifying that the change must take place because of experience and/or practice.

Psychologists differentiate three types of learning:

1. **Classical conditioning,** the process by which two events become associated so that they can substitute for each other and cause the same or very similar reactions;

2. **Instrumental learning,** which is when the context and consequences of behavior either affects its rate (increases or decreases it) or shapes it to become more expert; and

3. **Observational learning,** which is when we learn by observing others.

We will consider ways in which each of these affect the patron in the movie theater or the person at home watching a movie.

At least some of the time, movies do make "relatively permanent changes" in the audience. They make us sad or happy in the short run, but there is evidence that they can frighten us for long periods of time (Vincenzo, Hendrick & Murray, 1976). Some movies help change our attitudes and beliefs. They teach us new ways to talk and interact with others. They motivate us to go places, do things, and acquire skills.

Classical Conditioning

Psychologists give the Russian veterinarian Ivan Pavlov credit for discovering the principles of classical conditioning. Pavlov was studying digestion in dogs when he noticed that they began salivating when the caretaker who brought them food arrived. He believed that the dogs came to associate the arrival of the caretaker with food, and since food made them salivate, over time the arrival of the caretaker made them salivate. Pavlov devised a famous experiment to test this observation more formally. Instead of a person who, as you know if you've seen *Cujo* (1983), can be eaten by dogs, Pavlov used a bell. The bell initially brought about no salivation. He would ring a bell and then put meat directly into the dogs' mouths. After a number of pairings of bell and meat, the bell alone would make the dog salivate.

The meat is called the **Unconditional stimulus (UCS)*** *because it always provokes the salivary response.* (Think: There is no condition when it does not lead to salivation.) It is a reflex. The bell is called the **Conditional stimulus (CS)** *because there are only a few conditions under which the bell leads to salivation.* Salivation can be either an **unconditional response (UCR)** when it is in response to the meat (UCS) or a **conditional response (CR)** when it is in response to the bell (CR). While it seems like needless fussiness on the part of Pavlov to distinguish a UCR and a CR when they are both salivation, a UCR and a CR are different in two important ways:

　　1. The conditional response is always weaker and may be different from the UCR in other important ways; and
　　2. The conditional response gets weaker over time if the conditional stimulus is not paired with the unconditional stimulus; that is, if we stop putting meat in the dog's mouth, eventually the bell will stop making the animal salivate. After we get out of the theater, what has frightened us will affect us less and less over time. The process is called **extinction.** It is another example of why we say learning in *relatively permanent.*

　　This is how classical conditioning works in the laboratory. How does it work in the "real world" of the movie theater? You come in to see a movie. You see a POV shot of an underwater scene. This leads you to have some sort of reaction. Maybe you like oceanographic documentaries. This previous experience makes you look forward to what you are going to see. Or maybe being underwater makes you feel anxious. You worry about breathing. Then at the same time, you hear music that is deliberately chosen to make you feel anxious, maybe even frightened. Now the music is associated with being underwater and being underwater is associated with the unsettling music. And this is all associated with the POV shot of our underwater character. You're probably going to feel unsettled, even though you haven't seen anything genuinely disturbing yet.

　　Suddenly, you're on the beach. The music is familiar and tonal. Your anxiety goes away. You are ready for the blond couple to run down the beach shedding their clothes for a midnight swim and some lovemaking afterwards. Actually, it won't be completely anonymous because the girl tells the boy her name, Chrissie. The beach is beautiful. The sea is calm. Off in the distance in the moonlight, there is a buoy with its bell ringing. Chrissie urges her companion to come into the water, but he is drunk, falls, has difficulty re-moving his clothes, and eventually passes out on the edge of the water. Chrissie swims. Back and forth. Doing an underwater pirouette. All seen from land.

---

*Some textbooks will use the terms Conditioned and Unconditioned instead, but the terms used here are what Pavlov actually proposed and make more immediate sense.

At this point, the third musical motif is introduced as we watch her from the land. It is a tinkling, swirling sound with no melody: shimmering strings, high woodwinds, and a vibraphone playing arpeggios. This music could go either way—shimmering water music or the ominous calm before the storm.

Then we have a return of the underwater moving POV shot, this time looking up to the surface of the water and Chrissie's tantalizing legs treading water. Our character rises from the ocean floor toward her. The bass strings growl the half-step motif, the three-note melody is played in the winds. This is foreshadowing on steroids.

We return to Chrissie. Something has grabbed her. She has lost control. She screams. She is pulled one way and then the other in the water. Then there is a short cut to the half-naked boy on the beach and absolute quiet. We return to Chrissie's struggle as the music crescendos, interrupted by unexpectedly loud whacks from the xylophone. She screams out for help one last time and is pulled under. And then there is silence, except for the bell in the buoy Chrissie had tried to hold onto for protection, now seen at a distance from land in the middle of the peaceful water.

In these first few minutes of *Jaws*, director Steven Spielberg and composer John Williams have created for themselves an arsenal of sounds and visual images with which they can manipulate the audience. The dissonant intervals of the music are unnerving in themselves, but when paired with what will be increasingly graphic and disturbing images, they become terrifying.

* * *

Some psychologists who specialize in learning do not like the term, but classical conditioning primarily explains changes in *involuntary behavior*. Classical conditioning is not about learning to read or becoming more expert at chess or basketball. It has to do with reflexes like salivating and closing your eyes when you see something disgusting, like Chrissie's crab-covered remains on the beach the next morning, and it has to do with emotional responses, such as being frightened or laughing. These behaviors are said to be involuntary because you cannot produce them entirely at will. If you are like most people, you cannot salivate or stop salivating when you want to. And we have limited ability to laugh and cry at will. It is possible to get better control over your emotions by taking an acting class or undertaking behavioral therapy. In both situations, you will learn to recapture past experiences that were associated with strong emotions.

One involuntary reaction we have in the movies is our initial assessment of characters. We know that such assessments are based on at least three things:

1. Their physical appearance;
2. Our past experiences with the actors; and
3. The sounds and images that are associated with their introduction.

Let's consider how the three main (human) characters in *Jaws* are introduced.

Chief Brody is introduced immediately after Chrissie's death. It is a blazing sunny morning and the first image we see in this scene is the blank horizon—blue sky above, blue water below. Brody sits up in bed, coming into the frame of the horizon. When he stands, he is in his underwear and he walks stiffly. He kids around with his wife, before receiving the phone call that will lead him out to what is left of Chrissie. They live in a small house. They have children who are already up. We discover he is a newcomer to the community. All of these details lead us a) to identify him as a likely hero of the movie; b) regard him as likable and concerned; and c) view him as ordinary.

Some of this is necessary because of the actor portraying Chief Brody, Roy Schieder. Many audience members in 1975 would have had associations with him from action-adventure roles in other movies. He is not that kind of hero here. In fact, one of the plotlines in the film, which may be more important than killing the shark, is Brody overcoming his deepest fear—the water. The origins of this fear is so private his wife, with whom he shares pre-teen children, does not know them. "A drowning," is all the chief says. So it is important immediately to establish him as an ordinary person who loves his family and who is quite content to be leading a peaceful life. We like him. We worry that he might not be up to the job, whatever it is.

Captain Quint is introduced in a completely different manner after an additional shark attack and several unnerving scares. The second attack occurs while Brody watches anxiously from the beach, having been talked out of closing the beach by local politicians and business leaders. A young boy is killed while rafting just beyond a large group of children, including Brody's son. The musical set-up for the attack is the same: tinkling water music; POV shot of the boy's legs kicking the water from the air raft as we add the half-step and three-note motifs. While in Chrissie's attack we saw nothing but her head above water in the dim light, here we catch a glimpse of something large and dark before the boy turns into an exploding fountain of blood. Brody runs to the beach ordering the children out, but what happens is that the adults run *into* the surf to gather their children. He is as powerless with this crew of sunbathers as he was with the city officials. The scene ends with the image of the deflated raft bobbing in the bloody surf, a huge half-circle chomped out of it.

A meeting is called. The business community is still against closing the beaches. But Brody is firm. There is general talk about the $3000 bounty that has been offered. Over the general conversation comes an unpleasant sound—fingernails being dragged across a blackboard. The crowd parts and we see Quint for the first time. He is still scratching the board on which he has drawn a cartoon shark with a stick figure in its mouth. He is scruffy and emotionless. He sits alone. The Classical Conditioning paradigm here is:

> UCS (nails on board) → UCR (shiver, discomfort)
> CS (Quint) ————→ CR (shiver, discomfort)

Quint says that he will find the shark for the $3000, but he will kill it for $10,000.

Did Pavlov discover Classical Conditioning? The answer to this question is *no*. Pavlov was the second person to describe the phenomenon in the laboratory, which he did when he received his Nobel Prize in 1904 for the discovery of cortisone. The first was Cornell University graduate student Henry Tinklepaugh in 1899. Before either of these, the philosopher John Locke did a good job analyzing the phenomenon based on everyday observation in 1699 in his *Essay on Human Understanding*. Much of the idea of association had been proposed by Aristotle 2000 years before.

But we might owe the conditioning procedures in *Jaws* and other movies more to the work of the German composer Richard Wagner (Cohen, 1990). In his last seven operas, Wagner began using musical motifs, small snatches of melody and/or harmony and/or rhythm, to represent everything from *the* Dragon to the love potion to ecstatic love. In his epic *Der Ring des Nibelungen*, there are more than a hundred motifs. Here's how they work:

> A sword is going to be important in the story. Every time we see the sword or it is talked about, the motif is used, either in the singer's melody or in the orchestra. In *Die Walkure*, Siegmund escapes a mob into the house of his sister. He doesn't know that Sieglinde is his sister, but that's a very long story. Suffice it to say, his life is in danger and he is weaponless. He sings that he wishes he had a sword. The sword motif is used in his melodic line and in the orchestra. As he scours the house for something to help him, he notices a sword above the mantel. "Great," he sings. "Not so fast," sings Sieglinde, "That is a magic sword left by a stranger who said it was for his son." As she sings this, she uses the sword motif and the father motif to construct her tune. "I've got to try," says Siegmund, and he pulls down the sword, using both sword and destiny. Later in the cycle, when we hear these motifs again, they will bring along with them their associations from the earlier operas.

Matt Hooper. Before the introduction of the third of the heroes of the movie, oceanographer Matt Hooper, we have another conditioning episode. Looking to collect the reward, two locals lure the shark at night with a hunk of roast beef. The shark has other plans: He will take the roast beef and the pier to which it is attached out to sea; and then as the music gets much more intense, he will turn back to the shore and just barely miss a taste of one of the bounty hunters.

Hooper's introduction can almost be missed. This is due in part to the fact that in 1975, Richard Dreyfuss was almost an unknown actor, and he does not have the looks of a traditional movie star. When we first see him, he is getting off a boat assisted by a townsman who towers over him. He is incapable of getting anyone to pay attention to him. Moreover, chaos has broken out at the harbor as everyone with a small boat and a bucket of chum wants to go trawling for the killer shark. They even take their dogs along for the ride. It is a funny scene except for the looming presence of the shark. The conversations are light and comedic, but they are actually about death.

All three main characters have been introduced in ways which activate our emotions. We want Chief Brody to succeed, although we don't know if he is up to the task. Quint is annoying, and Hooper is comedic, although as we get to know him, we become impressed with his knowledge. He is considerably more than a spoiled rich kid with an unusual interest in sharks.

Instrumental Learning

Instrumental (or operant) learning refers to how we acquire and refine voluntary behavior like reading a textbook, riding a bicycle, or gardening. Psychologists conceptualize these voluntary behaviors (B) as being signaled by their antecedents (A) and strengthened or weakened by their consequences (C), leading to the analytical paradigm of

$$A \to B \to C$$

For example, being in a movie theater (A) means that if you talk out loud (B), you will be shushed and possibly evicted (C). This relationship is a **contingency**: *If under A conditions, you do B, then C will happen.*

The focus of discussion about instrumental learning in psychology is often on the consequences. Essentially, five things can happen after a behavior:

1. You can receive something that you like, such as attention from a valued colleague or a can of soda; this is often called **reward** or *positive reinforcement*. Rewarding a behavior *strengthens* it, making it more likely to occur in the future.

2. You can receive something that you do not like, such as negative attention, a slap, or being called a name. This is referred to as **punishment**. When behavior is punished, it is less likely to occur in the future.

3. You can lose something you like, such as being fined $125 for speeding or having your championship ring taken away from you because you bet on the outcome of the championship game. This is called a **penalty**

(sometimes called positive punishment) and it, too, makes behavior weaker, less like to occur in the future.

    4. You can lose something you do not like, as when a hockey player is let out of the penalty box; or when someone says "uncle," you stop wrenching his arm behind his back. This is called **relief** or *negative reinforcement*. Like positive reinforcement, negative reinforcement strengths behavior it follows.

    5. Nothing. When nothing happens following a behavior, it is said to be **on extinction**. Behavior that is on extinction gradually weakens over time. This extinction is a little different from the extinction in classical conditioning, where the CS loses its potency over time when it is not paired with the UCS. But both involve gradual weakening of what was newly learned.

But the "A" and the "B" in the ABC contingency are important as well. In the example above, the antecedent of being in a movie theater tells us what will happen if we talk, but it does not mean that we will be shushed anywhere but in the theater. You have learned that if you are watching a movie with a friend in his recreation room, you can talk a little, but if you move around too much, he will turn the movie off, which is a penalty if you are enjoying the movie. Music in a movie that *foreshadows* can be thought of as an antecedent.

Sometimes what the antecedent signals is that something will happen if a behavior occurs, but at other times, particularly in schools, the antecedents signal a level of performance. For example, you will get an A (a reward) if you know 90 percent of the material; in addition, you will also have no homework (relief). If we gradually raise our expectations for the quality of behavior, we are said to be **shaping** it. Another way we may change the ABC contingency is to move from rewarding a behavior every time it occurs to only rewarding it occasionally. This is called **thinning.** Behavior which is only occasionally rewarded is resistant to extinction. That is, if we reward every behavior and then stop rewarding it, the behavior will stop quickly. But if we move from rewarding behavior every time, and then only occasionally, when we stop reward altogether, the behavior will continue for some time.

Instrumental learning and classical conditions can be disaggregated in the laboratory and are usually studied separately, but in the real world, even the real world of the movie theater, they are interconnected processes. Money is a good example. It's one of *the* most powerful rewards, and therefore is part of instrumental learning. But money acquires its meaning and ability to influence us by becoming associated with merchandise and services that it can buy, which is done though Classical conditioning. Money is powerful because it has been associated with perfume, hamburgers, movie tickets and new trousers. It not only substitutes for those things, it brings along the emotions we associate with those things. Before any of those associations, money has little power over people. Children would just as soon have a happy face sticker as a $50 bill. But once they have spent a few dollars, that changes.

Unlike the internal emotions that are manipulated by Classical Conditioning, instrumental learning most often involves overt behavior, that is, behavior that can be observed. So what behaviors take place in the movie theater that qualify as overt? One obvious one in connection with frightening movies is looking at the screen: By about 45 minutes into *Jaws*, many of us have had enough excitement and we may find ourselves looking away when we think something dreadful is going to happen.

Brody and Hooper team up, Brody drinking heavily, and they go on a night boat ride in the dense fog, looking for the shark. They share some personal details. They form an alliance. It is all very comfortable. There is no background music.

Then they see something ahead through the fog. The music starts again, more melodically, but using all three motifs, again and again. The music is the antecedent. In the past when we have heard it, it meant that something gross might be on the screen *if we continue to look*. We want to look away, but the music is somewhat restrained and goes on for quite a while, as Hooper prepares to get into the water to check out what turns out to be an abandoned boat.

Get into the water? He must be crazy! This is not going to be good. *I've got to look away*, you think. But the warning music isn't strong enough to make you stop peeking. You look. Nothing bad. You look again. Nothing bad. In fact, the views of the flashlights in the fog and the underwater shots are actually quite stunning. Keep looking. Keep looking. Keep looking…

There is one important aspect of instrumental learning that is often left out: the rewards, punishment, relief and penalty all depend on the person. What might be a reward for one person might be a punishment for another. For example, people high on sensation-seeking who kept looking might be beside themselves with delight when the half-eaten face bobs out of the hole in the side of the boat and Hooper screams in shock, dropping his knife and inhaling water; while someone who is high on empathic concern may close his eyes and not open them until the movie is over.

Observational Learning

Observational learning allows us to acquire new behavior and information without having to experience the contingencies directly. By watching others successfully or unsuccessfully attempt a trick on a skateboard, we may maximize the chances of doing it ourselves without pulled muscles or broken bones. After observing the effects on another person of eating unknown food, we may avoid poisoning or find a new source of nourishment. In a new neighborhood, we observe which pets are approachable and which are to be avoided. By the time we graduate from college, we have acquired tens of thousands of words by observing them in use. We may decide not to wear the shirt our aunt gave us for Christmas after hearing the comments made by our friends when someone wears one similar to it. These are all examples of observational learning.

Observational learning is sometimes thought of as a third class of learning, quite dissimilar to Classical Conditioning and Instrumental Learning, but it can also productively be thought of as special cases of each. When we watch someone else become frightened by a shark, we too become more frightened of sharks (classical conditioning). If we see someone go off recklessly into shark-infested waters and get eaten, then our propensity for entering shark-infested waters is diminished (instrumental learning). In fact, in the summer following the release of *Jaws*, going to the beach decreased dramatically in the U.S., and when people went, they sunned on the beach rather than swam in the ocean. People learned to be afraid of sharks by watching *Jaws*. There are unconfirmed stories that people stopped showering in 1960 after seeing *Psycho*.

Psychologists like to differentiate observational learning from **imitation.** Imitation is immediate and then gone, while observational learning can last for very long periods of time. If you are talking to someone and you lean toward him, he is likely to lean toward you. This is imitation. If you put your hands behind your head, he might imitate that, too. If you say "hello" to a perfect stranger on campus, she is likely to say *hello* back, while if you say "hey," she is likely to say *hey* back. These are all examples of imitation. There is a lovely scene in *Jaws* in which Brody's young son sits at the table while his father drinks heavily and the boy *imitates* his actions. Imitation does not imply a *relatively permanent change in behavior.* It you go to a soccer match and people around you are screaming and cheering, you too may scream and cheer. But it does not mean your rate of screaming and cheering in your everyday life has increased: Imitation is bound by time and place. If you scream when Chrissie screams, you are imitating. If, the next time you get asked to go skinny-dipping in the ocean, you politely decline, you may have learned through observation.

But merely observing something is not a guarantee we learn. There are conditions under which learning is more likely than others:

> We are more likely to learn if we are motivated to learn the behavior. If we watch someone do a trick on a skateboard and *we want to learn to do the trick,* we will learn more than if we are merely a casual observer. When we are motivated, we pay attention to the relevant details. If we watch *Life Is Beautiful* in the context of an Italian language course, we will pick up more vocabulary than if we are watching it on a date, unless our date is Italian.

We are more likely to learn from characters in movies that are like us than from those who are different from us. Brody is more like most of us than either Quint or Hooper. Therefore, we are more likely to learn to avoid sharks than to chase them in our boats or to dive in the water with them. Children imitate children, not adults or even cartoon characters.

Related to the last issue, we are more likely to learn from characters with whom we identify than from those with whom we do not. It is possible to identify with someone who is quite different, in many respects, from ourselves. In viewing *Psycho*, most people, men and women, identify with Marion Crane. It is probably a good thing that few identify with Norman Bates. So, in *Jaws*, the story is mostly told from Brody's perspective. We see him at work, with his family, in his interaction with businessmen and politicians. Most people will identify with him, although some viewers will identify with Hooper, particularly those who want to be scientists or more specifically oceanographers.

We are more likely to learn from a character who has good outcomes than from one who ends up badly. There was a strongly held belief that for the good of the audience, in movies good behavior and good people should be rewarded and bad behavior and bad people punished. This was part of the Motion Picture Production Code from 1930 to 1968. The Code also prohibited detailed representations of crimes like robbery, safecracking, dynamiting, murder, arson, rape and use of drugs because it was feared that they would cause some people to be afraid and would instruct others in how to commit these crimes.

Chief Brody (Roy Scheider) is about to meet the star of *Jaws* (Universal Pictures, 1975).

It is also the case that we do not have to actually *see* the activity to learn from it. We see very little of the shark in *Jaws,* and yet we become afraid of sharks. Much of the horror in the movie is supplied by our imaginations. To some viewers, the final, graphic gulping down of Quint by the shark seems less frightening than things that have come before. We can also learn by merely hearing about something (if that was not the case, there would be little point in school). For many, the movie's most harrowing episode is when Quint talks drunkenly about his World War II experience of being in shark-infested waters after his ship capsized, waiting his turn as the predators picked off his shipmates one by one.

Music in Movies

We described in some detail how music plays a critical role in *Jaws.* But it is worth asking whether what we are describing is the exception or the rule. We think that *Jaws* is a particularly clear example of how music can be used to heighten a film's emotional impact, but music does more than add chills or tingles to a movie.

Since the beginning of the movies, there has been music (Wierzbicki, 2008). The earliest moving pictures, exhibited in the late 1890s and early 1900s, were accompanied by music partially because they were part of traveling vaudeville shows where musicians were part of the entourage, and partially because music masked the sound of the projectors (Fuller, 1996). These were in fact "moving pictures," shots from a stationary camera, lasting a minute or so, that showed amazing things like water pouring over Niagara Falls or people strolling on the Atlantic City boardwalk. When movies started to tell stories, music became part of the filmmakers' arsenal of techniques. Theaters had, at a minimum, a pianist or organist who accompanied the movies, often improvising scores for movies they had not previewed. D.W. Griffith popularized the idea of a specific score for his epic films. The most prestigious silent films came with scores for small house orchestras. Less important films came with *cue sheets,* which were suggestions for melodic content to be played at cued spots in the film. Very early on, the film studios tried to get a song to be associated with a film, so that if the film became popular, there would be interest in buying the sheet music or records for the songs; and if the songs became popular in their own right, it would create an interest in seeing the movie (Silent Film Sound and Music Archive, 2018).

Then as now, music has two primary functions in films: It helps tell the story, which may be said to be its cognitive function, and it enhances our emotional reaction to films, which is its affective function.

There are a number of cognitive roles music plays in movies (Boltz, 2001). Music can help locate the movie or a scene in time and place. For example, the bebop opening of *Rear Window* let the audiences in 1954 know that what they were about to see was set in the present and that the location was likely to be urban and *avant-garde*. This was music that most people were only vaguely aware of, but they knew it was contemporary and the kind of thing the denizens of small Greenwich Village apartments would listen to. Likewise, the music being played on the beach in *Jaws* lets the audience know this was a drama being played out in the present among the idle young. In both cases, as we watch these movies decades from their making, the music helps locate where, when and who we are watching.

Music can set the tone of a movie or a scene. Bebop jazz has a nervous energy to it, and *parts* of *Rear Window* have that energy. It perfectly reflects Jeff's urge to get out of the scorchingly hot confines of his little apartment. Offenbach's *barcarole* provides a romantic envelope for Guido and Dora at the opera: It tells us in advance something about how the scene will play out.

Music is used to let the audience know that the scene is changing. The guitar and harmonica music in *Jaws* and the swelling orchestral music that leads into the Paris flashback in *Casablanca* would be typical examples. A more unusual and famous example would be the sudden intrusion of loud, peppy "newsreel" music that begins the quick cinematic review of Charles Foster Kane's career, after the slow, moody opening sequence in *Citizen Kane* (1941) in which we have witnessed Kane's death

Music can tell us what a character is thinking. The music that plays while Marion is driving through the rainstorm before pulling into the Bates Motel lets the audience know that she is anxious and conflicted. Before Rick tells us what he is thinking ("Of all the gin joints in all the world..."), the modulation of the melody of "As Time Goes By" into a minor variation in a low register lets us know all we need to know: He is thinking angrily about Ilsa.

Music can guide an audience member's selective attention to certain aspects of the imagery on the screen, to attend to the *right* information. If the music becomes restless, we know to look around. If we hear shark music, we look for the shark.

Music can help us make up our minds about characters quickly and accurately (or not). We meet Marion Crane and her boyfriend just as the agitated music of the credits in *Psycho* has become slow and sensual. Marion is sensual—and slow to see the consequence of her impulsive theft.

Similarly, in its capacity to affect our emotional state, music has a number of different functions (Ellis & Simons, 2005). In and of itself, music can produce an emotional impact. In general, it has been found that tempo and tonality directly bring about emotional responses. Fast music energizes, while slow music calms; music in a major key is happy, while music in a minor key is sad. This is summarized in Table 5.1.

Table 5.1.
The Impact of Aspects of Music on Mood

	Minor	Major
Fast	passionate scary	joyful happy
Slow	sad	relaxed routine

This table may look familiar, as there was a similar one in Chapter 2 when we were describing mood.

But this diagram is overly simple. While minor key music is usually sad and major key music happy, tonality is also affected by a consonance-dissonance dimension. Very dissonant music that is in a minor key might well be thought of as *agonized* or *angry* rather than sad, and dissonant music in a major key might well be described as *ominous*.

The effect of the speed of music is also modified by whether the meter is regular or irregular. Irregular meter creates anxiety. So regular, major-key music might be thought of as joyful, but irregular, fast, major-key music might be thought of as *energetic*. Minor key music that is regular is *sad* or *passionate*, but when minor music is irregular and slow, it becomes *suspenseful*. When it is fast and irregular, it is *frightening*, as in the *Jaws* shark-attack music.

Inserting a sad song (slow, minor key) at the right point in a movie can make the scene sadder, even if we have had no experience with the song. Even if a character is shown standing perfectly still, if there is loud, dissonant, irregular minor-key music playing in the background, audiences will not think, "He is standing still." Rather, they will assume that he is stymied, trying to make up his mind, and the decision he is about to make is a dangerous one.

But what we've spent most of our time describing thus far in the chapter is how a composer can take a song or a motif and though repetition and pairing it with emotional content in the film, the music will take on additional meaning. In the psychology laboratory, we identify one thing as the conditional stimulus and one as the unconditional stimulus. But in the movies, it is not just that the "shark music" takes on more frightening qualities as it is paired with more disturbing shark imagery: It is also the case that the music produces its own emotional response, and that by pairing it with the images of the shark, the shark becomes more disturbing. It is not a one-way process. Combined, the music and the shark images strengthen each other.

But instead of developing a rich series of associates inside the film as in *Jaws*, filmmakers can also bring music into the film that already has those associations. *Casablanca*'s use of the French national anthem "La Marseillaise" is a good example. "La Marseillaise" is an emotional song, and even if you don't recognize what it is, it will have a certain impact on someone hearing it. But in 1943, hearing "La Marseillaise" could bring tears to one's eyes. More subtly, the film uses a number of Nazi-associated tunes to create a mood of anxiety, include repetitions of the opening nine notes of Germany's national anthem "Deutchland uber Alles."

The use of Offenbach's *barcarole* in *La Vita è Bella* is a brilliant use of existing music. First, the scene at the opera is brought to a perfect mood by the sweet, slow rocking of the music. But when Guido subsequently finds the recording while he is serving the German officers in the concentration camp and puts it on the loudspeaker as a way of communicating with Dora, we have music that has associations both outside the film and within the film. The music has a strange, transformative effect on the interior shots of the camp, making them almost beautiful. In addition to the emotional impact, there are thought-provoking aspects to the music. The lyrics are about the fragility of love and the beauty of the night. Additionally, many will know Offenbach was Jewish, and the German officers would not have had access to this music had they been in Germany.

Finally, we may ask: Why is music such a ubiquitous part of movies? In a 2014 study by Pehrs *et al.*, young adults watched romantic movie clips, with and without musical background, while having their brain activity monitored by fMRI scans. The scenes without music activated visual and speech areas in the brain plus, to some degree, areas associated with emotion. Music alone activated different, music-perceiving areas of the brain and to a degree the emotional parts of the brain. But together, they simultaneously activated not only speech, music and visual perception areas, but all the areas that connect them as well. And the emotional areas were much more active than with the clips seen without music.

One of the hot topics today in psychology is called **mindfulness**—the pursuit of activities that fully engage a person, particularly as a means to relieve stress. Mindfulness involves not only becoming fully engaged in an activity but eliminating other activities, turning off your cell phone, getting away from friends and family for a time, having time completely devoted to regeneration and being well. Movies are a mindful activity. The goal is to be transported and fully involved, leaving daily hassles behind. And this study suggests that quite literally, when we attend to a screen with a musical soundtrack, our minds are full.

Key Psychological Terms

Conditional response: An acquired reaction to a neutral stimulus that has been paired with a stimulus that reflexively brings about the response.
Conditional stimulus: A neutral stimulus that comes to elicit a response because of pairing it with a stimulus that reflexively brings about that response.
Extinction: The loss of learned behavior. In Classical conditioning, when a CS and a UCS are no longer paired, the CS gradually fails to elicit the conditional response. In instrumental learning, when a response is no longer rewarded, it gradually loses strength.
Instrumental learning: Learning that is shaped or maintained by its context and consequences.
Learning: Relatively permanent changes in behavior brought about through practice or experience.
Mindfulness: The pursuit of activities that fully involve the person as an avenue to well-being.
Observational learning: Learning by watching others.
Unconditional response: The behavioral part of a reflex.
Unconditional stimulus: The situation that triggers a reflex.

Key Cinema Term

POV: Point-of-view shots representing what one character is seeing.

6

Cognitive Psychology and Understanding Movies

Guido is stuck in traffic in a tunnel. There is something off kilter about the traffic and the people in the stalled vehicles beside him. There is a bus where all we can see are the arms of the passengers. Many of the people in other vehicles are staring at Guido. He wipes the windshield. We see that in another car, an older man is pawing a woman who is dressed in lingerie.

Something catches fire in Guido's car. It fills with smoke. He cannot roll down the window. He beats against the window glass. People stare at his panic. Eventually he gets out and climbs to the top of the car and then floats away over all the traffic, into the sky, into clouds. He passes by a structure covered with scaffolding. Perhaps it is a rocket ship.

Then we see a boy in an old-fashioned school uniform on horseback riding on a beach. He rides past a man lying in the sand. The man rises and says that they must get him down. He finds a rope and the rope is tied to Guido's leg. He is a kite, flying over the beach. He unties the rope from his foot. He falls slowly and silently into the sea.

* * *

In this chapter, we will look at some of the cognitive processes that are involved in comprehending the plot of a film and making judgments about characters. We will use Frederick Bartlett's (1932) Schema Theory as a way of understanding how we put together the bits and pieces of information that filmmakers give us into a coherent plot, and Lev Vygotsky's idea of the Zone of Proximal Development and Jerome Bruner's (1983) idea of scaffolding to help understand how we form schemas. And we will rely on Piaget's (1928) ideas of assimilation and accommodation to help us understand how we decide whether the schema we are using is the right one. We will look specifically at montage, the arrangement of shots in a scene, and sequencing of scenes to see how plots are formed. We will conclude the chapter by considering how we organize conflicting information about characters.

* * *

There is a classic study of memory by Bartlett, done in 1932. Bartlett had his participants read a Native American story called "The War of the Ghosts" and then recall it at different times after reading it. Not surprisingly, one of his findings was that over time, people remembered fewer and fewer details of the story.

What may be surprising was that people remembered the story as more and more "logical" over time. For example, while the title of the story is the "War of the Ghosts," when his British university participants recalled the story considerably later, they tended to eliminate the supernatural details and to include more rational motivations, or perhaps more European motivations, for the characters, motivations that were totally absent from the original story. For our purposes, the most important finding of the "War of the Ghosts" study is that our mind is actively creating a coherent narrative out of the bits and piece of information we get, either from a story, a movie or real life; and that the coherency comes from other patterns that we have previously learned.

Cognitive psychologists today call Bartlett's ideas **schema theory**. Schema theory says that new information interacts with old information, and old information is kept in memory in rather large bundles called schema. As we are being exposed to new information, one's mind searches for a schema into which to fit the new information. It looks for the best fit, even thought that fit may not be exact. We have already encountered a very similar idea when we discussed *scripts* with regard to teenage girls' learning norms for dating from watching favorite movie stars in romantic encounters in movies. The differences between *scripts* and *schemas* is small: Scripts to some degree are provided for the person by the culture, while a person's schemas are often uniquely his own.

We see this mental activity in many places. A person who has had too much to drink the night before may have a perfectly coherent memory of leaving the party and coming home, because she has a well-developed schema for leaving parties. Some additional information, such as the later knowledge that someone had taken her car keys, makes her have a different, coherent memory, which itself may not be accurate: If Jane took my car keys, then she must have given me a ride home. Patients with various forms of dementia also seem to "fill in the gaps," creating a narrative of the day based not on what they remember but on what has been normal in the past. This is called **confabulation** which basically means "storytelling." It is also very likely that this ability to make logical narratives out of bits and pieces of information is what writers are talking about when they say that at some point in writing a novel or movie script, "the characters take over" and they just record what they say and do.

This ability is not just for artists and people with temporarily or permanently damaged brains. It happens all the time when we read stories and we watch movies. As we look at a movie, we actively create the plot based on what the director chooses to tell us and what he or she chooses *not* to tell is. When people are asked to recount the plot of a movie at a later time, they very often have clear recollections of scenes that didn't occur. Gaps in the narrative are filled in by their working brain to make sense of what they did see.

For example, Meischke (1995) showed college women R-rated movie clips and then had them tell what happened when the scene faded out: Did the characters have intercourse? Did they use safe sex? She found that her participants relied on existing schema (e.g., promiscuous people have sex on the first date) to make the predictions. Most of the schema came from watching other movies or TV programs. Also using schema theory, Boltz (2001) found that accompanying music helped create expectations about characters and how the plot would work out. While she used a very complicated research design, it is of some interest that one of the clips she used came from the Alfred Hitchcock movie *Vertigo*. In this segment, a retired policeman is secretly following a friend's wife for him because she may be in danger. She drives to the San Francisco flower mart and buys a bouquet and then goes to the Mission Delores and visits an old grave. Three conditions were examined: "positive" music, in this case Samuel Barber's "Adagio for Strings," a slow and sad piece for orchestra; "negative" music, in this case the dissonant and irregular music of Tangerine Dream; or no music.

For those that heard the positive music, 88 percent of the viewers thought that he was romantically infatuated with the woman and described him as caring, loving, romantic, nice and shy. For those who heard the negative music, 94 percent thought he was going to harm her, and described him as cold, lonely and secretive. Of those that heard no music, 77 percent thought he was a private investigator and described his as intelligent, analytical, curious and honest. When asked at a later date to remember whether certain items had been present in the clip, music enhanced recognition, but those who saw the clip with music also "remembered" a number of items that had not been in the clip, but which were congruent with the mood of the film the music had established.

Another example of how schemas help us understand film would be to return to the opening three minutes of Federico Fellini's *8½*. It is probably safe to say that until 1963, no movie ever opened this way, and therefore we have no schema on which to assimilate the strange events of this film. But when, suddenly, at the end of this opening sequence, we see and hear a man who will turn out to be a movie director waking up in bed, as a member of his production staff begins talking about the day's schedule, we know that what we have just seen and heard has been a dream.

The developmental psychologist Jean Piaget used schema theory in a more dynamic way. He also believed that we ordinarily use existing schema to understand new information. When the material matches the existing schema or is very close, he called this process **assimilation.** For example, in an early scene in 8½, the movie director, who is staying at a spa as he gets ready to make his film, goes and "takes the water." He has a brief word with a representative of the cardinal about his new film, and then he goes to the springs, wrapped in a bathing sheet. All of this fits neatly into a kind of film about well-to-do individuals.

But sometimes the new information does not fit in with any existing schema, and we have to either modify the existing one or create a new one. This is called **accommodation.** As is often the case in 8½, things start out easy to assimilate and then they begin to go haywire. The walk to get the mineral water becomes a grand procession, with Wagner's "Ride of the Valkyries" playing in the background. Finally, a beautiful woman comes silently from the spring, bringing Guido his own pitcher of water. We have moved from reality, to exaggeration, to fantasy. We assimilate only part of this movie, because it keeps changing the ground rules; that is, we don't know what schema to apply.

Learning to Understand Movies

At the end of Chapter 4, we asked: "How immediate is the perception of images in film?" We suggested that film theorists might overestimate the difficulty of image perception. Some images, at least, seem to be understood at a simple level, without any particular education. Other kinds of images may need some learning.

Jerome Bruner and his associates (Bruner, 1983; Nunio & Bruner, 1978; Wood, Bruner & Ross, 1978) have elaborated on an idea by the Russian educational psychologist Lev Vygotsky to describe what might be going on when parents, grandparents, teachers, friends and siblings talk to children as they are reading stories, solving problems or watching movies. Vygotsky pointed out that people who know us well are aware of what we know and what we don't know. They also have ideas about what we could learn easily, given our state of knowledge and ignorance. Vygotsky called those things that we can learn readily, the **zone of proximal development.** *Proximal* means "next," so the zone of proximal development are the things we are ready to learn.

Bruner suggested that not only do skillful people know what we can learn next, but that they can assist us in learning more remote things through a process he called **scaffolding**. A scaffold is a support structure. Clarke-Stewart and Beck (1999) suggested that a parent's scaffolding of a movie might include: focusing the child's attention on important elements in the film as it is being watched, asking questions to see whether the child is understanding the movie, correcting misunderstandings, giving the child emotional support, particularly if the content of the movie might produce negative feelings, drawing the child's attention to similar stories or events that they know the child has experienced, e.g., helping the child find the right schema, discussing the movie, particularly critical aspects of it, afterwards, and, in some cases, reminding the child why they are watching a movie, for example, they have to learn specific content for a class assignment.

Scaffolding has been well researched in watching mothers and children reading together. Children whose mothers do many of these things remember the plots better than those whose mothers do not provide a scaffold for them. Clarke-Stewart and Beck (1999) did the same thing, but using a movie clip. Thirty-one five-year-olds watched a five-minute clip from the movie *Prancer* (1989) with their mothers. Fourteen other children watched the clip alone. After watching the clip, mothers discussed the clip freely with their children. These conversations were videotaped and scored for elements of scaffolding. Some mothers talked extensively with their children, while others talked very briefly. Then the child told a researcher what he or she could remember of the clip.

The five-minute segment was a highly emotionally charged one. The main character, a little girl, is in the woods looking for one of Santa's reindeer, Prancer. Her father finds her and is upset that she is in the woods alone. He tells her that she may have to move in with a relative because things are not going well for him. A shot is heard. Prancer has been wounded. The father goes to his truck to get a gun to put the reindeer out of its misery. The little girl tries to argue him out of it, but before anything can be done, Prancer disappears.

The researchers kept track of two kinds of information recalled: objective facts and comprehension of internal states. For example, "the girl is in the forest" is an objective fact, while "she is looking for the deer" is an internal state. Children who discussed the clip with their mothers included more objective information (about five events) than those who did not discuss it with their mothers (about three events). The authors used a scoring procedure that listed 18 events the child could have remembered, so these five-year-olds left out a considerable amount of information. Perhaps more telling, however, was the findings that the children who discussed the movie with their mothers included an average of 2.4 internal states, while not one child who did not discuss the movie with his or her mother included any internal states when retelling the story to the researcher.

6. Cognitive Psychology and Understanding Movies 117

The authors then analyzed the conversations of the 31 children who watched and discussed the clip with their mothers and compared what was discussed to the amount of objective and internal state information the children reported. Three aspects of scaffolding were significantly related to recall of objective facts: drawing children's attention to important events, correcting mistakes, and having extended exchanges about important aspects of the clip. These three aspects of scaffolding, as well as the overall length of the discussion, the number of questions the mothers asked, and the number of emotional words (the father was *angry*) the mothers used predicted how many internal states the child remembered. Perhaps it becomes apparent here one way in which empathy develops. A key component of empathy is understanding what another person is feeling, and those kids who did not discuss the film with the mothers gave no evidence that they understood what was going on inside the characters' heads.

This is the only study of scaffolding that we have been able to find about children watching films with their mothers, and as useful as it is, there are several limitations. The authors do not report on the mistakes that children make in telling the story. Similar studies done with storybook reading indicate that scaffolding not only helps children remember details, but it helps them avoid inaccuracies. We would also be interested in how much children remember at a later date. The authors also did not track whether parents made references to other stories that the children knew, which is a primary part of scaffolding. And the authors did not look at the kinds of things that parents scaffold for five-year-olds, compared to older or younger children. This would be important because the zone of proximal development would be very different for older children.

Scaffolding has largely been studied in young children, but it is likely that it continues throughout our lifetimes. One of the main reasons we take college film classes or read film criticism is to provide a scaffold for the movie-watching experience. In class, the teacher may spend 15 minutes introducing the day's film. Some of what she does is to tell students a few things to look out for (focusing attention); she draws parallels to other films (helping find good schemas); she anticipates some things they are likely to misunderstand; she often talks about the characters' internal states. For example, in preparing students to watch *Casablanca*, they need to be reminded about America's non-interventionist position in World War II prior to the bombing of Pearl Harbor. Because one of the film's most poignant subplots is about a young Bulgarian couple, students need to know about the tragic circumstances in Bulgaria at this point in history. She may want to be sure that the students know the German and French tunes that are used effectively in this movie: If you know what they are, they are more effective in conveying the emotional content of the film. She needs to be sure that the students know what the Vichy Government and Vichy water are, etc. This is certainly scaffolding.

As adults, we scaffold movies for each other all the time. If you discover your date hasn't seen *Hangover II* before you go to see *Hangover III*, you tell her about the previous movie. If you are going with a friend to see one of your favorite films, you mention things to look out for that you think will enhance his viewing, and as especially interesting moments are about to come up, you focus his attention on the screen. And after we watch a movie, we often have lengthy discussions, in which we try to correct misunderstandings and help our friends find pleasure in watching movies.

Developing the right schemas that allow us to understand a movie is important in gaining pleasure from the moviegoing experience: It is difficult to imagine getting much enjoyment out of a film that you barely understood. In Chapter 1, we discussed some research that indicated that personality is related to the kinds of film genres people like. But the kinds of genres people like is also related to their familiarity with the genre. For example, in mystery movies you have to know that the fun is trying to figure out who committed the dirty deed, usually a murder. Usually in a mystery, the director gives out a few pieces of information, and the viewer finds a motive ("Follow the money") and believes that one person is the likely culprit. Then the director gives a few more bits of information, and another motive seems the more likely ("It's usually the jilted lover") and then a few more bits of information and another possible motive lets us think, for a period of time, that someone else did it. If you understand that this is the way these kinds of films are organized, they can be great fun. If you have had no experience with this kind of film, they just seem to be an example of chaotic storytelling. A student wrote the following, bewildered response to *Vertigo*:

> This was a really awful movie. I can't understand why people think it's so good. First it seems to be a movie about this detective who develops a psychological problem. Then you think it's about ghosts, and then it's about a suicide. Then the main character goes crazy. Then it turns out the woman who died, didn't die, and there was some sort of plot for this man that you've completely forgotten about to kill his wife. And there's a love story tacked on to it that turns out terrible. I was confused and bored all the way through.

But after seeing several such films, listening to her classmates talk about them positively, and getting pointers about what to look for and how to watch a mystery, this student began to like them.

Understanding Montage

The plot of a movie is presented to us in units that are called **shots**. The order of the shots is called **montage**. The order is important. For example, suppose we see two different shots. In the first, we see the exterior of an apartment building with the Dome of Florence's cathedral in the background. In the second, we see a man standing in a room reading a letter. Most of us would assume that the man is inside an apartment in Florence, although the movie didn't actually tell us that. But if the order of the shots is reversed so that we see the man reading first and then the apartment building and the Dome, we are likely to think that the man has received a letter from Florence or from someone he met in Florence. Film theorists suggest that montage creates a **third meaning**, independent of the literal meaning of two shots that are juxtaposed.

Montage does other things besides **locating** the action and showing us what people are thinking or seeing (usually referred to as **character perspective**). Two events may be happening at the same time. A car is driving down the street. The next shot is of an ambulance racing down another street. The montage cuts back and forth. We would not be surprised if the ambulance runs into or narrowly misses the car. This can be referred to as **simultaneity**. Montage often simplifies and shortens the action. We have a shot of a man holding a car door for his wife. We then have a shot of his face looking pleased. In the next shot, he is driving. We have left out him going around the car, getting in, turning on the ignition and pulling out into the street. This kind of shortening is called **ellipsis**.

One other thing that can happen between shots is that we can change scenes. Often there is a cue to this change. It can be a **dissolve**, where one scene merges into another, or it can be a **fade**, in which the scene just disappears into black. Music, surroundings or another location shot can cue us that we are now in a different time and place, potentially with different characters. Usually we move from one scene to another one forward in time, but we can also move backward in time, in a scene that is often called a **flashback**.

Often a scene begins with what is called an **establishing shot**, which is another term for a *location shot*. In an imaginary scene, the establishing shot could be looking in through a plate glass window into a diner. Helen is sitting in the booth alone. She's looking at the menu and then at her watch, in close-up. It is 6:15. Our next shot is Henry running down the street, looking at his watch. This would be an example of *simultaneity*. In the next shot, we see a lot of bustle around Helen, and she looks at her watch again. It is now 6:25. This would be an example of ellipsis. Then Henry walks in, kisses her on the cheek and sits opposite her. We then have a medium shot from inside the diner so that we see both of them. Helen and Henry's positions are now reversed on the screen. He says, "Sorry. I got held up in traffic." We then go to a close-up of Helen. She looks down sadly. This is what Henry is seeing, so it would be a *character perspective* shot. We see Henry's hand come into the frame and hold her hand. We hear Helen say, "You could have left earlier if you wanted to be here on time." We have a close-up of Henry. Then a close-up of Helen. Then back to a close-up of Henry. He wipes his cheek. He says: "I was in a meeting and I couldn't get away." We now have another close-up of Henry. He's in another place. There has been a change in location and we are not in the time frame of the rest of the scene. The back of a woman's head comes into the frame and kisses him on the cheek, and when it pulls away, there is lipstick on his cheek. He takes a handkerchief and wipes away lipstick from the same spot that he wiped in the previous shot. This is a flashback. Finally, there is a medium shot of the two of them in the diner again. "Sorry. It won't happen again."

This scene would last about 45 seconds, although it accounted for about 15 minutes of action. It consists of nine shots, one of which is from another time and place. No adult used to watching TV or movies would have difficulty understanding it. Yet it clearly involves a fairly sophisticated ability to understand narrative. When we remember the events in this scene some time later, we may actually remember it as if it all was done in one shot. He comes in. They talk about his being late. And we now know that the reason he is late is that he was with another woman.

Adults have been shown to prefer scenes that are told using montage techniques over the same scenes being told without many cuts (Kraft, 1981). They report that they find the cut sequences more interesting, more active, quicker and, paradoxically, longer than the uncut sequences. They do not, however, remember the cuts very well. Just as Bartlett would have predicted, they remember the scenes differently from the exact images they were presented with, and they remember seeing the emergent "third meanings" conveyed by montage. For example, in our imaginary scene, you may even "remember" that Henry has broken up with the other woman, or that he is lying to Helen, even though there is nothing we literally saw that tells us this. You also are likely to "remember" this scene as happening before the scene in the diner, not that it was a brief flashback within the scene.

To return to our question about how hard is it to understand a movie, psychologists want to know whether our understanding of montage is innate or whether it is learned though watching a lot of TV and movies (and reading stories that use similar techniques). They want to know how difficult is it for children, for example, to understand plots told using sophisticated montage techniques. Do people from cultures that do not have TV or movies have difficulty following the narrative in movies? The assumption among early cognitive psychologists was that it was difficult for children and others unfamiliar with movies to follow montage. Film theorists, who generally believe that watching a film is a complex and highly symbolic act, even more strongly believe that one must learn to comprehend movies through a long process of learning how to read the symbol systems of a movie.

Some cognitive psychologists such as Rogers (2005) suggest that much of movie imagery and montage is accessible to us without a great deal of sophisticated learning. A child or a person from another culture who cannot read the watch in the imaginary scene described above may not know that ten minutes has elapsed, but if we had seen Helen sitting before a full plate of food and then seen her sitting before an empty plate, wiping her mouth, it may be easy for almost anyone to know that time has passed. So when children or people from other cultures have difficulty understanding a film narrative, it may be that they do not understand the specific content, rather than that they do not understand the process of montage.

Film critics may think learning to understand movies is very difficult because they are often interested in very sophisticated films. If we try to understand how an adult or a child processes the information in a straightforward drama or comedy, it may require very little specific learning on their part. Theoretically, the image in our diner scene from the outside turns everything around when the image is shot from inside. That would seem complicated, but from the time children can crawl, they watch their parents from different parts of the room. As they move, their perspective changes, just like shots from a moving camera. They may become interested in something else, and get back to their parents after a few minutes of inattention. This is like ellipsis. They may look back and forth at two simultaneous actions.

If we are interested in a complex film, such as 8½, it may require some special knowledge to understand what is going on. This film is about a director, Guido, who has the equivalent of writers block. He is making a movie about a cellist who is preparing to go into space, but he is really trying to make sense of his personal life, which is unraveling. Some of the time in the movie, we are in reality. Guido is talking to potential actors and giving them screen tests. He is talking with his scriptwriter. He is trying to get some publicity shots of himself with a local cardinal, because his previous movie was condemned by the church. Other times he is in his memory. He remembers his childhood. He remembers when he was a school child going down to the seashore to see an obese prostitute who lived in a bunker there, and having her dance for him. Having no real interest in the movie he is pretending to make, he shoots a screen test of this episode from his life. He is also having difficulty sleeping, so he is also remembering his dreams. We often see the same scene in four versions: the actual action; a memory of it; the version he is shooting; and the dream version. It's pretty complicated.

There is also a fifth level. In 1963, Fellini was a celebrity, and Italians would have known a good deal about him professionally and personally. A few years before, he had actually abandoned a movie project about sending a cellist into space. 8½'s rocket set, seen at the beginning and end of the movie, was actually built for the failed movie project. To obtain funding for

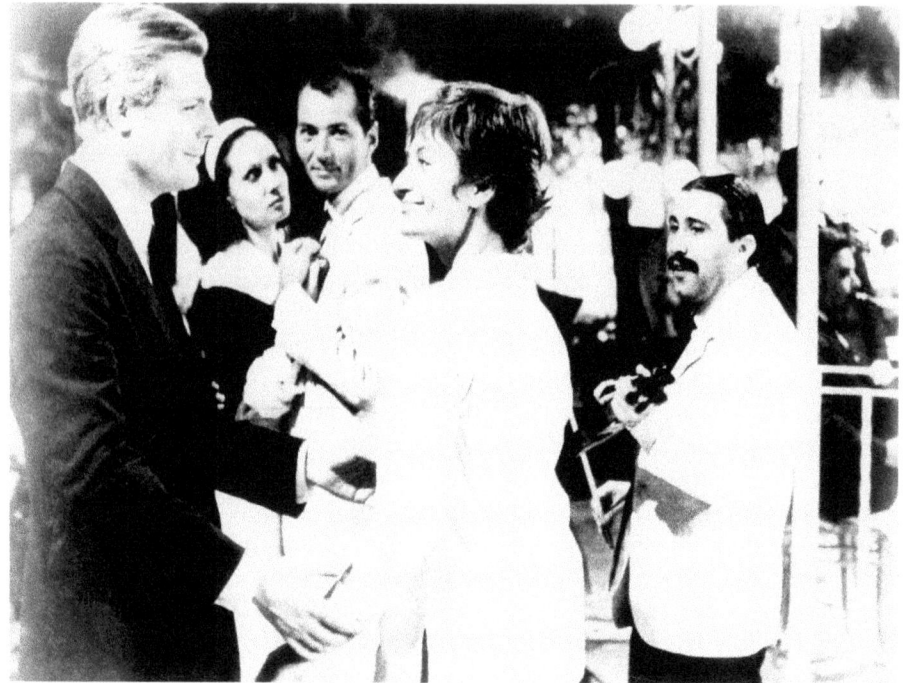

The movie director, Guido Anselmi (Marcello Mastroianni), unexpectedly bumps into his wife (Anouk Aimee) in the resort town where he is preparing to shoot his new picture in *8½* (Embassy Pictures, 1963).

8½, he had to agree to incorporate this expensive set into the plot of the movie (Bondanella, 1991). His mistress is playing his mistress, etc. So, while it is a movie that may not be fully understood by children or people from cultures without a rich media tradition, it is also a very interesting and very funny movie.

Children and Montage

When we do research on children's cognitive abilities in any area, there are a lot of complications. One is that they often do not understand the questions we are asking, or perhaps they do not understand that in a research setting you give factual, not fanciful answers. For example, Troseth and DeLoache (1998) describe an anecdote in which a colleague's three-year-old daughter was told that she was going to be on television. She asked, "Will I still be here?" and when told that she would still be there, she commented that there would be two of her then. This kind of confusion between the image on a TV screen and reality was also found in a study by Flavell, Flavell, Green, and Korfmacher (1990) in which a substantial number of three-year-olds said that if you tipped over a TV on which there was an image of a bowl of popcorn, the popcorn would fall out. Troseth and DeLoache's main study, however, suggested that very young children quite readily grasp that images on a TV and reality are different, although there can be a relation. They showed two-year-old and two-and-a-half-year-old children a video of someone hiding an object in a room. When the two-and-a-half-year-olds went into that room, they easily found the object, but the two-year-olds had difficulty doing so. When the video was arranged so that the children thought they were actually looking into the room, however, the two-year-olds easily found the object! It is difficult to make absolute sense of these findings, but they suggest that the way we pose questions to young children will influence the answers we get.

The first studies of montage and young children suggested that children did not really understand that various shots told a coherent narrative. Children seemed to be telling the researchers that they viewed each shot as separate and unrelated to the shots that came before and after them. And yet, if you watch any Disney movie, montage plays an important role, and young children seem to understand these movies.

Smith, Anderson and Fischer (1985) conducted two studies that examined the way that children understand montage. In the first study, they used familiar toys to tell a short series of events. They edited the films in three ways:

1. The events were seen by a stationary camera; no montage was used.
2. The events were seen by a stationary camera that panned (moved over the scene) and zoomed (became close-up).
3. The camera not only panned and zoomed, but cut for close-ups and different perspective shots.

Three- and five-year-old children were then given the same toys used in the stories and asked to act the stories out. Five-year-old children remembered about twice as much information as the three-year-olds, but within each age group, there were no significant differences among the three editing techniques.

In the second study, the researchers constructed 12 films using toys, which used location, ellipsis, character perspective or simultaneity. They then asked four-year-olds and seven-year-olds to use the toys to tell the story. They scored whether the children, in retelling the story, included material that was part of the "third meaning." For example, if an establishing shot placed a character in one location, did the children put the toy in the correct location? If the shots moved between two actions, when the children performed the story, did they show the two actions happening simultaneously and continuously? Did they show things that were left out in an ellipsis, e.g., if a character was standing near an object and a second character asked for the object, did the children show the first character pick up the object and bring it to the first character? If something was shown from a character's perspective, for example, looking out a window, did the child have the character say, "Now I see the moon," even though he didn't say that in the film they watched?

Again, while seven-year olds did a better job than the four-year-olds, the younger children showed considerable ability to understand montage. Table 3.1 summarizes the data, combined for the different montage techniques. What this table does not tell us is that in some individual films, the younger children have very hard times interpreting a specific film. Because the article is short, the authors do not address this issue. Perhaps it is a question of knowledge. As we suggested in our imaginary diner scene, if children couldn't tell time or read some other important factual element, they would not know that ten minutes had elapsed.

Table 6.1.
The Percentage of Time Children Provided Information That Existed Only in the Montage.

	Four-Year-Olds	Seven-Year-Olds
Location	59	86
Ellipsis	78	98
Simultaneity	42	94
Character Perspective	62	67

Anthropological Studies of Montage

Forsdale and Forsdale (1966) reported incidents when individuals from non–Western, media-limited cultures had difficulty telling when a montage indicated a change in scene vs. one which was just a different shot of the same scene. Their participants saw many more scene changes than were actually represented in the films. Their results have been interpreted to suggest that one has to learn how to read a film. But if very young Western children can read films with little exposure to films, why can't adults from these cultures?

The answer is probably that they *can* understand montage, but that they, like young children, do not have the information that signals a change of scene or just a change in perspective. For example, we know what is in an apartment and what is in a diner. So when we have the interpolated scene in our hypothetical scene above that is clearly in an apartment, we know that we are now in a different place and time. Likewise, if you have never been in a diner, a shot of two persons in a booth, behind which are other booths, and a shot of two people in a booth where there is a plate glass window and a lunch counter behind them, might signal to you that the location has changed.

The classic German film M (1931) is based on a serial killer from that time who preyed on children. The police become very vigilant and they close down the bars, brothels and drug dens. The city's criminals, upset about this, decide to form a vigilante squad themselves to catch the killer. A lengthy montage sequence uses simultaneity as it cuts back and forth between a meeting of police officials and a meeting of mob bosses. They are discussing similar issues, and there is a kind of ironic humor that comes out of this sequence. The problem is, most contemporary American viewers cannot tell when we have moved from the police office to the mob boss meeting. Both are in rather bare rooms. Everyone in both rooms is chain smoking. Everyone in both rooms is male. They look the same, because we cannot recognize the importance of the ways the people are dressed and talk. If we really understood how a criminal boss in 1931 Germany and police officials dressed, or recognize street German from 1931, we would understand the irony in his scene. Here, instead of assuming that there are two locations, many people think that the cuts between the two meetings are different shots of the same group.

Sequencing

It has been a staple of storytelling from at least the time of Homer onward to begin the story in the middle, and at a strategic point to go back and supply the beginning. Odysseus's story in the *Odyssey* begins during the ninth year of his return trip home from the Trojan War. About a third of the way through, at a dinner party, Odysseus gets a chance to tell the story of the first nine years of his travels.

Being able to understand the sequence of events in an important cognitive skill. For many years, there was a subtest on intelligence tests that measured this ability. Children or adults were given what amount to frames of a cartoon that are out of order, and they are asked to arrange them in their proper sequence. While we get better with this task with age, very young children can do simple examples of this task. For example, if you gave children four pictures, one of a child halfway up a slide, one of the child sliding down the slide, one of the child at the back of a slide on the ground, and one of the child at the top of the slide, most four-year-olds can arrange this sequence of events in the proper order, particularly if they have had any exposure to a slide. You can even change the view of the child in each picture, so that one might be seen from behind the slide and another from in front of the slide.

Psychology researchers study how we comprehend plots and how different kinds of storytelling devices affect our understanding of plot in several ways. One of the most common is to develop multiple ways of telling the same story and seeing how the different ways of telling the story affect our ability to remember and understand the plot. Cowen (1988) completed a study in which he edited a story in four ways, from a simple straightforward telling of the story with few shots, to having many shots and telling the story somewhat out of sequence. The adults in his study had little trouble sorting out the sequence of events, but contrary to expectations, the use of multiple shots seemed to help the audience understand the motives of the individual characters better. Perhaps it is because changing shots would keep our attention better, or that by using montage, third meanings are created.

Most commercial films tell stories in a linear way, in chronological order. Certain kinds of stories, however, cannot be told that way. Mysteries, for example, often begin with the circumstances immediately after a crime has been committed. Chronologically, this would be time C. Then we begin the investigation, which is time D. The detective investigates the relationships among the principal suspects, which is time A, which leads to the actual crime, which is time B. It's an elaborate example of the card arrangement task. The same structure can be seen in *Casablanca*. While the main story takes place over roughly two or three days in December 1941, but about halfway through the film, there is a flashback to 1939.

Another kind of film that tells stories out of sequence will be discussed in the last chapter: films that represent the process of psychotherapy. The classic form of this genre of film begins with a client who has problems (Time C). Therapy (and life) go on (Time D) with occasional flashback to earlier events in the client's life (Time B), until the most critical events that created the client's problems are discovered (Time A), which allows the client to heal (Time E). Movies like *Good Will Hunting* (1997) and *Spellbound* (1945), discussed in the last chapter, follow this structure. There is no other way to tell these stories. Fortunately, few people have difficulty following them.

The Primacy Effect: Does It Work in Movies?

What happens in a movie when conflicting information is presented? This is a particularly important question to ask when we are discussing our evaluations of a character. For example, in a very early scene in the classic *Gone with the Wind* (1939), as we first see Rhett Butler, one of Scarlett O'Hara's friends tells her several stories about how he is a bad person, his parents have disowned him, he has behaved badly toward a woman, he has an irregular occupation. When we actually see him shortly thereafter, he behaves in a very different way. For 70 years, film audiences have ignored Scarlett's friend's warnings, and they like Rhett Butler very much.

This is an area of research where it become clear that storytelling is very different in the movies than it is in text. Beginning with classic studies by Hovland (1957), text descriptions have found what is called a **primacy effect**, that is, the first information is generally believed for a long time, despite subsequent information that contradicts it. For example, an introductory description of a policeman might be that he is tired, lazy and inattentive. He then goes on to discover major evidence to solve a crime. When we ask readers to tell us how he solved the crime, they are more likely to say that he was "lucky" than that he was "actively using his intellect." We could create a similar scenario that initially described our policeman as smart and driven to solve cases and then describes a series of accidental discoveries, and usually readers will say that he "solved the crime because he was active and able to tell good evidence from bad."

Another use of the idea of the primacy effect has been found in studies of college lecturers. If a guest lecturer is introduced as an expert, her lectures are generally rated as highly organized, informative and interesting and the speaker is regarded as smart and skillful, while if she is introduced as a person with a lot of experience in the field, but students are asked to bear with her because she is not a teacher or researcher, students will generally rate the lecture as disorganized and not very smart. Even if the two lectures are exactly the same and delivered by the same person.

Cowan (1984) made brief movies representing some of the exact stories used in the original Hovland studies. He was not able to find a primacy effect. In the movies, he found that viewers' ratings of the character were based on their most recent behavior.

What accounts for the differences in findings between text and film? It is perhaps the fact that in a text, almost everything is up to your imagination. You get to decide what characters look like, what they are wearing, and what their personalities and motivations are, except when the author has given us specific details. As we read a book, we may revise our opinions and views of characters as the author gives us more information. But so much of how we see a character has been invented by us at the first moment the character has been introduced, it will take a lot for us to change our minds significantly. In a movie, many things are settled from the first shot onward. A particular actor is playing the part. He or she is of a certain body type, age, physical attractiveness, etc., and these actors have prepared to present their character in a specific way. They may have prepared to come off as confident at first, only to allow you to see the cracks in their façade. There will be surprises along the way. For example, there are only hints in the first half of 8½ that there is no movie. We know that Guido is anxious about something (why

Guido (Marcello Mastroianni), wrapped in a bath sheet and wearing his signature hat, attempts to get his fantasy memories under control in *8½* (Embassy Pictures, 1963).

else would he have a dream about confinement and escape at the beginning?), but the potential for his wife to encounter his hard-to-control mistress could account for that. But why, we wonder, does he refuse to tell the actors anything about their roles? Why does he avoid the producer? Why is he filming screen tests of actual events in his life rather than scenes from the movie?

We are prepared to believe Guido until we have caught him in too many lies. For some viewers, it is not until the scene where Claudia Cardinale, playing herself, directly asks him whether there really is a part for her in his movie or even a movie that some viewers understand that the movie is a sham.

* * *

The end of *8½* is a comic catastrophe. At a press conference that is forced on him by his producers, Guido can no longer keep his secret. The world will see that he is a fraud. There is no movie. After imagining a number of ways out, including a quick suicide under the VIP table, he admits it and the clowns and extras who were scheduled for the press conference begin marching around the rocket ship. Before he leaves, his insufferable script co-writer informs him that the purpose of art is to create silence. What is finally left is the shy, curious schoolboy he once was, the lonely boy from the beach, the erotically charged boy who visits the enormous prostitute, the spoiled boy who is bathed by all the adoring women of his family in the film's central scene.

There is no ready schema for *8½*. It is therefore a bit of a struggle to understand, at least the first time you watch it. We believe that this is a film that is enhanced by a second viewing. (Did you notice that the woman in the lingerie in the opening scene was his mistress? Did you see the rocket ship? Did you notice that the woman bringing him water at the spa was the actress who saw through his scheme?) But even if much of it remains a mystery, this is a one-of-a-kind movie about moviemaking and anxiety and sleep and the long-remembered comforts and agonies of childhood.

* * *

The three chapters in this section were about the experience of a movie: how we attend to the sounds and sights; how we may learn from a movie; and how we piece all this together to form an entire meaningful experience. We have had to rely a good deal on tangential research—research on picture-looking, TV-watching and plot construction from written text—because research in a theater has been so hard to do that it has never really been done and because movies are inconveniently long for the typical psychological experiment.

And yet all of this does come together to help us make sense of the movie-watching experience. Today we watch more movies on TV screens than in theaters, so the research on TV is directly useful. We talk about cinematography with the same terms we apply to photographs, drawings and paintings. Stories are stories, and we understand them in very similar ways, whether they are told to us or they unfold to us on stage, screen or the written page. But there are some interesting differences that may affect the outcomes. Films are set while plays happen differently in each performance; plays and movies supply everything you see or hear, while text leaves most things up to one's imagination.

Now, the movie is over and we get on with our lives. In the next section, we will look at what happens after the movie.

Key Psychological Terms

Accommodation: Developing new cognitive structures so that new information can be understood. (Piaget)
Assimilation: The ability to understand new information with existing cognitive structures. (Piaget)

Confabulation: Constructing a narrative in real life from fragments of memory, often associated with brain injury.

Primacy effect: The finding in prose narrative the readers stay with information they first receive about characters. There is some evidence that this does not apply to characters in movies.

Scaffolding: Building a series of efficient steps to learn content that is well beyond the zone of proximal development.

Schema: A cognitive structure, associated with both Piaget's theory of thinking and Bartlett's theory of memory.

Zone of Proximal Development: Those things that can be learned next. (Vygotsky).

Key Cinema Terms

Character perspective shot: A shot that shows us what a character is thinking or seeing.

Dissolve: This occurs when the final shot in a scene gradually blends into the first shot of the next scene.

Ellipsis: Leaving out part of the action in a scene.

Establishing shot: The first shot in a scene which "establishes" the characters and location of the scene.

Fade: This occurs at the end of a scene when the last shot gradually disappears, signaling the end of the scene.

Flashback: A scene that comes after another scene in novel or film, but antecedes it in the sequence of events of the film.

Location shot: An establishing shot showing the location of a scene.

Montage: The sequence of shots in a scene.

Third meaning: Generally agreed upon meanings in film that arise from the way a film is cut rather than directly stated in the film.

PART III

After the Movie

The processes that we had to go through in choosing the movie are forgotten; the movie has been seen, the popcorn eaten; we have discussed it with the friends we went with; we are home later that evening, or a few days later, or even years later. Has the movie had an effect on us? That is what we are going to discuss in these final two chapters.

Some movies no doubt have lingering effects, at least for some people. Johnson (1980) studied two samples of adults and asked about movies that had caused them extreme distress. This research was prompted by reports that in 1973 and 1975, several individuals had to be hospitalized by extreme reactions to *The Exorcist* and *Jaws*. These reactions were called traumatic neurosis (Bozzuto, 1975), but today we would refer to them as PTSD, post-traumatic stress disorder. Johnston found that about 40 percent of the people he interviewed could remember being very disturbed by a movie for more than 48 hours; that the stress reactions following a movie had all of the characteristics of other stress disorders; and contrary to expectations, the main reason the respondents gave for their disturbance was not the portrayal of graphic violence but the overall intensity of the movie. This kind of research has been taken seriously. When preview audience were struck by the graphic portrayal of the landing sequences in *Saving Private Ryan* (1998), the Veterans Administration staffed 125 additional counselors on their phone lines for the movie's opening weekend (Bauman, 1998). The demand for phone time was so great that they continued offering enhanced phone counseling for several additional days.

There are two chapters in this section. In the first, we will look at whether manufacturers who pay to have their products placed in movies are spending their money wisely, and we will consider how movies influence us for bad (smoking, suicide and violence) or good (tolerance, political beliefs and romance). The second chapter, on the portrayal of psychologists, the mentally ill and psychological treatment, will discuss how movies may influence our view of different professionals and atypical individuals. In this chapter, we will abandon talking mostly about a single movie and consider a few different movies that may have helped shape our cultural knowledge and expectations about mental illness and therapy.

7

Selling Watches, Changing Hearts and Minds

Movies get a lot of criticism. We are not referring to film criticism, which tells us whether films are entertaining and well made. We are talking about the fact that hardly a month goes by without some special interest group telling us that a particular film, director, actor or studio has an agenda to make us think more positively or negatively of African-Americans, gays, Arabs, Evangelicals, etc. Sometimes this is obviously true. Michael Moore's 2004 documentary *Fahrenheit 9/11* was certainly designed to influence the presidential election, and Mel Gibson's same-year film *The Passion of the Christ* had as one of its goals increasing interest in Christianity. The question here is: Are movies effective in changing our attitudes about products, behaviors and beliefs?

Most of the time, it is difficult to separate the economic intentions of the filmmakers—attracting a large audience and making money—from the values the film seems to espouse. *The Lion King* (1994) was resoundingly criticized because 1) the female lions did all the work, while the males took all the glory; 2) the evil hyenas were portrayed by voice actors of color; and 3) the principal wicked lion "sounded gay" (e.g., Chethik, 1994).

Of course, in nature, female lions do most of the hunting and childrearing, regardless of prevalent views on gender roles at Disney. One also suspects that the wide variety of accents and vocal timbres in the cast was a decision to make the story intelligible (and likable) to young children, rather than to have them associated with good or bad characters. Which is not to say that some children might not become frightened of an educated British accent because of Jeremy Irons' creepy portrayal of uncle Scar. And it should be remembered that, at other times, Disney has been accused of being too pro-feminist, pro-gay and anti-majority values.

There are striking examples of how, in small ways, films have altered the way we live. One example of this has to do with the films of the silent movie star Rudolph Valentino. Valentino was one of the original gender-benders, and in several of his films he did things that were uncommon for men to do. In one film, for example, he wore a bracelet. That caused a small bubble in the men's bracelet business, but it passed. In *Son of the Sheik,* however, Valentino wore a Cartier Tank wristwatch. Until that time, men carried pocket watches and women wore wristwatches. The following Christmas season, wives and girlfriends bought men wristwatches, and this change was permanent, or at least until the smartphone replaced the watch. James Bond films are credited with making American consumers more interested in French food, wine, foreign sports cars, casino gambling, the martial arts and international travel (Chapman, 2008). Almost every Bond film, too, has occasioned groups to speak out that his treatment of minority groups and women may have a detrimental effect on the way we view these people. There are no public available data about whether applications to the CIA increase after the release of a Bond film.

But the question remains whether movies affect us in larger ways: Do they alter our political ideas or our understanding of justice or our view of our fellow man? One film that is likely to get an affirmative response to those questions is *The Best Years of Our Lives* (1946). Begun mere months after the end of World War II, it details the first few weeks home of three returning servicemen: a mature, married banker who had spent the war as a sergeant; a drugstore clerk who had become a pilot and an officer and impulsively married a woman he barely knew; and a sailor who lost both of his hands in a fire aboard his ship, who returns home to his shocked family and the girl he left behind. None has an easy time of it. This film provided a new way of viewing returning servicemen and led to the adoption of many current ideas, including PTSD.

In this chapter, we will look at some of the research on how movies influence us. We will begin by examining the issue of product placement, the practice of having the well-liked stars of films use specific branded products. We will then shift our attention to the issue of how movies may affect rates of smoking, sexuality, violence and suicide in teenagers, before looking at how movies may influence us on social and political issues.

Product Placement

We work about 35 miles from the plant that makes Reese's Pieces. When the candy was first introduced, it did not catch on. Not until 1982 when Elliott used them to lure E.T. out of the shed in his backyard. Perhaps people thought, if extra-terrestrials like them, I might, too. Sales increased 65 percent. Of course, the parent corporation mounted a huge tie-in advertising blitz, which certainly accounted for some of that increase.

If you look at films from the 1940s and 1950s, most of the products that were being consumed by the actors were not real brands—although even in the 1930s, the MGM studio had an office for soliciting placements. Today, however, companies routinely pay large sums of money to have their branded products placed in movies. Lexus paid more than five million dollars to have its product featured in Spielberg's *Minority Report* (2002). This practice helps defray the huge costs of making films. Both movie critics and social critics are outspoken against the practice, but according to research by DeLorne and Reid (1999), American moviegoers generally find that the practice makes films more realistic. Viewers in other countries may not be as accepting (Gould, Gupta & Grabner-Krauter, 2000).

There are two competing theories behind product placements. One is the idea from social psychology called **mere exposure**. Mere exposure suggests that by simply being exposed to something in a normal situation, one becomes more positive toward it (Zajonc, 1968). The theory is based on the observation that almost all animals are wary of novel stimuli and tend to avoid them. Thus, for a commercial product, it is a good idea to have potential consumers become familiar with it. This might occur in a scene in a grocery store where a sign for a new soft drink is conspicuous. No one purchases one or drinks one with enjoyment. We just see the product logo, preferably for a long time, and the idea is that the next time we go to the store, we might pick one up because we are no longer wary of its newness.

The other theory is derived from observational learning. We discussed this idea in Chapter 4 and will return to it later in this chapter when we describe research on the relationship between aggression and watching violent movies (Bandura, Ross & Ross, 1961; 1963). Here the product is used (a car is driven, food is eaten) and audience members may be influenced to want to use the product themselves. Rather than "merely" being exposed, and forming an **implicit memory**, in this situation the advertiser wants the audience member to have an **explicit memory** of the product and imitate the actor, remembering where he or she saw the product and remembering its name. *Some* of the general findings from this area are:

Children (and people in general) will copy specific behaviors more if the person they observe is one they identify with. We identify with characters on the screen who are like us in terms of age, sex and other characteristics; we also identify with people we would like to be like. If we see James Bond go into a bar and order a vodka martini, we are more likely to try a vodka martini if we identify with James Bond. It also helps if we are watching a genre of film that we like (Redker, Gibson & Zimmerman, 2013). We tend to imitate "good" characters. If James Bond is perceived as a good character, we are more likely to imitate his drink choice.

We tend to imitate behavior that is rewarded by others or is effective. If James Bond offers a stunning woman at the bar a vodka martini and she accepts it and then leaves the bar with him, we are more likely to drink vodka martinis.

Observing behavior on the screen that leads to punishment or ineffective outcomes or behaviors performed by the "bad" characters may lead to those behaviors being less likely to be adopted. That is, if we see a bad guy drinking a vodka martini, we are less likely to drink vodka martinis in the future. If he drinks a vodka martini and gets violently sick, we are even less likely to drink vodka martinis. If he offers a vodka martini to an attractive woman at the bar, and she tells him that his taste in drinks is disgusting, and she leaves alone, we are less likely to order vodka martinis in the future. We are picking on vodka martinis because in the 1960s Smirnoff's paid the producers of the Bond films a substantial amount of money to have him change his drink of choice from gin martinis, which he drank in the Ian Fleming novels, to vodka martinis (Chapman, 2008).

Karrh, McKee and Pardun (2003) conducted a survey of members of a professional group, ERMA (the Entertainment Resources and Marketing Association), which is responsible for placing products in movies and TV shows. These authors asked these professionals what they wanted in a placement. In order of importance, what these individuals wanted was:

1. The product is portrayed in a favorable light.
2. The product is shown in use.
3. The brand name is mentioned in the dialogue.
4. The brand is shown for a long period of time.
5. The placement receives publicity in the press.
6. Competing brands are *not* shown.
7. The movie achieves box office and critical success.
8. Lead actors are associated with the product.

We can see here that the ideas behind those who place products in movies are a combination of mere exposure (the brand is mentioned or shown for a long time) and observational learning (it is shown in a favorable light, it is shown in use, it is associated with the lead actor, its use leads to pleasant outcomes). The issues of the product being in a successful movie relate to how many people are exposed to it, while publicity in the press would include the product being shown in trailers for the movie, etc.

Of course, too, manufacturers want to avoid their product being associated with a negative scene or even being placed a movie that is dark, depressing or violent. Coca-Cola was not happy when their polar bear ad was interspersed with a violent murder in *Natural Born Killers* (1994) rather than in the scene where actors were watching the Super Bowl, for which permission had been given.

Product Placement and Children

Critics are more vocal against product placement in films aimed at children. There are two reasons for this. First, children often view films again and again. Therefore, what for an adult may be a very subtle message, may be repeatedly hammered home on children. Second, some people think that children are more easily led by advertising messages than adults. Other researchers, however, are less concerned, as they point out that children have limited processing and memory skills.

Auty and Lewis (2004) tested several hypotheses about children and product placements by showing children one of two two-minute clips from the movie *Home Alone*. Both scenes showed the family eating. In one, a Pepsi was prominent in the scene. It was talked about by name, and it was spilled. In the other scene, the family ate an unbranded meal, and Kevin (Macaulay Calkin) draws attention to what they are eating by saying "Bless this highly nutritious macaroni and cheese microwavable meal that the supermarket had on sale. Amen." Younger (six- and seven-year-old) and older (11- and 12-year-old) children were studied. Most of the children had seen the movie before, some several times.

After watching the clip, but before asking questions about it, the children were allowed to choose between a Coke and a Pepsi. Forty-two percent of the children who saw the macaroni and cheese clip chose Pepsi, while 62 percent of the children who saw the Pepsi clip chose Pepsi. This suggests that the clip influenced their choice.

The researchers then asked the children to remember what the characters were eating and analyzed these differences by age. Fifty percent of the younger children who saw the Pepsi clip remembered that they were drinking Pepsi, while 67 percent of the older children who saw the Pepsi clip remembered Pepsi. Although somewhat more of the older children remembered Pepsi, it was not sufficient to say that they remembered significantly better.

The researchers then analyzed the data by those who remembered Pepsi by name and those who did not, and they found that there was no difference in their choice of Pepsi. That is, being able to remember explicitly that the characters had been drinking Pepsi did not affect their choice. Merely being exposed to the clip was the critical factor.

The researchers also examined whether the children had seen the movie before the session. Children who had seen the movie before and who saw the Pepsi clip were far more likely to choose Pepsi than those who had not seen the movie before and saw the Pepsi clip, those who had seen the movie before but saw the macaroni clip, or those who had not seen the movie before and saw the macaroni clip. In fact, all of the last three groups were more likely to choose Coke.

The researchers drew several conclusions. First, the memory that children have does not have to be explicit to influence their behavior. It was "merely" that they had exposure to the product. They also concluded that the processes are similar in the younger and older children. We might urge caution on accepting this idea. Statistical comparisons are influenced by the number of participants in the analysis. This study began with 96 children. When the comparison between choice of Pepsi and Coke was made between those who saw the Pepsi clip and those who saw the macaroni clip, all 96 children were included. When the comparison was made between age groups for the explicit memories for Pepsi, only half of the participants (those who had seen the Pepsi clip) were used. So there were only 48 children in this analysis. Twelve out of 24 younger children remembered Pepsi, while 16 out of 24 older children remembered Pepsi. With these small numbers, there is not enough statistical power to say conclusively that there was no real difference between the two groups.

Brown *et al.* (2017) put a twist to this issue by examining the effects of watching whole movies on children's snack choices immediately following. These 9- to 11-year-olds watched either *Alvin and the Chipmunks* (2007) or *Stuart Little* (1999). These movies, the authors tell us, were selected because they were similar in length, were live-action–computer animated movies, did not have health as their primarily focus, and featured a rodent as the main character. *Alvin* showed 36 different foods being consumed. Thirty-four of these were human foods, 17 of which were branded. *Stuart Little* contained 13 food items, 11 for humans, only two of which were branded. While children were more likely to select items they had seen in the movie, these authors found that when they compared the caloric intake between the two groups, there was no difference. While caloric intake is not the only important health-related aspect of food, this study does suggest that just imitating a movie in the short term might not be as disastrous as some claim.

Smoking (and Other Substance Use)

One concern about product placement is when the product is harmful, as in the case of cigarettes. Anti-tobacco groups have lobbied hard to get cigarette smoking removed from movies, but it is still there. Particularly it is still there in films that are not designed to be seen by children and young adolescents (PG-13- and R-rated films).

Because there has been substantial government funding for research in this area, there is plenty of literature on this topic. An example of research that looks at the risk of watching movies in which favorite actors smoke was conducted by Dalton et al. (2003). What is impressive about this study is its large sample size and the fact that it is a prospective study. In a **prospective study**, data is collected at one stage and further observations are made later. Other studies, called **retrospective studies**, have participants try to remember what they were like in the past. These are often flawed because, as we discussed in Chapter 3, our memories are actively trying to create meaningful stories and are not always accurate. In this case, students in grades five through eight in 14 schools in Vermont and New Hampshire completed a written survey about smoking behavior and attitudes in 1999; 3547 indicated that they have never smoked, not even a "few puffs." These students who had never smoked were then contacted one to two years later by telephone, and 2603 completed the interview. Two hundred-fifty-nine (ten percent) had initiated smoking. The students were then asked whether they had seen a list of 50 movies. Each student got a unique list of movies drawn at random from 601 popular movies that had been coded for the number of episodes of smoking in them. It was estimated that 52 percent of the smoking initiation could be attributed to the amount of smoking they had seen in the movies. Because this was a statistical analysis, the margin of error was that somewhere between 30 percent to 67 percent of the instances of smoking initiation could be linked to viewing smoking in the movies.

These results seem astonishing—more than 50 percent of the risk of starting smoking in early adolescents can be linked to seeing smoking in the movies! One would think that having parents who smoked or siblings who smoked or friends who smoked would be more important.

Of course, these were adolescents who had never smoked by the time they were 10 to 14, not even a "few puffs." Most of the adolescents who were at risk because of friends or parents who smoked were not included in this analysis—they had already taken a few puffs. It is also worth noting that of those adolescents who "initiated smoking" in this study, 80 percent said they had only had "a few puffs." Only two percent said they had smoked 100 or more cigarettes during the year or two since the study had begun.

What is compelling about this study is the amount of smoking in movies these adolescents had seen and compare that to how many started smoking. The participants were divided into four equal-sized groups (called **quartiles**) based on the amount of smoking they had seen. Of those who had seen the least amount of smoking, only three percent had initiated smoking. In those in the next-to-lowest quartile, nine percent had initiated smoking. Among those in the next highest quartile, 11 percent had initiated smoking, while in the quartile that had seen the highest number of smoking incidents, 16 percent had initiated smoking.

There is some other interesting information in this study. The total list of 601 movies consisted of the 25 most popular movies each year from 1988 to 1995, the most popular 100 movies each year from 1996 to 1999 and some additional movies popular with young teens. Forty-five percent were R-rated, while only 24 percent were PG or G. The respondents averaged saying that they had seen 16 of their sample of 50, so out of these 601 movies, students had seen about 200. Many must have been seen on TV or video. Most of the participants, then, had seen quite a few PG-13 and R-rated films.

It is also of interest that in the 16 films the students had seen, the average number of smoking incidents was 95. That's about six incidents per movie. That seems high to us, but the research cited in the previous section and in Chapter 4 suggests that we don't really have to be aware of such incidents for them to have an effect on us. We are just not paying particular attention to the amount of smoking when we watch most movies. After reading this research report, we watched the movie *Good Will Hunting*. We remembered that there was a little smoking in that movie. When we got to the 12th incident about halfway through the movie, we stopped counting.

Finally, some of the data collected in the original written surveys also correlated highly with initiating smoking. The group that were more likely to initiate smoking: adolescents high on sensation-seeking and rebelliousness, students doing average or poorly in school, adolescents with parents, friends or siblings who smoked, and children whose parents did not disapprove of smoking. Older adolescents were more likely to initiate smoking than the younger adolescents.

After this study was published in the highly influential journal *The Lancet*, several researchers wrote letters to the editor suggesting different interpretations of the data. One of the problems with correlational research is that it is very difficult to establish cause and effect relations. If two variables are correlated, one cannot determine whether A causes B, B causes A, or the relationship between A and B is caused by a third variable. Because this is a prospective study, however, we can rule out some of the possibilities, because events in the present cannot *cause* events in the past. So, for example, if sensation-seeking in 1999, when none of these particular participants smoked, is correlated with smoking later, it cannot be that the later smoking caused the earlier level sensation-seeking.

Responding to the critics of the study, the authors made clear what their interpretation of the data was. When children who are at risk for smoking are exposed to role models in the movies smoking, they are likely to start experimenting with smoking.

But there are other interpretations. Perhaps parents who don't care if their children smoke, also don't care if they watch R-rated movies or associate with other adolescents who do smoke. Perhaps teens who are high on sensation-seeking and rebelliousness watch a lot of films made primarily for adults and also try smoking for reasons other than they have seen smoking in the movies. They want to act grown-up or to defy rules.

Yet, when taken with other studies on smoking, and the literature on product placement, it is probable that watching people whom a young adolescent likes, such as movie stars, smoking in movies, makes it more likely he might try smoking (Distefan, Gilpin, Sargent & Pierce, 1999). And there is strong evidence that people who experiment with smoking when they are younger—even a few puffs—are more likely to become smokers later than those who do not.

It's no surprise that very similar questions about teens viewing movies showing alcohol and other drug use have been asked, often by the same researchers (e.g., Sargant, Wills, Stoolmiller, Gibson & Gibbons, 2006). The findings are similar, but there are important differences, largely because of how the use of different substances has been portrayed in movies. In general, though, children of parents who restrict R-rated films have less substance use than those whose parents do not restrict access to films made for adults. Tobacco use in movies is casual. Wedding and Niemec (2014) describe only two movies where tobacco use and tobacco addiction are mentioned, *The Royal Tenenbaums* (2001) and Jim Marmusch's quirky *Coffee and Cigarettes* (2003). Mostly, the characters in these two films struggle with their reliance on tobacco humorously.

That is not the case with alcohol. There are many films that treat the issues surrounding alcohol use seriously and show the near and far outcomes of heavy alcohol use. Excellent films such as *The Lost Weekend* (1945), *Days of Wine and Roses* (1962), *Leaving Las Vegas* (1995), *House of Sand and Fog* (2003) and *Smashed* (2012) feature portraits of alcoholism that are stark and thoroughly negative. It would be hard to imagine that many would want to adopt the behaviors of the main characters in these films. But there are also a lot of films that show casual alcohol use. Sargant *et al.* (2006) report that in those 601 films mentioned above, 52 percent of the G-rated and 90 percent of the PG-, PG-13- and R-rated contained some alcohol use, with the average amount of screen time increasing from just over a half-minute in G-rated movies to five minutes in R-rated movies. Watching a lot of drinking in movies was associated with teen drinking, controlling for age, sex, parenting style, smoking and sensation-seeking.

Marijuana use in movies is rarely either casual or psychologically problematic. Using marijuana will often get you in trouble, with your supplier, in comedies, or the law, in more serious films. *The Big Lebowski* (1998), for example, portrays Jeff Bridges' "The Dude" as an amiable, irresponsible weed addict whose recklessness leads to a series of situations that if this were not a Coen Brothers comedy would be life-threatening. But "The Dude" became and remains a icon whose phrases have become part of popular culture. Other drug use—heroin, cocaine, methamphetamine—is portrayed in movies as psychologically, physiologically and legally dangerous.

There is strong evidence that watching marijuana use in movies leads to marijuana use in teens (Cox, Gabrielli, Janssen & Jackson, 2018). Marijuana use is rarely found outside of R-rated films, so children whose parents restrict their watching R-rated films have a decreased risk of using marijuana. Cox et al. (2018) found, however, that not all viewing of marijuana and alcohol led to increased risk of use: Viewing substance use content *with parents* not only mitigated the risk of substance use onset but provided some resistance to later use.

Early Sexuality

In the present time of high scrutiny of the tobacco industry, it is highly unlikely that any cigarette company is paying a studio to include their brand of cigarettes in a movie aimed at children. It is also highly unlikely that people making movies are deliberately trying to make young teens experiment with their sexuality. But that does not mean that movies do not have that effect. One issue uncovered by Dalton et al. (2003) was that many children and young teens are watching a lot of movies not intended for them.

National surveys of teenagers (e.g., Roberts, Foehr & Rideout, 2004) find that they use different types of media about seven hours per day. At the time of this particular study, TV was the most used, about three hours a day, and teens watched videos and movies about an hour a day—about as much time as they spent reading. If a teenager reads novels for an hour a day, she may read 20 or 30 novels a year. If she watches movies in theaters and on video for an hour a day, she can see 175 movies per year. That creates a lot of opportunity for young teens to be exposed to inappropriate content.

Pardum, L'Engle and Brown (2005) conducted an ambitious study of over a thousand seventh and eighth grade students in North Carolina. They ascertained how much time students spent using specific media (specific movies, TV shows, Internet sites, musical artists, newspapers and magazines) by having the participants keep a media use journal, and then they coded samples of each of these specific sources for sexual content in terms of nudity, relationships, sexual innuendo, touching and kissing, pubertal issues and intercourse. They then interviewed the students about their sexual activity and their intentions to have sex.

Overall, 11 percent of the media units, for example a scene in a specific movie, contained sexual content. In the movie category, 12 percent of the units contained sexual material. Forty-six percent of the time that a scene in a movie was coded as "sexual," it was because it contained nudity or partial nudity; 21 percent of the time it was because it was about relationships, and 17 percent of the time it was because there was touching and kissing. In 11 percent, there was sexual innuendo, and in only four percent was intercourse suggested or portrayed. The raters noted that only two percent of the sexual coded units in movies contained "sexually unhealthy" messages, and only one percent of the sexual movie units contained images or talk of sexual violence.

Having rated the most used media for their sexual content, the sexual media exposure of each participant was computed for each of the media studied and compared statistically to their reports of current sexuality and intentions to have sex. Thus, if an adolescent watched ten hours of movies which were rated as having 45 percent of their scenes having sexual content, their sexual exposure due to movies would be 4.5 hours. If they listened to 40 hours of music where 60 percent of the time the content was sexual, their sexual exposure due to music would be 24 hours. These authors found that there was a significant relationship between both current sexual behavior and intentions to engage in sex and the amount of sexual content in movies. Music produced somewhat higher relationships. TV and magazines produced no significant relationships to current sexual behavior, but did with intentions to have sex, while newspapers and Internet sites had no relationship to either current behavior or intentions.

In a follow-up analysis in this same research program, Brown, Halpern and L'Engle (2005) compared the difference in sexual media use by early maturing and late maturing girls. Early and late maturation was determined by the girls' self-reports of when they had begun to menstruate; 17 percent had not yet had their first period. Early maturing girls had more exposure and interest in sexual movies and TV, had seen more R-rated movies, and were more likely to report that they believed the media message was that it was okay for teenagers to have sex, compared to later maturing girls.

These authors suggest that for early maturing girls, TV, movies and magazines may serve as a "sexual super peer." That is, the portrayal of intimacy and sexuality in movies, TV and magazines serves as a source of information about how to act around members of the opposite sex when you are the only one in your class interested in the opposite sex. Later maturing girls, on the other hand, have real peers they can ask questions of. This study refines the ideas we discussed earlier concerning Engle and Kasser's (2005) ideas that girls who idolize male stars use watching their movies as scripts for how romantic encounters should take place. Those girls were more interested in and trusting of boys and more likely to be dating. It is possible that they were also early maturing.

As in the studies of substance use, watching movies with sexual content with parents has been found to dramatically reduce the risk of early sex in teens (Parkes, Wight, Hunt, Henderson & Sargant, 2013)

Suicide

Suicide is a common theme in movies. Some social critics and mental health practitioners have argued that representations of suicide, particularly in media available to adolescents, is irresponsible (Stack, 2005). The imitation of suicide representations in media is called the **Werther Effect**, because after the publication of Goethe's novella *The Sorrows of Young Werther* in 1787 there was a dramatic increase in suicide by gunshot throughout Europe. There are four questions here:

Do media representations of suicide increase suicide attempts?
Are there aspects of the presentation that increase or decrease the likelihood of imitation?
Do media represents of suicide only lead to individuals already likely to commit suicide imitating *the methods* presented in the media?
Even if the effect is only in imitating a method among those already likely to commit suicide, is the method shown more likely to lead to a "successful" attempt than other methods?

Historians believe that in the case of the Werther suicides, the answers are: Yes, suicide attempts seemed to increase overall because the suicide was portrayed as glorious and romantic (see Hittner, 2005). In *The Sorrows of Young Werther*, the hero fell in love with a woman who had made a deathbed promise to her mother to marry someone else. The novella consistently portrays Werther as a man who had missed his one opportunity for love, and it only gives his side of the story. The book closes with his suicide, and there is no description of the effects of his actions on others around him. The third question is difficult to answer because of when the novella was published, but it is believed that the actual rate of suicide went up, not just the imitation of the method. The answer to the last question is Yes, one of the problems with the method used by Werther in the novel is that a gunshot to the temple is a particularly effective method of moving a suicide attempt to a suicide. So, overall, the number of suicide attempts increased and more attempters used guns. Both contributed to a substantial increase of completed suicides.

We have many ideas of suicide, many of which are incorrect. One is that teenagers, particularly teenage girls, are at high risk for committing suicide. Depending on age, women are four to eight times *less* likely to commit suicide in the United States than men. Women's rates of suicide are relatively constant over ages, while men increase their rates with age. While about one in 5000 males commit suicide between the ages of 15 and 25, the rate triples by old age (Elnour & Harrison, 2008). What makes teenage suicide of great concern to psychologists is that most of the reasons for suicide, from an adult perspective, seem irrational. While one can understand the suicide of an older man who is facing disability, chronic pain and/or has experienced the loss of a spouse of many decades, it is frustrating to see a young person commit suicide over a break-up of a month-long relationship he identified as "the love of his life" or a failure to make an athletic team or getting into a first choice of college.

Another misconception about suicide is that people who are going to commit suicide have made up their mind: They will not talk about it, and even if they do, talking about it makes it more likely they will carry out their intention. The decision to commit suicide is often based on an incomplete examination of a situation. A teenager may feel she has no friends, has a bad home situation, and has missed out on some opportunity in her life that will make the rest of her life meaningless. Pointing out that in a year or two she may go to college, where she may make friends, be away from her home, and find other important aspects of a life may help direct her away from her suicidal intent. So some mental health workers think that a movie about teenage suicide and particularly suicide attempts, properly couched, can bring about positive results, if it gets those prone to suicide to seek professional help (Niederkrotenthaler *et al.*, 2010). If one seeks out help after thinking about or attempting suicide because he or she has seen representations of similar behavior in movies or other media, it is referred to as the **Papageno Effect**, after a character who stops a suicide attempt in Mozart's opera *The Magic Flute*. Thus, movies could have a negative, positive or maybe even a neutral effect on suicide rates.

Shoval *et al.* (2005) looked at the effects of a heavily promoted documentary on a teenage girl in Israel who planned to commit suicide and subsequently did so by jumping off a cliff. They looked at the number of attempted and successful suicides and the methods used for the two months before the broadcast and the month afterward, and compared them to the previous year. There were more "jumpers" following the documentary than in the two months before, but when they compared the data to the previous year, there were no differences in rates of attempts, suicides or methods. What was different, was that the age of suicide attempters decreased dramatically during the last week of the promotion. If the number of younger teens increased, the number of older teens had to decrease. Thus, this particular movie had a modest effect, but there was something about it that led younger teens to higher rates of suicide attempts.

Till *et al.* (2014) did a large online survey of adults and measured the psychological traits of suicide ideation, depression, psychoticism and life satisfaction and correlated scores on these traits with genre preferences and ratings of movies with and without main characters' suicides or suicide attempts. High suicidal ideation, high depression, high psychoticism and low life satisfaction were associated with preferences for *film noir*, tragedies and horror movies, but these traits did *not* predict either an interest in or avoidance of movies with suicidal content, except, unexpectedly, life satisfaction. Individual *high* in life satisfaction rated the movies with suicidal content higher than movies without suicidal content. The authors suggest that those with high life satisfaction may be better able to cope with such content.

The Effects of Watching Violent Movies

Pennell and Browne (1999), summarizing the potential links between watching aggressive media and serious violence, list five concerns that have been expressed by psychologists. First, frequent exposure to violence may lead to a reduction in empathy, as we discussed in Chapter 1. People low in empathy are more likely to victimize others, because they do not understand the effects of their actions on their victims. It is easier to steal from someone or assault them if you do not understand what the loss of specific objects may be or that being a victim of a theft or assault might make people fearful. A second result of watching a lot of media violence is that people may become desensitized to violence. **Desensitization** *is a process by which the negative associations involved with a behavior are removed.* Most of us would be alarmed if a friend violently attacked a stranger, but the concern here is that individuals who have been exposed to a lot of violent media material may not react in that manner. A third, more direct result is that those who see a lot of violence in the media may copy these violent behaviors. Fourth, individuals predisposed to aggression may have that predisposition unleashed by watching violent media. Fifth, concern has been expressed that those who watch a lot of aggressive media may come to regard violent behavior as much more common than it really is. Eron (2001) lists these as probable results of watching a lot of media violence and adds a sixth concern: children, adolescents and adults who watch a lot of violence may develop fantasies that include violence.

Of course, these same processes would occur for people who encounter a good deal of real-life violence. Police are at risk for this, as are people who live in crime-ridden neighborhoods. Pennell and Browne indicate that whether media are to blame for high rates of violent behavior among adolescents or whether real-life aggression is the culprit has not been demonstrated. Let's look at a few studies on the topic.

Albert Bandura and the Bobo Doll: Direct Imitation

The first of these processes to be studied was direct imitation. In a series of classic studies, Albert Bandura and his colleagues (Bandura & Huston, 1961; Bandura, Ross & Ross, 1961; 1963) looked at how young children reacted to an aggressive model. In Bandura, Ross and Ross (1961), the models were an adult male and adult female who aggressed for ten minutes toward a five-foot tall inflatable Bobo punching bag while children were in the room working on an art project. A third of the children in the study saw what was described below.

> ... [In] addition to punching the Bobo doll, a response that is likely to be performed by children independently of a demonstration, the model ... laid Bobo on its side, sat on it and punched it repeatedly in the nose. The model then raised the Bobo doll, picked up the mallet and struck the doll on the head. Following the mallet aggression, the model tossed the doll up in the air aggressively and kicked it about the room. This sequence of physically aggressive acts was repeated approximately three times, interspersed with verbally aggressive responses such as, "Sock him in the nose...," "Hit him down...," "Throw him in the air...," "Kick him...," "Pow...," and two non-aggressive comments: "He keeps coming back for more" and "He sure is a tough fella."

A third of the children saw the same adult models sitting placidly playing with Tinkertoys, while another third had no experience with the model. The experimental design used is outline below:

> 6 girls watched the male model being aggressive
> 6 girls watched the male model playing with Tinker toys
> 6 girls watched the female model being aggressive
> 6 girls watched the female model playing with Tinkertoys
> 12 girls saw no model
> 6 boys watched the male model being aggressive
> 6 boys watched the male model playing with Tinkertoys
> 6 boys watched the female model being aggressive
> 6 boys watched the female model playing with Tinkertoys
> 12 boys saw no model

The children were matched across conditions on the basis of teacher ratings of their normal aggressiveness in the nursery school they attended. That is, in the five groups of girls and the five groups of boys, there were a balance of high-, medium- and low-aggression children

The children were first taken to another building and a room filled with expensive toys. After a few minutes of playing with these toys, they were told that not all children could play with these toys, and then they were taken to another room which contained another group of toys, including a three-foot Bobo doll, the mallet, dart guns and a variety of non-aggressive toys. The reason the children were first taken to the room with the expensive toys was to arouse them slightly,* to see whether watching the placid model, the one playing with Tinkertoys, would *reduce* aggression, compared to the no-model control group.

The study found that the children who had seen the aggressive models imitated them, and they had the highest rates of all the kinds of aggression observed. Boys were somewhat more likely to imitate the male model, while the girls who saw the aggressive female model were substantially more aggressive than those who had watched the male model, particularly in the area of verbal aggression. More than half of the children in the placid model condition and control group exhibited no aggression at all. The only difference between the placid condition and the control condition was that the children in the control condition were more likely to use the mallet aggressively, although not necessarily toward the Bobo doll. Gunplay among the boys was about the same across all conditions.

Of course, this study does not involve movies. That was done two years later in a follow-up study (Bandura, Ross & Ross, 1963). In this study, there were three conditions. The first condition was a replication of the aggressive model from the previous study, with boys and girls distributed equally with a male or female model. The second condition had children working on the same art project while films of the adult models were shown on a color TV six feet away. It might be remembered that color TV was a novelty at this time and might have been expected to draw the children's attention more than it would today. The third condition had the same aggressive acts toward the Bobo doll, but it was done by a cartoon cat who spoke in a high-pitched voice and whose behavior was accompanied by cartoon music. There was, as above, a control group that saw no aggression.

Table 7.1 shows the comparisons of the boys and girls who saw live aggression, vs. filmed human aggression, compared to the control group that saw no aggression. The data presented are the percentage of five-second intervals in which aggression occurred. There are two types of aggression listed, total aggression and the aggression that was specifically viewed in the videos, called imitated aggression, although clearly the control group could not be

---

*The correct term here would be frustrate. Freud's views of aggression included the idea that aggression is always linked to being frustrated, and that frustration always leads to aggression. A number of social psychologists and learning theorists had by this time convincingly shown that frustration sometimes leads to aggression, but not always. Some of Bandura's work would show that not all aggression is caused by frustration. In fact, in Bandura and Huston (1961), imitation alone could account for aggression.

imitating it. Hitting anything other than the Bobo doll with a mallet would be part of total aggression, while hitting the Bobo doll with the mallet or saying "Pow!" would be considered imitated aggression. Boys were more aggressive than girls. Girls were more aggressive when they had watched the female model than when they had watched the male model. But what is most striking is that there were few differences between watching the live model or the filmed model.

Table 7.1
Percent of Five-Second Intervals in Which Aggression Was Present.

	Watching Live		Filmed		Control
	Male	Female	Male	Female	
Boys					
Total Aggression	55	32	35	48	30
Imitated Aggression	16	8	6	14	2
Girls					
Total Aggression	24	27	33	36	15
Imitated Aggression	4	8	3	4	<1

In table 7.2, we have combined the male and female model data and compared the live, filmed human, cartoon and control data for boys and girls. By combining the data, we see the small differences between the filmed vs. the live models, and we also see that the cartoon condition had about as much total aggression as these two conditions. But the amount of imitated aggression was lower in the cartoon condition. Since the emphasis in this study was on imitated aggression, the effect of the cartoon condition was minimized in this report. But remember that the fourth idea about the effects of watching aggression is a general unleashing of aggression, and when comparing the cartoon condition to the control condition, we see that the cartoon condition had twice as much aggression as the controls. Different researchers interpret the cartoon data differently (Blumberg, Bierworth & Schwartz, 2008).

Table 7.2
Percent of Five-Second Intervals in Which Aggression Was Present.

	Live	Filmed	Cartoon	Control
Boys				
Total Aggression	44	42	49	30
Imitated Aggression	12	10	7	2
Girls				
Total Aggression	26	34	34	15
Imitated Aggression	6	4	3	<1

There are several aspects of these studies that have made them among the most frequently cited studies in all of psychology. First and foremost, they showed that children will imitate what they see in the media, even if that behavior is contrary to the behavioral guidelines they have been raised to follow. Even if you are wondering at this point whether aggression toward a Bobo doll is real aggression, it is at least an antisocial behavior that most children have been taught not to do: behaving roughly toward someone else's toys.

Second, by looking at the male vs. the female model, these studies gave us a way of understanding why not all children imitate everything they see on the TV or movie screen. Bandura used the idea of *identification*. He presumed that boys were more likely to imitate male role models and girls more likely to imitate female role models. And they were less likely to imitate cartoon characters than real-life people. As we have discussed, later research on film aggression found that we are more likely to imitate "good guys" than "bad guys." One of the reasons that Americans may have more gun violence than the Japanese, even though both cultures view a lot of gun aggression, is that on Japanese TV, the bad guys far more often use guns than the police, while in the U.S. we often see images of good guys using guns. We are also more likely to imitate people with whom we share characteristics, like ethnicity and social class, but also things such as historical time. We are more likely to imitate someone in a contemporary drama than in a historical or fantasy one.

Far more importantly, these studies began an attack on the Freudian version of *catharsis*. This is the idea that we have a lot of pent-up emotions that are bad for us, and that by watching a film, or a play, or a TV program and by having these emotions come to the surface, we may rid ourselves of these bad emotions. This is sometimes referred to as the Flatulence Theory of emotion: Emotions hurt us like pent-up gas and when released, we feel better. The Bobo Doll studies have changed the way we look at the idea of catharsis. Today, it seems incredible that in the 1940s, it was believed that one way of treating aggressive inmates or psychiatric patients was to have them view aggressive movies and afterwards act out their aggressive feelings.

The Drabman and Thomas Studies

In a series of four studies published in the mid–1970s, Ronald Drabman and Margaret Thomas (Drabman and Thomas, 1974a, 1974b, 1976; Thomas and Drabman, 1975) found that while imitation of violence was modest, watching televised violence made children tolerant of violence in the real world. These studies used various ways of demonstrating the point. We will describe the earliest of the studies (Drabman & Thomas, 1974).

The researchers divided a group of third and fourth grade students so that half of the boys and half of the girls saw eight minutes of a Hopalong Cassidy movie that depicted several gun battles, shootings and fistfights, after being shown a trailer room that was filled with toys. The children who saw no movie were shown the trailer room and then were escorted to the lab. In the lab setting the experimenter told the children he had a problem: He had promised to look after two younger children who would be in the trailer that they had been shown. Then the researcher turned on a TV monitor and said:

> There's no one there now. Well, I might get back before they arrive, but if I don't, could you watch the children for me? Thanks a lot. Just watch the TV, and if the children get there before I get back, then you keep an eye on them. I imagine they'll be okay but sometimes little kids can get into trouble and that's why an older person should be watching them. If anything does happen, come and get me. I'll be in the principal's office.

Two minutes after the researcher left, a four-year-old girl and a five-year-old boy were seen on the monitor being escorted into the trailer room Actually, this was a videotape and it was the same for all children. An adult escorted them in and then left. Then, after 60 seconds of coloring, an argument ensued. The girl criticized the boy's block structure and coloring ability. The boy knocked down the girl's block tower. The girl began chasing the boy, mocked him, and then began to hit him. The camera was knocked over and the video went dead but yelling was still heard until finally the boy screamed, "Watch out" and there was a loud crash, after which nothing further was heard.

The dependent variable was how long the children in the experiment waited before they went for help. Children who had seen the Hopalong Cassidy clips waited, on average, more than a minute longer than those who had not seen the clips. Importantly for the authors, 15 of the 18 who had seen the film waited until after physical fighting broke out before going to get help, while of the 19 who had not seen the film, 11 went for help *before* physical aggression.

Later Research

Funk, Baldacci, Pasold and Baumgardner (2004) looked at 150 upper elementary schoolchildren and examined whether empathy and desensitization to violence were affected by exposure to real-life violence, TV violence, movie violence and violent video games. Children with the lowest empathy scores played violent video games. Desensitization to violence was influenced by playing violent video games and by viewing violent movies.

In their sample, TV violence and real-life violence did not predict either low empathy or desensitization to violence, but they observed that the children in their middle-class sample were probably not exposed to much real-life violence, and as elementary school students, most of the "violence" they saw on TV was probably in cartoons. These authors suggest that the higher influence of video games comes from their highly active nature: While watching a movie, we are less involved in the violence than we are in a video game where we may get points for our own violent behavior. Additionally, the rate of violence in video games is much higher than in moves, although in many video games at the time it was also less realistic than in movies.

Berry, Gray and Donnerstein (1999) examined the effects of the actual amount of violence shown in a film on college students' reactions in three experiments. In each experiment, they showed either an uncut, violent film or the same film with some or all of the violence cut. In experiment one, the film was a 90-second clip from *Reservoir Dogs*, in which either one graphically violent shot or two violent shots were cut and compared to the uncut version. In experiment two, it was a four-and-a-half-minute clip from *Cliffhanger* (1993), in which a shot where one actor struck another 13 times was cut (British version) or left in (American version). In experiment three, they showed the American version of the entire movie *Cliffhanger* which was compared to the British version, which had two graphically violent scenes changed. After each viewing, the clip or the movie was rated on an 18-item questionnaire that produced Enjoyability, Anxiety-Producing and Violent subscales. Men and women were compared.

In the first experiment, women found the uncut version more anxiety-producing and less enjoyable than men did. Both men and women rated the uncut version more violent than the cut versions. With the longer clip in experiment two, students again rated the American (uncut) version more violent than the cut British version. Again, women found the uncut version more anxiety-producing than the men. Enjoyability scores were not significantly different for the two groups.

When an entire film was used in experiment three, the students rated the American version as more violent, but the difference was not statistically significant. The authors of the study use an interesting phrase in describing their results: They say that differences in ratings "approached significance." But as one of our statistics professors liked to say, *Statistics isn't horseshoes, and so almosts don't count.* In fact, if you look at the three studies, the differences in the ratings of violence decreases with the length of the movie they looked at. As the films get longer, there is more non-violent content, so the ratings get weaker when you cut a couple of shots from a whole movie than from a 90-second minute clip.

Despite the fact that the violence ratings were not significant, women enjoyed the cut version better than the uncut version, while men enjoyed the uncut version better. Both of these findings were statistically significant. Women found either version more anxiety-producing than men, and women, but not men, found the uncut version more anxiety producing that the cut version.

Changing Attitudes and Beliefs

After reading about studies of teenage smoking, early sexuality and suicide, you may wonder whether psychologists ever study anything positive. We wish the answer were a clear *yes*, but within psychology there are critics who argue that we don't. They also argue that we should. Their approach is called **positive psychology**, and they point out that while it is useful to discover what leads to unhealthy behavior, it is equally important to discover what leads to positive behavior. For example, in Dalton *et al.* (2003), the ten percent of the kids who initiated smoking saw a lot of smoking in PG-13- and R-rated films. They also found that these kids' parents didn't disapprove of smoking. To a positive psychologist, the message might be more valuable if you say that if you want to keep your children smoke-free, let them know you disapprove of smoking and monitor their movie choices. For example, these researchers found that even parents who smoke can help their children be smoke-free if they strongly indicate that they do not want their children to smoke.

In looking for studies of what people do on dates for Chapter 3, we went to the psychology database PSYCINFO, computerized search engine maintained by the American Psychological Association that looks at research studies published in the thousands of psychology research journals around the world. It also includes books and dissertations. You can put in key terms like "dating" and "adolescent" and it will generate a list of hundreds of summaries of articles, books and dissertations that deal with the topic of dating in adolescents and you can get direct access to many journal articles that are published online. Of the first 300 articles that we found on adolescent dating, 268 had to do with dating violence. That's a very negative bias. Presumably, adolescents have positive experiences while dating, but one would be hard-pressed to discover what they are by reading the psychological research literature.

In the material that follows, we will try to be more of a positive psychologist. That is going to be difficult, because there are more studies, for example, of how watching media may create stereotypes than there are studies of how watching movies may make people more tolerant.

Pornography and Attitudes About Women

In the area of movie research, pornography is one of the most contentious topics. Some people believe that pornography is a release valve and that watching pornography makes most people less sexual, while others believe that it is the breeding ground for sexual crime and that watching pornography makes people prone to sexual violence. Some people take the position that all pornography, include male gay pornography, degrades women, while others see the pornography industry in the United States as a hallmark of First Amendment rights. Sharp and Joslyn (2001) looked at results from an annual large-scale national survey (General Social Survey) done in 1975 and again in 1986 to see whether people believed that exposure to pornography made individuals more prone to sexual violence toward women. They chose these two years because they felt that the discourse in the media had radically changed: In 1975, the media generally looked favorably on efforts to lift restrictions on pornography, and X-rated films were routinely advertised in major newspapers and sometimes reviewed by the papers' film critics. By 1986, the idea that pornography was violent toward women was current and most newspapers had stopped advertising pornographic films.

What they found was that there were virtually no differences in the findings between the two times, so the authors suggest that the changes in the discussion in the media had little effect on most men and women. Age, income and political ideology were not predictors of whether people believed that pornography led to rape. Being a woman, being less well educated, being religious, and *not* having any direct experience with X-rated films all led to higher endorsements of the connection between pornography and rape. At both times, holding feminist ideas led to *lower* endorsement of the relationship, despite the fact that the most vocal leaders of the anti-pornography movement at the later time considered themselves feminists.

Because of the very strongly held beliefs of many of those who do research on pornography, much of the research is biased toward finding results consistent with the preconceptions of the researchers. You may wonder how this is possible. Isn't research supposed to be a neutral ground where competing ideas are put to the test? Indeed, that is an idea that many researchers have. But others feel it is their duty to find evidence that supports their strongly held convictions.

Consider this finding: Most violent sexual offenders report very high rates of pornography use (Purcell & Arrigo, 2006). Most report that they became addicted to pornography and that pornography drove them to their sexual violence. Most used highly violent pornography. It is thus conceivable that by watching sexual acts involving violence again and again, because of their addiction, they were vicariously reinforced to engage in the behaviors they watched. But it is important to remember when reviewing this data, that the people who make these claims have a vested interest in changing judges' and juries' perceptions of them from victimizers to victims. Some researchers take these statements about addiction to pornography literally. Others are much more willing to consider the possibility that people who kill may also lie, if by lying they might not get the death penalty.

Pornography use, for most people, is a private behavior, and in many places in the U.S., it is in some ways illegal. So we must take any finding from any single study with a grain of salt. When people are reporting private behavior that is potentially illegal, they have strong motivations not to tell the truth or at least not the whole truth.

We want to describe one study that we think balances both positions. Jansma, Linz, Mulac and Imrich (1997) felt that there were many problems with earlier research on pornography and they conducted a study that addressed some of those issues. First, they wanted to consider the issue of whether *all* pornography made men likely to sexualize women. They began by accepting that pornography that showed violence toward women did so, but they examined two kinds of non-violent pornography: sexually explicit films that showed mutual concern and interest between two individuals, and films that degraded women. The authors noted that in many previous studies, the films selected to view as "degrading" and "mutual" were chosen by the researchers and one had to accept the researchers' definitions. Before accepting their independent variable of degrading vs. non-degrading, they showed films to panels of men and women. They selected two films, one of which showed a couple interested in mutual pleasure and one showing a woman as sexually insatiable and objectified by dress (only jewelry and spiked heels) and activity with several men wearing leather and masks based on the reactions of their panels. A third of the male participants watched a non-sexual movie.

Second, for the dependent variable, they wanted to examine real behavior rather than paper-and-pencil attitude measures. After viewing a movie segment, the men were invited to be a part of another experiment where they were matched with women volunteers. They were asked to briefly converse with the women, sitting near each other on a sofa, about which of 15 objects would be most useful if you were in a plane crash in the wilderness. After this conversation, both the men and women completed questionnaires, two of which focused on their attitudes toward their partner and their assessment of the interaction.

Third, they wanted to determine whether the effects of watching pornography were observable in all men or only in some. They administered a questionnaire that measured traditional masculine attitudes. Men were divided into those who were sex-typed (believed they were masculine, dominant, aggressive, decisive, goal-oriented, etc.) or non–sex-typed (believed that they were more helpful, nurturing, emotional, etc.). Overall, they found no differences between men in their views of the women as a function of which movie they watched. When they examined the sex-typing of the men, however, they found that those with "traditional" rated their partners as less smart and more sexually interested in them.

Attitudes About Minorities

While many people have criticized specific movies for their portrayal of minorities and have suggested that these movies contribute to the continuation of racial and ethnic prejudice in the U.S., it is equally likely that other movies have contributed to the development of positive attitudes toward minorities. The most widely studied period of movies for this material are films made during World War II. All over the globe, movies were made that glorified one's friends and vilified one's enemies, both within and without. German films of this period portrayed Jews and others disliked by the Third Reich as degenerate criminals and these portrayals are often regarded as having had a significant influence on the general populace's willingness to stand by as the Final Solution was carried out. But such historical studies are only suggestive, and not based on any clear scientific evidence acceptable to a psychologist.

Likewise, there were many American films made during this period in which Japanese are portrayed as lunatic mass murderers, willing to sacrifice their own lives to further their country's imperialistic designs on the rest of the world. Germans were not as ruthlessly portrayed in films. During this period, however, some studios, notably Warner Brothers, produced movies in which the Japanese were viewed more sympathetically. Interestingly, these more balanced films got higher box office receipts than those where the propagandistic "yellow peril" was portrayed. It would be nice to think that American audiences rejected the jingoistic propaganda films, but it may as likely be that Warner Brothers' films had more theaters that showed its films and people went to see actors like Cary Grant.

One of the great box office hits of World War II was Laurence Olivier's film version of Shakespeare's play *Henry V.* In addition to glorifying a nationalistic king, this play has many scenes in which soldiers from various parts of the United Kingdom (Scotland, Wales, Ireland and England) come together, learn that each other are not the enemy, and forge working relationships. This film became the template for many films, both British and American (Harvardi, 2014). There was a good deal of regional prejudice in the U.S. before the war. Often these films, like *Henry V,* began with stereotypical representations of southerners, New England Yankees, New York Jews and ethnic groups such as Italians and Hungarians, but the final resolution was that they were all Americans (or Brits) who shared many values and were in the military for the same objectives. These films were shown to men in the service and are also believed to have helped overcome much of the regional prejudice. But again, there is only anecdotal evidence for this.

Hollywood seemed to realize its responsibility in helping the country come to terms with minority issues toward the end of the war and immediately afterwards. For example, when President Truman integrated the military in 1945, the studios reshot some scene to show African-Americans fighting alongside Caucasian soldiers and sailors, with the assumption that mere exposure would be helpful in changing attitudes. In the decade after the war, Hollywood made a number of serious films examining the problems of servicemen who returned to the States with Asian wives.

Eno and Ewoldsen (2010) examined both implicit and explicit prejudice and their role in reactions to films with racial content. **Implicit prejudice** is measured using indirect means such as reaction times, while **explicit prejudice** is measured using questionnaires in which specific statements about racial (or other) groups are rated as true or false for the individual. In their first study, they found that the movie *Remember the Titans* (2000) was interpreted differently depending on racial-prejudicial states before watching the movie. Specifically, those who explicitly stated self-motivation not to be prejudice tended to see the movie as being about football rather than civil rights, while those who indicated external pressure not to be prejudiced saw the movie through a highly racial lens. In a second study which examined the effect of watching *Rosewood* (1997), a film about a massacre in a black town in 1923, viewing the film brought about reductions in prejudice measured both implicitly and explicitly.

In a related study, Mazur and Emmers-Sommer (2002) examined attitudes toward non-traditional families and homosexuality before and after watching two films, *Father of the Bride II* and *The Object of My Affection*. The former is about a young married couple announcing that they are expecting a child. Their families are supporting. The wife's mother and father also discover they are expecting a child. All characters are white, middle-class, heterosexual and married. *The Object of My Affection* involves a complicated relationship of a woman who comes from a stepparent family. She becomes pregnant by a man she does not want to marry. She has a lesbian roommate to whom she is attracted. But her roommate has a relationship of her own. Eventually, the mother develops a romantic relationship with an African-American man, and the biological father, her boyfriend, her lesbian roommate and her significant other all become involved in raising her daughter.

The authors measured attitudes toward homosexuality and non-traditional families before and immediately after watching the films. Prior to watching the film, the authors found that women held more favorable attitudes toward both non-traditional families and homosexuality than men did. They also found that people who held traditional attitudes toward the family had negative attitudes toward homosexuality. The group that watched *Object of My Affection* had a significant change in attitudes toward non-traditional families, but watching this film did not change attitudes toward homosexuality.

While there are many studies of the effects of other forms of media on attitude change, there are very few of movies. Adkins and Castle (2013) provides an exemplar of how this research might be done. First, they had their participants watch whole movies. One of the three they chose was *The Rainmaker* (1997), which is centrally about a young man with leukemia and an insurance company that fails to authorize his bone marrow transplant. Another was *As Good as It Gets* (1997), which has a subplot in which a main character's son needs allergy treatments and gets them through the generosity of a writer. The third, *That Thing You Do!* (1997), is about a small-town rock band and has no health-care content. The authors described these films as overt message, subtle message and control films, respectively.

The authors measured participants' attitudes before the study, even though they used random assignment to movies. Normally, one either uses pre-assessment *or* random assignment. The problem here that was addressed by using both, was that when people agree to come at a later time to watch a whole film, there is a good deal of attrition: At the last minute, people do not show up. And those who do not show up are not just a random chunk of the population: People with certain attitudes might well say that they do not want to watch a liberal movie about health care.

Finally, the authors measured attitudes immediately after the movies and then again, using computers, two weeks later.

The results were not startling. When attitudes toward government-run healthcare were measured, there was no difference in the three groups prior to watching the movie, but significant differences were seen immediately after the movie, with those seeing the subtle message movie becoming more in favor of government-run healthcare than those in the control condition, and those in the overt message group changing to being more in favor of government-run programs than those in the subtle message group. While some of these attitudes are attenuated by the two-week follow-up, the differences among the groups still were statistically significant and in the same direction. It was also noted that by the follow-up wave of data collection, those who began with favorable or neutral views on government-run healthcare generally remained consistent with their post-movie views, while those

7. Selling Watches, Changing Hearts and Minds

who had negative views prior to the movie were more likely to return to less favorable views, but they did not return to views as negative as those with which they had started.

* * *

Even though we tried to be positive, this chapter failed to be an exemplar of positive psychology. Most of the research literature is focused on the marketing of things that are bad for us. It seems that in psychology, there is a bias toward problems and their possible solutions rather than toward finding ways of avoiding the problems in the first place.

The Best Years of Our Lives is in its own way problem-focused. It made a whole generation of Americans more aware of the issues facing returning servicemen, particularly those who had had combat experience and those

The wedding that concludes *The Best Years of Our Lives*. Fred Derry (Dana Andrews), the psychologically damaged aviator in the left foreground, looks on as the minister awkwardly places Wilma's (Cathy O'Donnell) hands into Homer's (Harold Russell) hooks. In between we can see the Stephenson family, Peggy (Teresa Wright), Milly (Myrna Loy) and Al (Fredric March) (Samuel Goldwyn, 1946).

who came back with injuries that altered their lives. The banker has learned to drink a little more than is socially acceptable. His children have grown into adolescence and young adulthood without him and while they love him, he is really not functioning as their parent any more. At work, his bosses want to put the war behind them and go ahead with business as usual. But he is in the best place of the three returning veterans.

The Navy seaman who lost his hands may seem the most vulnerable. In one of the movie's most emotional scenes, he takes his girlfriend to his room, not for a romantic interlude, but to show her how incapacitated he is when he removes his prosthesis. He is trying to break up with her, but at least for the time being, she is standing beside him.

The pilot may be the most lost of the bunch. He became a successful adult in the military and now must return to being a boy from the other side of the tracks. He suffers from nightmares and finally decides to commit suicide. But there are people around him who want to help him recover, if he will let them. It is not altogether clear whether he will.

The Best Years of Our Lives changed the average American's view of military veterans. It was thought to be instrumental in setting up rehabilitation programs for World War II vets. It is even speculated to have been a player in the decision of the Veteran's Administration to go ahead with the Boulder Conference, which led to the creation of the occupation of Clinical Psychologist.

The moviemakers had such changes in mind, but *The Best Years of Our Lives* influenced us in other ways. The discussions about domestic servants is seen to be one of the reasons this occupation decline rapidly after World War II. The movie depicted women's desire to remain in the workforce, even after the men returned from war. The film is also one of the earliest positive portrayals of divorce in the American cinema.

Key Psychological Terms

Desensitization: Becoming insensitive to stimuli; specifically, becoming insensitive to real-life violence because of exposure to media aggression.
Explicit memory: An explicit memory can be brought into consciousness.
Implicit memory: This refers to an experience that had taken place but is not accessible to consciousness.
Mere exposure: The belief that by having very passive exposure to a person or product, the natural tendency to avoid the novel will dissipate.
Papageno effect: Seeing images of individuals who fail to complete suicide and then go on to happy lives decreases the number of suicide attempts.
Positive psychology: A movement in psychology to steer away from the pathological and focus on prevention and well-being approaches.

Prospective research: This is developmental research where data are collected at two points; this research does not rely on memory.

Quartile: A statistical procedure in which a rank-ordered sample is divided into four equal groups.

Retrospective research: Developmental research where the temporally first data are collected by having participants recall past events.

Werther effect: A prominent suicide is thought to provoke copycats.

Cinema Term

Product placement: The practice of paying to have branded merchandise seen or used in movies.

8

The Depiction of the Mentally Ill, Therapists and Therapy

Aristotle pointed out that good drama is about flawed characters. Few of us would be very interested in a movie that told the story of a successful middle manager in a department store who did her job well, loved her family, and volunteered at a local literacy center on Wednesday nights. The story becomes more interesting, or more entertaining, if she has a secret drinking problem, one of her children joins the skinheads, or her husband is a vigilante who goes out at night killing muggers on the subway. Movies, novels, plays and TV programs do not give us role models. They give us, more typically, problems. In discussing why Shakespeare focused on falling in love rather than on living happily ever after, Stephen Greenblatt (2004) noted: "There are few happy marriages in all of literature, just as there are rather few representations of goodness."

This is a prefatory remark to the idea that we should not always look to fiction films to understand the mentally ill, the profession of therapist, or how therapy works. Entertaining movies take liberties—sometimes, extreme ones—with each of these things. In the movies, the mentally ill are often much more dangerous and much more aware of their problems than they are in real life and many of their more unpleasant, routine symptoms are ignored. Delusions are entertaining, while Irritable Bowel Syndrome is not. Therapists often seem to have more problems than their clients, to whom they disclose much more of their personal lives than would be ethically acceptable. Therapy in the movies most often involves transformations in the clients so remarkable that if they were common in the everyday work of psychologists and psychiatrists, there would be little need for clinics, let alone mental hospitals.

There are a lot of movies that feature the mentally ill and therapists. The only professions seen more frequently are criminals, policemen, lawyers, writers and actors. Wahl, Wood, Zaveri, Drapalski and Mann (2003) found that one out of four *children's* films has a mentally ill character in it, and nearly two-thirds have references to mental illness or therapists. Even before the twentieth century, we have found glimpses into the world of madness entertaining. Shakespeare gave us Lady Macbeth's dissociative reaction after killing a king and Lear's foray into depression and dementia. He gave us a ridiculous version of institutionalization and treatment in *Twelfth Night*, and he created a series of amiable drunks, from Sir John Falstaff to Sir Toby Belch, whose alcoholism catches up with them in the end. Nineteenth century opera is filled with crazy sopranos. And novelists from Dostoyevsky to Patricia Cornwell have created fascinating portraits of the mentally ill, usually the criminally mentally ill.

What movies cannot do very well is create a genuine sense of time or scope in describing and dealing with these problems. A serious mental illness usually involves every aspect of a person's life, and most last for years, if not a lifetime. Giving a sense of the extent of mental illness and its impact on friends and family members can only be hinted at in the standard two-hour movie. And therapy is in reality more often a long series of small victories and occasional defeats, rather than the big, quick breakthrough that is common in descriptions of therapy in films. Freud believed in the big breakthrough, but even he thought it could only take place after years of therapeutic work.

In each of the sections below we have selected films that seem to be serious about showing the mentally ill, therapists and the process of therapy, and will discuss them in terms of what they help us learn about these issues. In guiding our choices of films, we have usually selected films that received a lot of media attention, received awards, or were box office blockbusters. In each category, we have also included a comedy.

The Depiction of the Mentally Ill in Films

Hollywood—or any other producer of movies—has no clear obligation to present mental illness in an accurate way. For those who have had careers treating the mentally ill, sometimes the ways in which mental illness is portrayed are ridiculous. Other times, filmmakers seem to try very hard to give an accurate picture of mental illness. There are also blends of the two.

In the United States, psychologists and psychiatrists most often use a diagnostic system called **DSM-V** (*Diagnostic and Statistical Manual of Mental Disorders, 5th edition*). The system is diagnostic as it lists the symptoms required for a clinical diagnosis of a mental disorder, and it is statistical in that it lists the incidence of the disorders. For example, Major Depressive Disorder is diagnosed when one has at least five of the following symptoms:

- loss of interest in most activities
- sleep disturbances
- loss of weight not explained by dieting
- physical agitation
- loss of energy
- feelings of worthlessness or guilt
- loss of ability to concentrate
- thoughts about death or suicide

DMS-V divides mental disturbances in 22 major categories, and then further subdivides these into specific subordinate categories (Major Depressive Disorder is a subordinate category of Depressive Disorders). The reason for mentioning this system is that it can help us get a feel for how representative portrayals of mental illness are, as well as their accuracy. While we will not review all movies ever made about mental illness, we will see, in those that we discuss, that certain mental disorders are very often represented, such as schizophrenia and sexual sadism. Schizophrenia, is a disruption of perception, thinking, personality, and emotions so significant that individuals with it lose touch with reality, affects about one percent of the population over their lifetime. *A Beautiful Mind* (2001) and *Shine* (1995) dramatized real cases of this disorder, although in extremely talented and advantaged individuals. Research consistently finds that while schizophrenia affects people in all groups, it is most common among the poor and poorly educated (Turner & Wagonfield, 1967). The incidence of sexual sadism is unknown, but a particular form of it, serial murder, is extremely rare. Hickey (2006) estimates that there have been only about 400 cases over the last two centuries. He points out that there have been more representations of the disorder in movies and on television than in reality.

Other disorders, which are very common (depression, sleep disorders, attention deficit hyperactivity disorder, etc.) are rarely represented. One of the reasons is that these problems do not translate readily into entertaining movies. For example, a masterpiece of Italian Neorealism, Vittorio De Sica's *Umberto D.* (1952), is about depression in a retired man in post–World War II Italy. Because of his middle-class background, he spends a great deal of time trying to protect the impression he gives when he is in public. He must have a clean if ragged shirt; he must have a dog to walk; he must always exhibit good manners, even when confronted with stupidity, violence and indifference. The film was a commercial disaster, and while it makes everyone's best film list, it is rarely watched (Bondanella, 1991). It is too accurate to make many viewers comfortable.

It is estimated, however, that over ten percent of the population will experience a major depressive episode. Sleep disorders rarely appear in movies, although highly fanciful depictions occur in Fellini's *8½*, *Groundhog*

Day and *My Own Private Idaho*. We can think of no attempt to serious depict ADHD, although the incidence among children and adolescents is about six percent. There is little to be learned by watching the child with ADHD in John Waters' 1998 farce *Pecker*.

Hyler (1988; Hyler, Gabbard & Schneider, 1991) indicates that in films, the mentally ill are portrayed in six stereotypes:

1. The homicidal maniac
2. The rebellious free spirit who is not really mentally ill, but finds himself or herself institutionalized
3. The enlightened member of society
4. The seductress
5. The parasite
6. The zoo specimen who is manipulated by a bad therapist. In their analysis of films for children, Wahl *et al.* (2003) found that while the mentally ill characters in children's films often got along with others and were often physically attractive, they were universally regarded as dangerous.

Of the five films discussed below, all have a mentally ill person as the central character. Three of these characters are dangerously mentally ill; one of these is a rebellious free spirit, and one is an enlightened member of society. None of the characters has received any treatment, so they may be regarded as portraits of mental illness full-blown.

M (1931)

M is a film about a homicidal maniac, one of the most chillingly portrayed in all of film history. Its historical context makes it worth watching, as well as its compelling picture of criminal mental illness and its effects on society. The film was made less than two years after the introduction of sound, and only a year before Hitler's rise to power, and director Fritz Lang's view of German society of the time is brutal. The film is also based on a real case, so even after 85 years, it rings true. The real killer's testimony at his trial was woven into the final scene where "M" (Peter Lorre) describes his obsession.

In a large German city, a man seduces and kills little girls. The film opens with parents anxiously waiting for their children to come home from school. One parent waits and waits, until she goes frantically into the streets looking for her daughter. But she has become another victim. The entire city is on edge. People who smile at children or even answer their questions are mobbed. Friends denounce each other. The police are at a loss as to what to do, so they begin to monitor activities in the underworld of prostitution, drugs and alcohol very closely. Simultaneously, they follow up, forensically, on letters they have gotten that they believe come from the killer.

Underworld leaders meet because their livelihood is threatened by the police crackdown. They decide that they can find the murderer more effectively than the police. They enlist pickpockets and beggars to be on the lookout for people who are cozying up to children. The beggars find a suspect and mark the back of his coat with the letter M (for murderer) just as the police discover the identity of the killer by tracing aspects of letters he has been writing to them. But when they go to his apartment, he is out, trying to find another child. The underworld forces M into a large, vacant building. Slowly they close in on him, and when they capture him, they hold a mock trial. One of them, who has obviously been in court frequently, acts as M's attorney, trying to ensure a fair trial. M is at a loss to explain why he has his obsession with little girls, and he gives a harrowing account of someone who is occasionally overcome by compulsions he cannot control. While the court demands his execution, it would be difficult for a viewer not to become somewhat sympathetic to him.

Part of *M*'s enduring appeal is that the filmmakers had learned their craft in silent films, and the visual images on the screen are often haunting. There is a long sequence when M looks at the toys in the windows of toyshops. The images of the toys are mesmerizing. We see M completely engaged in this activity. At some point it becomes obvious that this is a man who is obsessed with childhood, and it also dawns on us that this man is looking to find the most attractive toy so that he can seduce a little girl with it in order to kill her. This sequence is unsettling: We find the toys fascinating; he finds them fascinating. He is looking at them to find a way of harming children. Perhaps this makes us pause and examine our own motivations, even if just for a moment, for looking with such interest at the toys.

Over the last decade, with a spate of highly publicized horrible crimes against children, our society has become as unsympathetic toward pedophiliacs as the underground court in this movie. Yet many psychologists believe that many pedophiliacs were themselves victims of sexual abuse as children or have some sort of genetic problem that leads to their interest in children (Alanko, Gundst, Mokros & Santtila, 2016; Sullivan & Sheehan, 2016). Psychologists are split about whether pedophilia or sexual violence is treatable. But by giving us simultaneously the perspective of the grieving families, the tortured murderer and the hysterical crowd, this film makes the problem much more complex than the sound bites about child abduction on Fox News.

Harvey (1950)

Harvey is a classic comedy about alcoholism and institutionalization. Elwood P. Dowd (James Stewart), a convivial drunk, asks everyone he meets, from people he has known for years, to complete strangers, to join him for

8. Depictions of the Mentally Ill, Therapists and Therapy   167

a drink. He takes them to bars. He invites them to his home. This sociability poses a problem for his widowed sister Veta, who lives with him, because she is interested in finding a husband for her rather unattractive daughter Myrtle Mae. Whenever she plans any social activity at their home, her brother disrupts it with his merry band of drinking cronies.

Elwood's drinking has crossed over the line from social drinking to alcoholism. He has no job and is spending the family's money, and he has a peculiar delusion: He is usually accompanied on his alcoholic excursions by an invisible, six-foot-tall rabbit named Harvey. He talks to Harvey. He helps him across the street. He laughs at Harvey's jokes that no one else can hear. The soberest of those he encounters react with dismay when they watch him talking with an unseen rabbit, called a *pooka*. But many others, particularly other hard drinkers, just accept Harvey. Elwood doesn't have the stamina to keep real friends or achieve intimacy: He must create an imaginary friend and substitute having a drink with strangers for intimacy.

Elwood P. Dowd (James Stewart) talks with Harvey (unseen) as the staff of the psychiatric facility looks on in *Harvey* (Universal Pictures, 1950).

Elwood's sister decides to institutionalize him for treatment. The private sanitarium where he will be placed has a drug that will cure alcoholism. But we, and his sister Veta, come to realize that there will be a great cost if Elwood takes this cure. He will become like everyone else, self-centered and greedy and irritable, perhaps throwing Veta and Myrtle Mae out of the house. In the end, he does not take the cure, and he gives the *pooka* to the head of the institution, Dr. Chumley, who seems to need a bit of magic in his life. At the institution, Myrtle Mae meets an orderly and they become mutually infatuated. So while Elwood is still a drinker, he is no longer delusional.

This film tells us very little about the realities of treating alcoholism—that at best, only a small percentage of those who are involuntary committed for treatment remain sober for as long as a year. There is no such cure as the one depicted in this film. In the past, drugs such as Antabuse, which when taken regularly made alcoholics ill if they drank, were touted as cures, but alcoholics normally just stopped taking the drug, and there were dangerous side effects. Films like this unrealistically raise the expectations of those who have a friend or family member with a serious substance abuse problem that things will be solved once the individual begins rehab. It is not just narcissistic rock stars who relapse after treatment.

Yet this film does describe a certain kind of alcoholic well: the kind of drinker who has few demonstrable problems with alcohol early in life, but whose constant drinking finally catches up with him. Elwood has become completely passive. He recalls something that his mother said to him: that one has to make the decision to be "nice" or "smart." He finds nice to be better. Those around him have barely noticed how he has descended into a world of no consequence and delusion. He has given up his social standing and his career. He just drinks. There are so many touches that strike those who have dealt with alcoholics as correct that one suspects that the screenwriter, Mary Chase, must have known someone like Elwood. This kind of alcoholism is probably more common among the middle-aged. Younger alcoholics are more characterized by aggression, risk-taking and turbulent relationships. Elwood is completely non-assertive, does nothing but the routine, and has no relationships. But the idea that alcohol takes its toll on one's social life, one's social standing, and on one's intellectual ability is clearly here.

Dr. Chumley is little more than a joke, but he sets one pattern for the representation of psychotherapists in films: He's burned-out and longs for some magic in his life (see *Don Juan DeMarco* and *Good Will Hunting* below). They are transformed by treating a single client.

Writers of films about the mentally ill often confuse *delusion* and *fantasy*. Mentally ill patients with delusions are often tormented by their ideas and cannot come to grips with reality because of them. Their delusions are reality for them. A fantasy is something that a person would like but knows isn't real. Chumley fantasizes about lying in a hammock in Akron, Ohio, drinking beer, and having a beautiful woman mop his brow, comforting him by saying "My poor baby, my poor baby." This is a very funny scene, partially because of James Stewart's very funny reactions to the disclosure. He thinks beer isn't up to the fantasy, for example, and suggests whiskey. But Chumley is lying down on the psychiatric couch, and Elwood has assumed the position and role of therapist. When Chumley actually sees Harvey, we wonder how capable he will be in treating others in the future, or, for that matter, how capable he has been in the past. He has serious problems, another characteristic of therapists that we will see later.

Psycho (1960)

We have had a number of reasons to discuss Alfred Hitchcock's *Psycho* in earlier chapters because of its ability to attract huge audiences in 1960 and because of its manipulation of our sensory systems in the famous shower scene. Its final scenes make it of interest to students of psychology concerned with the portrayal of the mentally ill and therapists. The next-to-the-last scene is a very long and very dated account of Norman's transformation into his mother, delivered by a psychiatrist with a decidedly Freudian bent, while in the final scene we enter the mind of Norman-Mother as he-she sits in a cell deciding that he will not flick a fly off of his arm. Both scenes are genuinely creepy. But are they good psychology?

Yes and no. Freud thought at adolescent's discovery of his parents' sexuality was traumatic. But most of us accept the fact that our parents are sexual. Although it sometimes makes us embarrassed, it does not make us serial killers. Freud (1900–1911) thought that Hamlet's discovery of his mother's sexuality was why he kills Rosencrantz, Guildenstern, Laertes, Polonius and Claudius and drives Ophelia to suicide. But these are characters in a play, not real people.

When Norman assumes his mother's identity, he is ridiculing and controlling and threatens physical violence. Presumably, he is reliving her real way of interacting with him. These kinds of parental actions do affect their children's psychological wellbeing. A nagging mother, however, does not make someone a serial killer.

The touch of taxidermy is more accurate. Several serial killers, including Jeffrey Dahmer, had this as a hobby. Dealing with dead things in a routine may make some individuals insensitive to death. Also, studies of serial killers suggest that most of them are marginalized individuals. The Bates Motel has no customers because of a redirection of the roads. Norman spends his days alone with no real purpose. He has nothing else but to but indulge in his fantasies and there is no one to help him redirect his energies as his fantasies turn into delusions.

Monster (2003)

Monster is another film based on a real case, America's most famous woman serial killer, Aileen Wuornos. She was arrested in 1990 for seven homicides and executed in 2002. This is a disturbing film, and not recommended for everyone. Charlize Theron won an Academy Award for her portrayal of Wuornos. Perhaps even more disturbing is a documentary made the same year, *Aileen: The Life and Death of a Serial Killer*, not only because of the details of the case that are disclosed, but because the filmmakers seem to be traumatizing Wuornos and affecting the outcome of her death sentence appeal.

Wuornos, as portrayed in *Monster*, has narcissistic personality disorder, a condition where a person's immediate wants and gratification completely dominate her behavior, even to the point, in this film, of murdering others for seemingly trivial reasons. Her childhood sexual and physical abuse is so lightly hinted at that it is easy to miss. In the film, she was an adolescent who desperately wanted to be popular and was willing to use her sexuality to gain acceptance. In fact, she was probably prostituted by family members as a child. The origins of her pathology are too neatly tied up in this film to say much about the origins of her violence.

What this film does well is portray a person whose values are so far removed from most people's that she has become "a monster." At the beginning of the real action of the film, Wuornos is sitting under a bridge with a revolver, contemplating suicide. She later says that the reason she did not was that she had earned five dollars servicing a client, and that if she did not spend it on herself, then she would have gone to all that effort for nothing. She decides to spend the money on a couple of cheap beers, and ends up in a gay bar. At first she reacts angrily when a young woman makes a subtle pass at her, but then she enters into a long-term lesbian relationship with her. We normally think of decisions about suicide or sexual identity as decisions we take seriously, but Woumos makes them on the basis of five dollars and a bed for the night. Likewise, at least six of the murders of her clients seem not at all about self-defense, but about obtaining very small sums of money. In real life, after fighting her death sentence for some time, Wuornos changed her mind and urged her hasty execution for no apparent reason.

There are many controversies surrounding this film (see Miller, 2004). One was the decision to portray her lover as uninvolved at any level in her murders. She did turn Wuornos over to the police and testified against her. That she had knowledge of the crimes earlier seems likely in terms of her testimony. Miller also suggests that the label "paranoid," used frequently in the film, is not appropriate, as Woumos conveys a deep understanding of what is going on around her. Individuals who have paranoia have irrational thoughts that people are plotting against them. Additionally, describing the last six murders as "premeditated" seems inappropriate, as Wuornos seems to have planned nothing in her life.

The Aviator (2004)

Martin Scorsese's *The Aviator* is about the early life of moviemaker and entrepreneur Howard Hughes (Leonardo DiCaprio). The film depicts Hughes as having had obsessive-compulsive disorder, but OCD rarely has all of the symptoms Hughes expressed. His psychiatric problem was made worse by the fact that he was the richest man in America, and the people around him allowed him to spin out of control. Had people treated him more like a normal human being, perhaps he would not have spent most of his later life naked in dark rooms, eating the same three meals every day, worried about germs and the exact angle of the cut of his piece of chocolate cake with dinner. This point is most forcefully made in a sequence in which he is about to lose his whole economic empire because of a Congressional investigation. The actress Ava Gardner forces him out of his self-imprisoned madness, cuts his hair and fingernails, gets him to put on clothes, and coaches him about the investigation, so that by the time he gets to Washington he is the match for his political adversaries. This transformation seems unbelievable, but the events before, during and after the hearings are well documented. Shortly after the hearings, he slipped back into his private obsessive life.

The makers of this film worked very hard at making its representation of OCD realistic. DiCaprio not only touches everything with a tissue, he becomes locked into sentences that he must say with the exactly right inflection, and he repeats them without being able to stop. He washes his hands until they bleed. He cannot concentrate on a conversation, because someone has a speck of lint on his coat collar. He finds himself imprisoned in a bathroom, until someone comes in from outside, because he cannot touch the doorknob. He cannot eat a meal because the peas have rolled into the gravy.

In a highly eroticized sequence at the very beginning, Hughes as a young boy is bathed by his mother, who talks about a cholera epidemic. It is quite possible that the intention of the scene is to "explain" the origins of Hughes' OCD. But OCD is not brought on by being bathed by one's mother or living during a cholera outbreak. Current evidence suggests that OCD has a genetic basis, and biographic evidence suggests that Hughes' mother probably had OCD herself.

An A-List of Films About the Mentally Ill

Wedding and Boyd (1999) and Wedding and Niemiec (2014) have reviewed hundreds of films about the mentally ill in their comprehensive textbook series, and given them 1 to 5 ratings on their representation of different problems. Here is a short list of films that received 5 ratings, which are given to excellent films that depict psychology effectively. These are some of the best films ever made, including films by Hitchcock, Kurosawa, Truffaut, Huston, Polanski, Scorsese and Bergman.

Alcoholism or Drug Abuse	*Crazy Heart* (2009); *Long Day's Journey into Night* (1962); *The Lost Weekend* (1945); *Ray* (2004); *Under the Volcano* (1984)
Antisocial Behavior	*M* (1931); *Rashomon* (1950)
Anxiety	*Adaptation* (2002); *Batman Begins* (2005); *Vertigo* (1958)
Childhood Disorders	*The 400 Blows* (1959)
Depression	*Suicide Room* (2012); *Umberto D.* (1952)
Dementia	*Amour* (2012); *The Notebook* (2004)
Dissociative Disorder	*The Piano* (1993); *Psycho* (1960); *Twelve O'Clock High* (1949)
Head Injury	*Memento* (2002); *On the Waterfront* (1954); *Raging Bull* (1980)
Personality Disorder	*Blue Jasmine* (2013); *No Country for Old Men* (2007); *Taxi Driver* (1976)
Post Traumatic Stress Disorder	*The Deer Hunter* (1978); *Paths of Glory* (1958); *Shoah* (1985)
Schizophrenia	*An Angel at My Table* (1990); *Lars and the Real Girl* (2007); *Shine* (1996); *The Soloist* (2009); *Through a Glass Darkly* (1962)

Some of the films they rate as the worst are: *The Alphabet Killer* (2008), *The Bad Seed* (1956), *The Bell Jar* (1979), *Beyond Therapy* (1987), *Boxing Helena* (1995), *Bruce Almighty* (2002), *The Couch Trip* (1988), *Cruising* (1979), *The Deliberate Stranger* (1986), *Extremities* (1985), *The Fan* (1982), *The Fan* (1996), *House of Cards* (1993), *Luna* (1979), *Magic* (1978), *Poison Ivy* (1992), *Pineapple Express* (2008), *Raising Cain* (1992), *Tattoo* (1981) and *Visioneers* (2008).

The Depiction of Therapists in Films

No profession is really portrayed very accurately in movies or, for that matter, in novels or TV programs. Valentine and Freeman (2002) located 27 films from 1938 to 1999 showing social workers doing social work with children and families. They found the depiction of social workers to be very limited. Mostly social workers were white women. They frequently provided services to single parent families headed by men, although 85 percent of single parent families are head by women. They showed social workers mostly as either providing therapy (in positive portrayals) or as being rigid and anti-family rule enforcers (in negative portrayals). Their roles as policy makers, researchers and educators were not to be seen at all. Of course, not all the films were intended to be accurate representations of social work. Three of the films included in this analysis were *Follow That Bird* (1985), about a social worker removing Big Bird from his home on Sesame Street, *Addams Family Reunion* (1998), a dark-humored farce, and *Parents* (1988), a horror movie about cannibalism, a problem rarely faced by social workers. The authors, however, point out that these portrayals probably affect people's perceptions of the field anyway. Indeed, extreme films can influence views about professions and aspects of treatment in significant ways. For example, Walter, McDonald, Rey and Rosen (2002) showed medical students five short clips about electroconvulsive therapy (ECT), including one from *The Beverly Hillbillies*, and their negative endorsements (would not advise the treatment under any circumstances) went from nine percent before viewing the clips to 23 percent afterwards. It seems that seeing Granny Clampett become "a zombie" because of ECT is no real reason for physicians in training to turn away from a treatment option.

Bischoff and Reiter (1999) analyzed 61 movies released between 1988 and the end of 1997 which featured a psychotherapist in a prominent role and which were popular enough that they earned more than five million dollars. They specifically considered the sex of the therapist and found general stereotypes that women therapists were highly sexualized and that male therapists were portrayed as incompetent. They concluded that the sexualization of women therapists comes from the common connection between sexuality and intimacy, and the understanding that therapy is an intimate activity; men were seen as incompetent because of a general stereotype of men as being bad at intimacy. They also found high rates for both men and women therapists in non-sexual dual relationships, such as going to dinner with a client, hiring a client, or going into business with a client. Doing these sorts of things with clients is regarded as unethical. The larger problem is called **boundary problems**. For therapy to work effectively, there are certain boundaries that cannot be crossed. A therapist would not tell a client that when his own wife died, he had to seek counseling. A therapist would not strike up a conversation with a client at Wal-Mart. A therapist would not hire a client who could not pay her bill as his own secretary.

A specific boundary problem is called a **dual relationship**. A therapist at a university would not take on a student in her class as a client, or hire a client as a babysitter, or date a client. In what follows, however, we see that many boundaries are crossed in the movies, and many dual relationships exist. Remember, movies are about *flawed* characters.

What About Bob? (1991)

The first half of *What About Bob?* is very funny. Most of our clinician colleagues agree with that. And the film reminds us that when it comes to dual relations, it is not only the therapist who can cross over the line. Clients sometimes want to extend their relationship with their therapist beyond what is professional or healthy for either the client or the clinician.

Bob's (Bill Murray) problem is that he feels abandoned when his therapist (Richard Dreyfuss) goes on vacation. This is a misrepresentation in several respects. First, Bob isn't really the psychiatrist's client. He has had a single, very short interview, where the psychiatrist agreed to take on his treatment and gave him a copy of his new book *Baby Steps*. The idea behind *Baby Steps* is not particularly bad advice: If big tasks seem overwhelming, break them down into smaller sub-tasks. But, of course, the point of the title of the book is to ridicule self-help books. Bob has difficulty with almost everything in his life. He worries, for example, that his bladder might explode at any minute or that he might suddenly develop Tourette's Syndrome, a tic-like condition in which patients sometimes involuntarily shout obscenities. Bob takes the advice in *Baby Steps* literally. He leaves the office toward the elevator, which terrifies him, taking baby steps.

What is funny about this movie is the relaxed goofiness of Murray's character, contrasted with the rigid seriousness of Dreyfuss' uptight psychiatrist. Bob needs to talk. He tricks the doctor's answering service into connecting him with the doctor on vacation. Then he gets the psychiatrist's address in New Hampshire and joins the doctor and his family. He forces himself to take a bus to New Hampshire, despite his fear of buses and contamination, and his lack of funds. When he arrives at the right town, he just stands in the center of town, bellowing the doctor's name.

In this case, the psychiatrist is needier that his patient. Bob just needs a family, and when he connects with the doctor's family, his problems become less severe. That might work, at least to the level it works in this movie. Bob is neither delusional nor dangerous. In fact, it is difficult to really assess what is wrong with him. At times he has symptoms of OCD. At others, he has symptoms of anxiety, a condition characterized by a generalized fear that things are going to go wrong. Maybe he just spends too much time alone, ruminating. Bob trusts the psychiatrist and his wife and two children. He tries activities that he would never try in his lonely life in Manhattan. He appears to become somewhat more relaxed about doing normal things. But we must underscore *somewhat*. He goes sailing, for example, but only when lashed to the mast, screaming, "I'm sailing; I'm sailing."

It is also the case that psychiatry and clinical psychology are stressful occupations. But most therapists build in professional ways of dealing with that stress, not simply relying on a month in New Hampshire to relieve the previous 11 months of accumulated tensions. Many therapists seek therapy themselves, not because they have psychiatric conditions, but to avoid developing the bizarre behaviors that the psychiatrist in this film has.

Where this movie goes seriously wrong, about midway, is when the family decides they like Bob better than Dad, and the psychiatrist becomes absolutely nuts. He locks up on a TV interview promoting his book. He becomes abusive to his kids. Things are not quite as funny as they were. And then he tries to kill Bob by blowing him up. He even fantasizes about eating him.

The Silence of the Lambs (1991)

One thing we all hope for when we select a therapist is that it will not turn out to be Hannibal Lecter (Anthony Hopkins). Or, for that matter, any other of the therapists depicted in the movie. Lecter not only fantasizes about eating people, he does eat them: friends, clients, police. Yet he has an amazing understanding of the criminal mind, bits and pieces of which he is willing to dole out to the FBI agents and the psychiatrists in his institution for favors. Some of these favors are making his living arrangements more habitable, while others are receiving disclosures of personal information that he later uses to needle the people who have given them to him.

Clarice Starling (Jodie Foster), a young FBI Academy student, is sent to interview Lecter to see if he can help in the case of serial killer "Wild Billy," who skins his victims and then places a rare moth chrysalis in their

Hannibal Lecter (Anthony Hopkins) gets into Clarice Starling's (Jodie Foster) head in *The Silence of the Lambs* (Orion Pictures, 1991).

mouths. Lecter's insights help move the case forward, but he gets into Clarice's head. She's already dealing with a lot of issues: her dead father's reputation as a small-town law enforcement officer; her status as a woman in a male-dominated profession; a relationship with her boss. When Wild Bill's next victim is the daughter of a powerful politician, Lecter uses her political clout to get out of high security, and he escapes in a spectacularly brutal display of carnage. Clarice uses what Lecter has taught her to pursue Wild Bill in a taut, suspenseful conclusion. This is excellent, if gory, entertainment, which probably enhances our understanding of the profession of psychiatrist and criminal profiler not one bit.

Unlike the stereotype of male therapists as being incompetent, Lecter is portrayed as an expert in the processes of the criminal mind, and he is able to get Clarice to disclose the most disturbing moment of her childhood, from which the title is derived. The therapists in the smaller roles provide enough incompetence for several movies; how else could you explain letting Lecter out of maximum security? But is it common for psychiatrists to descend into this kind of madness?

Therapists, in general, are likely to experience depression, and their rates of suicide are relatively high (e.g., Kleepsies *et al.*, 2011). Because of their access to psychoactive drugs, psychiatrists—but not psychologists, who as yet do not have prescription drug privileges—have higher rates of drug abuse than many professions. Lecter, however, is described in this film as having schizophrenia, which usually first manifests itself in one's late teens or early twenties. It is highly unlikely that one could go through medical school and a psychiatric residency with this disorder. Serial killers usually are people on the fringes of society. They tend to have menial jobs. They do seem to have the ability of con people, which is usually necessary for them to lure their victims. Lecter is a fantasy.

Don Juan DeMarco (1995)

Therapist Jack Mickler (Marlon Brando) is retiring early because he is burnt out. But he is not just burnt out in the state psychiatric hospital where he works; he barely listens to his wife (Faye Dunaway) and his everyday life seems to be unraveling because of lack of attention. He is called in on an attempted suicide: A young man wearing a mask and cape (Johnny Depp) needs to be talked down from a billboard. The man does not want to jump, but he wants to die, by the sword of his most powerful enemy. Mickler tells him that his enemy is out of town at present but that he is his uncle, and he invites him to go to his villa to wait for his return.

A crisis intervention expert would *never* do that. While he would acknowledge the potential jumper's delusions, it would be a disaster to try to become part of them. How would he know that the imagined enemy has an uncle? Or what that uncle might mean to the potential jumper? Mickler even adopts the young man's Spanish accent. In a staff meeting, Mickler volunteers to treat the young man who calls himself Don Juan DeMarco. The head of the institution points out that Mickler will retire in ten days; Mickler responds that Don Juan is being held on a "ten-day paper." A young staff therapist is assigned the case, and when he is intimidated by Don Juan, he gives the case to Mickler. In their first therapeutic encounter, Mickler offers Don Juan medication from an unsecured drawer overflowing with prescription drugs. Don Juan respectfully declines, and they enter into an agreement: Mickler will try to convince Don Juan that he's not Don Juan, without drugs, while Don Juan says that he will convince Mickler that he is. Then Don Juan begins to spin a story of his life: his beautiful and religious mother, his romantic father, swordsman, professional dancer, and pharmaceutical salesman, and his beloved, beautiful and married tutor. Brando asks him questions about the implausibility of many points in the story—his name is Italian, he claims to have been raised in Mexico, but he speaks with a European Spanish accent, which Don Juan explains away. Don Juan also acknowledges the reality of his situation. He knows he is delusional and in a mental hospital. He prefers to live as Don Juan and to refer to the hospital as a villa. Delusional patients often do have an easy way of explaining away their delusions—Don Juan says that he has traveled a lot to explain his accent—but they are not delusional if they can differentiate their fantasy from reality.

By some extra-therapeutic sleuth-work, Mickler uncovers the truth about Don Juan. His family background is sad and the woman he idolizes is a centerfold he has never met. But Mickler's therapy sessions reawaken his own enthusiasm for living and his love for his wife, and at the end of the film, he and his wife, accompanied by Don Juan, still Don Juan, go off for a permanent island vacation.

Critics were mixed about this film. It may be an interesting story, and the performances by Depp and Brando are fascinating to watch, but it tells us nothing about the practice of public mental health. Even more ridiculous than the unlocked drawer full of pills and the attempt, through talking alone, to deal with a suicidal and delusional patient in ten days, is the idea that an indigent patient in a state mental health facility would receive daily, individual psychotherapy from a senior staff person. Persons on a "ten-day paper" are primarily being evaluated, not treated. And when treated, medication and nursing is probably all that would be available. We also have a strong reaction to the young therapist giving up on Don Juan after three or four minutes of rather polite intimidation. Every psychotherapist, particularly those working in state facilities, is subjected to far worse than this on a daily basis.

People who are institutionalized are there usually because they are aggressive, incapable of taking care of themselves, or likely to hurt themselves, not because they are polite and thoughtful and want to work through their problems.

Do Movies Portray Psychotherapists Accurately?

If these movies are representative of the depiction of therapists in movies, the answer is a resounding *no*. These therapists are socially and professionally inept, tormented, and tired of doing therapy. In fact, we do not really see them doing therapy. In *Don Juan DeMarco*, Mickler mostly just listens, putting most of his energies into finding out the truth about Don Juan and worrying about his vacation.

In these movies, the central therapists are psychiatrists and all of them practice a version of psychoanalysis. They jump into treatment without any kind of diagnostic process. Only Mickler tries medication, and he is readily talked out of that. We will get a more balanced and a more positive view in some of the films that feature the process of therapy.

The Depiction of Therapy in Films

Gordon (1994) suggests that one of the problems with the depiction of therapy in the movies is the nature of therapy itself:

> There is a problem, of course, in that psychotherapy does not lend itself easily to interesting visual representation.... The slowness of the process of establishing trust, of speaking, of listening, of reflecting and of coming to a joint understanding between therapist and client—these are not the stuff of popular cinema. Film, at least in its more popular variety, relies on pace, narrative clarity and some sort of linear progression.

Freud ventured his opinion in letters to his colleagues that therapy cannot and should not be represented in movies (Jakab, 2004). But therapy has become a staple of the movies. We will look at four films here and discuss their shortcoming, as well as their strong points.

Spellbound (1945)

One of the earliest films to depict the process of therapy was Alfred Hitchcock's *Spellbound*. It was the third highest grossing film of 1945 (Sackett, 1996) and most video reviewers give it four stars. It's revered for several of its features, including a dream sequence by Salvador Dali and an almost subliminal use of color in one of the film's final sequences when the real killer shoots himself in the head and there are exactly two frames of red (the rest of the film is in black-and-white). Its score received an Academy Award. It is well worth watching, despite some laughable skiing sequences toward the end.

Before looking at this film, one would do well to remember the state of psychotherapy in 1945. All therapy was provided by psychiatrists. Clinical psychology did not yet exist as a profession. Carl Rogers was just beginning to develop counseling, and behavior therapy was a decade away, as were effective drugs for psychiatric problems. What was available were hypnosis, which therapists today believe has very limited use, electro-convulsive therapy (ECT), which was widely used at the time, but now is typically only used with depression when medication has not proved worthwhile, and lobotomy, the surgical destruction of parts of the brain; it made volatile patients calm, but permanently interfered with their overall cognitive functioning. Lobotomy is not legal any more, except in one state.

And then there was psychoanalysis. By 1945, Freud (who had died in 1939) and his followers had been espousing a therapeutic approach for more than five decades that believed that almost all mental illness was caused by repressed childhood memories. By interpreting dreams, using word associations, and by talking with patients about their memories, it was believed that the critical event in childhood that was repressed could be found, and once uncovered, the patient would be cured or at least put on the road to recovery. We now believe that most of the major mental illnesses have a strong biological basis, and almost all psychologists are highly skeptical of Freud's ideas about therapy. In 1945, wealthy people who experienced mental illnesses went to resort-like asylums, as the one depicted in the movie and in *Harvey*, where individual psychoanalysis was sometimes practiced, but the main curative processes were more likely rest, exercise and being away from stress. At such private asylums, staff did live on the premises.

Those less financially able, went to state facilities that were packed and often chaotic. ECT and lobotomies were more likely the treatments of choice. With ratios of 500+ patients to one psychiatrist, the intensive nature of psychoanalysis was not feasible.

Whether or not Hitchcock believed in psychoanalysis in 1945 is up to debate. In his famous book-length interview with the French filmmaker and critic Francois Truffaut, Hitchcock said, "I wanted ... to turn out the first film on psychoanalysis. So I worked with [writer] Ben Hecht, who was in constant contact with prominent psychoanalysts." The film depicts psychoanalytic work accurately with two major exception, one of which is acknowledged in the movie. The other major exception is that the analysis seems to work. We would today doubt that once the childhood memory that was being repressed was discovered, any client would be as completely cured as the character portrayed by Gregory Peck appears.

Dr. Murchison, director of a private asylum, is about to retire. His successor, Dr. Edwards (Gregory Peck), arrives, but there is something not right about him. Psychoanalyst Constance Peterson (Ingrid Bergman) is immediately attracted to him, but also realizes he is not who he says he is. She discovers that he has amnesia. Today we would call his condition "dissociative fugue," which is a loss of autobiographical memory and identity associated with psychological rather than brain trauma. In "fugue," people leave their normal lives and may take on someone else's identity. Many psychologists believe that this condition does not actually exist.

Constance tries to help "Dr. Edwards" but he assumes that the trauma that caused his loss of memory and identity was that he has killed the real Dr. Edwards and assumed his identity, and he rejects her. When others discover he is not the real Dr. Edwards, the two of them escape in a quest for his memories. Constance uses traditional psychoanalytic methods (word association, for example) but all she gets are a few clues. She takes him to see her old mentor who does a very quick analysis, in which the Dali dream sequence is featured, and discovers that the Gregory Peck character only witnessed the death of the real Dr. Edwards while skiing. Later, the real cause for his amnesia is found in a childhood accident where he accidentally killed his brother.

Of course, this is a Hitchcock thriller, and there is a good deal more to the plot. The real Dr. Edwards was not killed in a skiing accident but murdered, and Peck's character is accused, hunted down, tried and found guilty of the murder, before Dr. Peterson eventually finds the correct answer to his dream and the identity of the killer.

The process of therapy as presented is ridiculously short, as the older analyst acknowledges. Psychoanalysis typically took years of three-times-a-week sessions. But the tools, the language, and the general feeling accurately portrays many aspects of psychoanalysis as it was practiced at the time.

A dual relationship is at the forefront of this movie: One does not do therapy with someone with whom she is romantically involved. Most therapists would also probably avoid a romantic entanglement with a psychotic murderer. At the beginning of the film, when Constance thinks Gregory Peck is the real Dr. Edwards, she probably should not be romantically involved with her boss, although in 1945 this was not regarded with as much disapproval as it would be today. Despite a reckless disregard for her own safety, Constance is portrayed as an involved, caring, scientifically infused individual. She seems to be a competent professional. Her romantic involvement with Peck reminds us of the findings of Biscoff and Reiter (1999) analysis of later films that found women therapists as highly sexualized.

Ordinary People (1980)

The critic Vincent Canby (1980) wrote of this movie:

> The Jarrets are not only ordinary people, they are also "nice" people. They wear the right clothes, read the right books, eat the right things and misbehave discretely. They put great store in self-control, as much in the privacy of their own house as abroad in the company of friends or strangers. The problem is that such niceness and control cannot accommodate the fear, furies and resentments occasioned when things go to pieces.

Ordinary People, Robert Redford's first film as a director, won the Best Picture Oscar for 1980. The story involves the problems of adjustment of high school senior Conrad Jarrett (Timothy Hutton) who had to be hospitalized for four months following a suicide attempt. The attempt followed a boating accident a year and a half earlier in which his brother Buck drowned.

There are several reasons this film can be highly recommended. Primarily, it faithfully portrays how the process of therapy often takes place, not only how the therapist works to get the client to re-establish his bearings and make sense out of the events that have triggered his problems, but how a person in out-patient therapy has to make sense of the different contexts of his life and how a therapist can help him do so. For example, of the two brothers, Conrad appears to have been less valued by his mother Beth (Mary Tyler Moore). She openly expressed her affection for her older son, but could not for her younger son nor, for that matter, her husband. She controlled Conrad and indulged Buck. Conrad's therapist Dr. Berger (Judd Hirsch) has to convince him that what happened was not that the wrong brother died or that his mother preferred Buck for any particular reason, certainly for no reason that was his fault. He must also help him make sense of the fact that, while he has always looked up to his brother as the dominant, more talented and stronger sibling, his brother quit trying during the ordeal on Lake Michigan. He has to accept the reality that he turned out to be the stronger of the two. He also has to deal with his anger at his brother for letting go of the boat—that he no longer has his best friend and because his best friend could not endure what he could. Coming to terms with each of these issues is a small victory in the therapeutic process. What is compelling about this movie's depiction of therapy is that there is no single breakthrough. It is a step-by-step process. The movie does not end with anything like a cure, but on a note that is both hopeful and still very sad.

And there are some backward steps. Because Conrad survived, because he attempted suicide, because he was institutionalized, because he had undergone ECT, his friends and teachers are wary of him. His swimming coach coldly tells him that he would not have let people put electricity in his brain, as if he were to blame for his therapy and for the events that led to a need for it. Shortly thereafter, Conrad quits the swimming team, but cannot bring himself to tell his parents about his decision. When his mother finds out, she reacts furiously. She was embarrassed to hear about his decision from a friend, and she simply will not tolerate another slip into depression. His father Calvin, who eagerly wants things to get back to normal, but seems clueless about what to do to help this happen, tries to negotiate, unsuccessfully, a truce between the two of them. Conrad feels betrayed, and Beth feels that, as usual, Calvin takes Conrad's side.

Another back step occurs when Conrad asks a young woman out on a date. At first things go reasonably well, but at a McDonald's his former swim teammates come in and make fun of him. He ends up the evening morose and uncommunicative. In a more critical back step, he goes to a swim meet while his parents are away for the Christmas vacation, and when the team has lost and his defection from the team is blamed for the defeat, he ends up in a fistfight with a former teammate. His best friend tries to connect with him, telling him he wants to help and that he, too, misses Buck, but Conrad rejects his help, saying that his friendship raises too many bad memories. When he gets home, he calls a friend from the hospital, only to discover that this time, her suicide attempt was successful. He panics and calls Dr. Berger.

In the late-night session that follows, much of the preparatory work from other sessions is brought to fruition. Here is where he can admit his anger at his brother, get rid of some of his anger at his mother, and learn that there are supports, including Dr. Berger, that he can rely on. So, what was a major backward step in his life, turns out to be another step toward recovery within therapy. He also learns from Dr. Berger that his friend, who seemed on the road to recovery, was not. This is a curious moment in the movie. Berger seems to be telling Conrad that he was his friend's therapist and that she stopped therapy, not because she was well, but because she was pressured to by her father. While this information is helpful to Conrad, there are still confidentiality issues even after a client is deceased that may have been violated here.

But things are not fixed. While Conrad goes to see the girl he had dated and she tells him that she would like to continue to see him, when he expresses his affection to his mother after his parents have returned from their golfing vacation, she cannot respond in kind to him. His father observes this, and later that night, Beth wakes up to find her husband crying in the dining room. He tells her that he has discovered that he no longer loves her and that he is miserable because his love for her was one of the things he counted on in his life. Beth goes upstairs and packs. Having said that she is not interested in changing earlier, the audience knows she is gone for good.

As Conrad's mother Beth, Mary Tyler Moore, best known for her roles as perky, resilient women in TV sitcoms, could be thought of as the villain in this story. She has emotionally distanced herself from her surviving son. But there are telling moments of her fragility underneath her emotionless facade. For example, she wrecks Conrad's Thanksgiving by refusing to be photographed with him, probably because she cannot tolerate an image being made of her broken family. She can tolerate no signs of her son's emotional problems or her husband's support of him. Conrad believes that she cannot forgive him for the literal mess he caused when he tried suicide: They had to re-grout the floor of the bathroom. He equates this with her firing a maid because she couldn't dust to her satisfaction. Yet as Beth packs, after her husband's revelation of his lost love for her, she is clearly just barely in control. There is a terrific sense of loss and sadness in her, but a complete unwillingness to do the necessary work to heal her family.

Conrad's father Calvin, who can express his grief over his lost son, his love for his surviving son, and his dismay in his wife's cold reactions to him, complicates the therapeutic process by wanting everything to get back to normal as quickly as possible. He cannot talk effectively about the past or the present. He wants to negotiate truces. But toward the end of the film, he seeks out Dr. Berger's help

The end of this movie, where Conrad and his father sit in the backyard and talk immediately after Beth has left, is very sad: they have accepted the loss of a son and brother and a wife and mother, but there is also a genuine pervasive feeling that together, they will survive. They begin the healing talk that they two of them have needed to engage in for a long time. Conrad wants to know why his father seemed so much more involved with Buck. Calvin says that he hadn't worried about Conrad because "you were so hard on yourself."

There are boundary issues here. For example, Conrad's father goes to see Berger and while they both acknowledge that what has gone on in therapy with Conrad cannot be discussed, Berger appears to take on Calvin as a client. Therapy can be either aimed at an individual or at a family system, but this blurring of the goals of therapy would prove problematic in a real situation. It is not particularly disturbing in the context of the film for Calvin to see Dr. Berger, but the problem is obvious if Beth could have been persuaded to see him. If Beth also became a client, then Dr. Berger would have had to resolve their conflicts, rather than just helping Conrad understand that his mother's reactions were cold and unfair and not his fault.

Good Will Hunting (1997)

Gus Van Sant's directed his co-stars' script, which won an Oscar for Best Screenplay. Our colleagues who do therapy are widely divided about this film. There are individual moments in it that are ludicrous, but many feel that, in general, it portrays the process of therapy well.

Will Hunting (Matt Damon), a spectacularly gifted young man, is crushed by a long history of abuse. He works as a janitor at M.I.T. and he can solve complex mathematical problems that the math doctoral students cannot. Nothing about his life works. He is headed toward prison for assault, petty theft and substance abuse, but an M.I.T. math professor steps in and suggests that before he gets sent to jail for his most recent offenses, an old classmate of his (Robin Williams), a clinical psychologist who teaches at the local community college, be given a crack at him. A judge agrees, and therapy starts.

Very few Ivy League–trained clinical psychologists teach at community colleges. Will knows this, and he resists becoming involved in the therapeutic process by constantly trying to turn the therapy sessions away from his problems to whatever has led his therapist to fail. Shortly into the first session, Will discovers that the psychologist's wife is dead, and he attacks the therapist's vulnerability so accurately that the therapist tries to strangle him. This is a boundary issue, or a whole series of them. The therapist discloses too much and allows the process to go on too long. And, although this is the third time in six films that therapists have tried to kill clients, it is important to note that such behavior is really rare.

Will has been in and out of therapy for most of his life, and he has decided that it cannot help him. The psychologist spends most of the time convincing him that he should let down his guard and give it a try. One of Will's problems is that his previous therapists have not been his intellectual equal, but this therapist is, and eventually he makes some small efforts.

Will has only one positive influence in his life, his best friend (Ben Affleck), but eventually he meets a Harvard co-ed who provides him a reason to get focused. Between the therapy and finding a romantic relationship with an intellectual peer, Will gets on the right track. Of course, that's the way things actually happen in real life. In *Ordinary People*, Conrad's relations with a girl also provide him with motivation to get his life in order. But Will rejects romantic relationships in the same way he rejects therapy. Why? Does he want to avoid getting hurt or does he feel he is not worth an emotional investment from someone else?

While we indicated that the shortening of psychoanalysis in *Spellbound* is, in some ways, just silly, the kind of intervention that Williams' character provides for Will, is of necessity time-bound, and is usually called **brief counseling**. He is not trying to fix Will in every aspect of his life, he is just trying to get the pieces together well enough that he can report back to the judge that he thinks that Will will not be showing up in his court again. Will's psychologist recognizes that Will intellectualizes everything and avoids anything that might have serious emotional costs. He also recognizes this as a typical aftermath of abuse and neglect. In their final session, the psychologist pushes Will to talk about his history of physical cruelty at the hands of an alcoholic parent, and then gets him to connect with his emotional response by repeatedly telling Will, "It's not your fault," until Will finally gets the message. The therapist continues to step over the boundaries by describing his own history of physical abuse along the way.

Everyone in this film seems excessively damaged, except for the carload of Will's friends from the neighborhood who tell dirty jokes, drink way too much, and work mind-numbing jobs. His M.I.T. professor is a shamble of insecurities. The psychologist has been bumbling along in a state of depression or angst for years, abused by a parent and bereft of his wife. Will's girlfriend is both emotional vulnerable and perking along into a prestigious medical school. But, in the sessions, that *process of establishing trust, of speaking, of listening, of reflecting and of coming to a joint understanding between therapist and client* is given a reasonable showing that makes for some interesting drama.

Analyze This (1999)

Harold Ramis' film is pretty funny, particularly the first hour, but it presents little more than stereotypes of therapy. A mob boss (Robert De Niro) cannot be ruthlessly violent any more, so he seeks out therapy to help him become violent again. A colleague of his has met Dr. Ben Sobel (Billy Crystal); Sobel rear-ended his car when there was a body in the trunk. De Niro demands therapy, whenever and wherever he needs it. He's like Bob, but with enforcers.

The cast of characters contributes to its humor. Most of the actors are well known from their serious work in Mafia movies, and it is just plain funny to see them reprising these roles in a comedy. De Niro is hilarious when he has panic attacks, even when he has a hospital psychiatrist beaten up for making that diagnosis. The end of the film, in which Dr. Sobel has to function as a mobster, falls flat.

The big gag and main point of the film is that everyone starts talking about their feelings. When Dr. Sobel discovers that as a boy, De Niro saw his father killed, he asks him, "How did you feel?" De Niro responds as if the question was moronic. "How did I feel? My father died. I was sad." But that is the point, and this is the critical moment, because De Niro was angry with his father at the time and now wonders whether he could have saved his father by warning him when he saw the gunman approaching.

One problem with this film as a way of understanding therapy is that psychoanalysis is not merely about feeling or even primarily about feelings. *Getting in touch with your feelings* is a mantra from counseling-derived interventions. Psychoanalysis is about making new meanings. Constance only asks Gregory Peck twice about how he felt in *Spellbound*.

So, what is recommended?

Psychotherapy exists in several forms today. Very few therapists practice classic psychoanalysis. Somewhat more practice **behavior therapy**, which is almost the exact opposite of psychoanalysis. Behavior therapists believe that most mental illnesses are neither illnesses nor mental, but they are the result of learning. Therefore, it someone has learned a behavior, such as depression, it can be unlearned by applying learning techniques. **Cognitive-behavior therapy** takes the position that mental illnesses are learned, but what is learned is not just behavior, but ideas, beliefs and attitudes. The psychologist in *Good Will Hunting* often uses cognitive-behavioral interventions. He believes that Will has learned that his is not worthwhile because there was something about him that merited severe punishment as a child. **Counseling** is a talking-based approach that helps people gain insights into their behavior, although it takes a less direct approach than cognitive behavioral therapy. Many psychiatrists take a much more **medical approach** to mental illness, doing most of their treatment by drug therapy.

About half of clinical psychologists today consider themselves **eclectic**, which means that they use techniques from all of the approaches. An eclectic approach is not just the idea of using a bag of tricks, but understanding that different problems have different origins and different routes in therapy. Some people are depressed because of events in their lives and an eclectic therapist would take a behavioral approach with them, while others are depressed for biological reasons, and a medical model may be more appropriate for them. Dr. Berger in *Ordinary People* fits the description.

Behavior therapy has not received much accurate representation in films. Its most extremely inaccurate version is in the futuristic film *A Clockwork Orange* (1971), in which conditioning is used to attempt to make a violent teenager incapable of violence and sexual aggression. Two costume dramas, however, give a good flavor of how rewards and punishments can be used to shape up behavior, *The Madness of King George* (1994), which concerns the treatment of the English monarch, George III, and Francois Truffaut's beautiful film *The Wild Child* (1994), based on the diaries of the physician who attempted to teach social behavior and language to a young teenager who had been left to fend for himself in the woods at an early age in the 1790s. Truffaut himself stepped in front of the camera and portrayed the teacher, Itard. While Itard may not meet modern American standards of warm and fuzzy, this film may be the most humane movie representation of the human impulse to help another person ever made.

Key Psychological Terms

Behavior Therapy: Therapy that is based on learning theory and ignores internal states like emotions.

8. Depictions of the Mentally Ill, Therapists and Therapy 187

Boundary Problems: An ethical violation that involves behavior that is outside the professional relationship, such as socializing with a client.
Brief counseling: Talk-based interventions which have a limited time frame, either because of practical reasons (court appearances) or based on research that counseling is most effective during the first three or four sessions
Cognitive-Behavioral Therapy: An extrapolation of behavior therapy to include thoughts and feelings.
DSM-V: The classification system of mental disorders of the American Psychiatric Association.
Dual relationships: Having more than one relationship with another at the same time (e.g., being a therapist and a family member).
Eclectic Therapy: An approach in therapy of using different procedures to match the disorder (e.g., using a medical treatment for a disorder that is organic and talk therapy with a disorder that grows out of a social situation).

Epilogue

While I cannot claim that we have reviewed here every psychological study of movies ever done, particularly in the areas of smoking and aggression, I feel we have been thorough. Now we want to revisit our original intent: to see whether the various areas of psychology shine a light on a common behavior, going to the movies. I believe that the answer is a qualified *yes*.

Psychology offers some insights into why people choose the movies they do. Some movies are just not stimulating enough for sensation seekers. Other movies are too much about the human heart for those who are low in empathy. Some movies require too mucgh rapt attention for the extravert who is all about interacting in the here and now. Other movies offer the possibility of unpleasant experiences, which the neurotic will avoid. In general, then, the personality characteristics of the viewer help more to explain why we *avoid* certain types of movies, than they help to explain why some of us choose zombie movies or some of us become fascinated with Hitchcock.

Media manages mood, and mood influences what media we choose. Psychologists have done a credible job examining the happy-sad vector in mood and its relation to media choice, but there are other aspects of mood: anxious-relaxed, bored-engaged, to name two of the usual suspects. These have not been explored to any real degree, and should they be, they likely will help us understand movie choice even better.

Most media psychologists have been looking for a general theory of media use with regards to mood that will account for how we choose what song to listen to on the car radio as well as how we choose movies, but movies are fundamentally different from pop songs in at least five ways:

1. Movies are much more of a commitment.
2. Going to the movies usually involve someone else.
3. Movies most often have a variety of moods and levels of stimulation within them.

4. When we choose a song, we usually choose one we have heard before; that is rarely the case with movies.

5. When we choose to hear a song, we hear it immediately; when we choose a movie, it may be hours, days, or even months until we see it.

We know very little about the actual choice itself, but we know that the outcomes are different when we choose a movie with a romantic partner, friends and family members, and with romantic partners, it makes a difference whether the relationship is one that is forming or one that is established and committed.

Our behavior in the theater—paying attention, processing, piecing information together—is something of a mystery, but there is considerable information on these issues when watching smaller screens, and we are watching movies, more and more, on smaller screens.

Finally, the degree to which movies influence us, to buy products, even those that hurt us, to entertain new ideas, to choose careers, and to understand those who are different from ourselves, remains controversial. Probably the best way of summarizing the current state of knowledge in this area is to say that movies contribute to our beliefs and attitudes but we are not media slaves. Movies are likely to influence children and teens more than adults because they have had less real life to temper their influence.

* * *

In closing, I will offer up 13 questions I would like to see explored in further research to fill in some of our holes in understanding:

1. Who doesn't like movies?

I have encountered such people, occasionally in my Psychology of Film class. They have enrolled because they needed a capstone course and the film course fits their schedule. They report that they don't go to movies, and they don't seem to like the ones shown in class very much. They say they are a waste of time, even though they are apt to admit they do things that are wastes of time (playing video games, binge-watching the TV news cycle, reading romance novels). To which I say, wasting time can be a good thing for your psychological wellbeing.

It makes sense in studying any behavior to get to know who does it and who avoids it. We have studies of sports junkies, high school marching band members and marathon runners. We don't have this kind of knowledge about who loves and who avoids movies. And this matters a good deal, if for no other reason than the fact that many of the studies we have mentioned involved mass communications majors enrolled in film courses, people who probably love movies more than the average person.

2. What role does boredom play in movie selection and attendance?

Boredom is frequently trotted out in the discussion sections of research articles with regard to film selection and rate of attendance. But it has really not been studied directly. Boredom susceptibility is a component of sensation-seeking, but as we mentioned, research on sensation-seeking has generally looked at its overall effect and not examined its components. People high in boredom susceptibility are both frequently bored and find boredom very unpleasant and will do almost anything to get it to stop. In a number of research areas, boredom susceptibility has been found to lead people to risky-taking behavior. Teens and young adults high in boredom susceptibility go along with others even when the outcomes are questionable. But it also leads people to try new things, to step out of the comfort zone. Someone who is bored may take a risk and go to see an Italian-language movie about a movie director who has begun a project without any idea where it will take him. Or an old-fashioned whodunit. Or a silent movie. While there has been some exploration of how boredom may lead some to watch too mature or too frightening movies, there is also the possibility that boredom is a horizon-widening quality.

3. How will we navigate the ever-broadening choice of movies?

In the small city in which I grew up where there were three movie theaters, there was almost always a movie playing that I could be talked into seeing. Making a choice among the three or four movies playing was relatively easy. And when movies started to appear on TV, while a little more complex, the decision was more about *when* to see movies. There would be a movie on TV I wanted to see on Thursday night, so we would have to go to the theater one of the other six evenings. Then cable. Then video stores. The Blockbuster in my city proudly announced that it had "over 2000 titles." I recall going there and on some occasions leaving without a rental. I was overwhelmed.

"Over 2000 titles" is small potatoes compared to what is available now. Being able to watch any movie at any time anywhere is an intoxicating possibility for movie buffs. And yet there might be a downside. Advocates of the Internet enthuse that all the libraries in the world are now literally at our fingertips, but reading is way down. Are the choices too complex? Will we just be guided by a search engine toward our favorite genre. What would happen if we ask Alexa to choose something outside our comfort zone?

One thing makes me slightly optimistic. Occasionally, Amazon or Google makes a suggestion that puzzles me. Usually it is because I have bought a DVD or CD or book for a friend who has very different tastes than I do. That purchase is then thrown into my usual pattern and something unexpected emerges.

4. How do people other than college students choose and process movies?

There are very few studies of middle-aged and elderly adults with relation to film. We have hints that their choice processes are different, but we know next to nothing about how they use movies and how movies influence them. To our knowledge, there are *no* studies of young adults who are not in college. Even studies of graduate students would be informative: They are a little older and have less free time and have to manage it more deliberately. I don't feel that *choice* has been looked at very effectively in children and adolescents. I would like to know about repetitive watching in these younger viewers.

5. How is behavior different watching a movie in a theater than watching TV?

When I go to the theater to see a movie, I sometimes find myself looking at audience members, and I see that they *do* look around, check in with their companions, pull out their phones, or fumble with popcorn. They do not look at the screen constantly. And, of course, when I observe this, neither am I.

There are all sorts of questions that come to mind here: How is a person's attention affected by the fact that he or she didn't choose the movie? How is our attention different if we are with friends or a romantic partner or a family member? Do children really mostly pay attention to children on screen, as the research on TV seems to imply? How do individuals with ADHD process movies? But most of all, for some of us at least, the experience of watching a movie in a theater and watching it at home are so different because of the theater's physical set-up and the difference in social rules, that it would be useful to deliberately make contrasts between the two situations: Are our emotional reactions to films *larger* in a theater? Is it easier to empathize with a character in the theater because we are not distracted by others? Will we remember a movie better when the images filled our whole retina and we were less distracted, than when occasionally looking at a small screen in our bedroom?

6. How are our childhood experiences with the movies linked to our later uses of the movies?

In a TV commercial making the rounds these days, a family in their open-concept living space cannot decide on what to eat or what to watch. Dad looks at the big screen, Mom looks at the laptop as she orders different take-out for everyone, and the two kids are watching on their phones. While I understand that the point here is to sell gadgets and to promulgate the myth that sharing space is the same thing as intimacy, I wonder whether these children will ever be able to make a social choice, extend their watching choice beyond what they are already comfortable with, or have a conversation about a genuinely shared experience.

This is a very different reality from how I grew up with movies. I watched them with my parents, in the theater and on TV. Sometimes the movies were made for kids—I recall having to be comforted after *Bambi* (1942) and *Old Yeller* (1957), and sometimes I was dragged along to very grown-up movies. The finale of *Vertigo* (1958) certainly impressed me as a ten-year-old who was taught by nuns. Going to the movies with my family, talking about what we would see beforehand, and discussing it afterwards, sometimes long afterwards, was a way of interacting with family members and learning to understand the benefits of stories, pictures and music.

7. Why don't we study comedies?

Comedies are the most popular genre of movies, and no one has given them any real attention, let alone the attention we have given to horror and violence. A focus on comedies would elucidate a benign and common aspect of moviegoing. I would like to know, when do we choose a comedy (and when do we choose slapstick or gross-out or farce or romantic comedies or musical comedies)? And I would like to follow up on the idea that comedies are actually good for us (Cousins, 1976). Maybe comedy is too benign and too common to get much attention.

8. Has anyone ever watched an entire movie on a phone?

I just want to know. I ask the students in my class, and no one admits to having done it yet.

9. Do movies about mental illness and therapy help or hinder the double stigma of being mentally ill and seeking treatment?

If watching Granny Clampett get "zombified" after electro-convulsive therapy makes MDs-in-training say they would not use ECT, what effect will spending two hours in a dark theater with Dr. Hannibal Lecter have on an anxious individual who is thinking about entering treatment? The fact is, we don't know. I have shown my classes the ludicrous portrayal of anxiety and the murderous rage of the therapist in *What About Bob?* and they report *more* willingness to seek treatment after watching it. I don't understand it, but that's what happens. This is a class demonstration, not controlled research, but psychologists particularly should investigate this issue, because a large segment of the population avoids getting help because they have negative opinions of the effectiveness of psychological interventions. That's not entirely the fault of movies, but I suspect they play a role.

10. Why do we find mental illness entertaining?

This may seem like a rude way of asking the question, but a lot of recent American movies have mental illness as a prominent theme. We must enjoy them.

There are two kinds of movies that focus on mental illness: movies of suspense or horror in which a deranged criminal is at work and movies that look closely at how mental illness plays out in other challenging situations. I would imagine that these two types of films appeal to different audiences. Having a a criminal character be "deranged," makes his or her actions unpredictable, which allows for more suspense and horror—although a methodical, sane person can also provide some gasps. It is the other kind of movie, the one that focuses on the reality of mental illness, that intrigues me. Who likes this kind of movie? What do they get out of it? Are these people who like to go to movies to broaden their perspective and learn things? Are these people who have personal issues they are trying to work out? Or is it a search for occasional novelty?

I would be very interested in seeing whether this is cultural. Do movies about deranged serial killers or returning veterans with PTSD play well in Sweden or Bahrain? Who watches these movies?

11. Why are we currently so obsessed with dystopic comic-book fantasies?

Just another thing I'd like to know, unless it presages the fall of civilization.

12. Politics aside, what really are the effects of watching pornography?

On the one hand, we were startled by how little basic research has been done in this area. On the other, we were not surprised, given how controversial it is. But if the often-made claim that one out of four log-ons to the Internet leads to viewing porn, this is an area that needs immediate attention. Unless, of course, watching XXX-rated films is psychologically equivalent to watching cat videos.

13. What about awe?

While writing this section, I caught *West Side Story* on Turner Classic Movies. This was a movie I loved as a teenager, and although I had forgotten the long, moving shot of Manhattan from above that accompanies the overture, even seeing it on a small screen brought back that sense of *awe* when I first saw it in a theater. This made me recall some other awe-filled moments in movies that still make the back of my neck tingle: the long entrance of Omar Sharif in *Lawrence of Arabia* (1962), starting as a wavering dot in the vast bleakness of the desert; Kong's first appearance in the 1933 version of the film that unsettled me for months as a child; the cityscapes of New York over Gershwin's music in Woody Allen's *Manhattan* (1979); Neville Longbottom killing the Slytherin snake at the end of the Potter films. Awe is why we pay to watch a movie in IMAX and why epics still have a hold on audiences. It is why John Ford shot in Monument Valley. It is why movies in theaters will probably never go completely out of fashion.

But there are also smaller, quieter moments of awe in movies: the sight of the bomber graveyard in *Best Years of Our Lives*; the drowning out of the Nazis' song at Rick's by the French refugees; groggy Jeff waking to find Lisa in his apartment in *Rear Window*.

Having these moments ... that's why I go to the movies.

References

Aash, S. D., & Byers, E. S. (1990). Effects of behavioural exchanges and cognitions on the relationship satisfaction of dating and married persons. *Canadian Journal of Behavioral Science, 22*, 223–235.

Adkins, T., & Castle, J. J. (2014). *Moving* pictures? Experimental evidence of cinematic influence on political attitudes. *Social Science Quarterly, 95*, 1230–1244.

Alanko, K, Gunst, A., Mokros, A., & Santtila, P. Genetic variants associated with male pedophiliac sexual interest. *Journal of Sexual Medicine, 13*, 835–842.

Allport, G. W. (1937). *Personality: A psychological interpretation.* New York: Henry Holt.

Aluja-Fabregat, A. (2002). Personality and curiosity about TV and films violence in adolescents. *Personality and Individual Differences, 29*, 379–392.

Alvarez, M. M., Huston, A. C., Wright, J. C., & Kerkman, D. D. (1988). Gender differences in visual attention to television form and content. *Journal of Applied Developmental Psychology, 9*, 459–475.

Alwitt, L. F., Anderson, D. R., Lorch, E. P., & Levin, S. R. (1980). Preschool children's visual attention to television. *Human Communication Research, 7*, 52–67.

Anderson, D. R., & Burns, J. (1991). Paying attention to television. In J. Bryant and D. Zillman (Eds.), *Responding to the screen: Reception and reaction processes* (pp. 3–25). Hillsdale, NJ: Lawrence Erlbaum.

Anderson, D. R., Huston, A. C., Schmitt, K. L. Linebarger, D. L. & Wright, J. C. (2001). Early childhood television viewing and adolescent behavior: The recontact study. *Monographs of the Society for Research in Child Development, 66*, vii–147.

Anderson, D. R., Lorch, E. P., Field, D. P., Collins, P. A., & Nathan, J. H. (1986). Television viewing at home: Age trends in visual attention and time with television. *Child Development, 57*, 1024–1033.

Anderson, D. R., Lorch, E. P., Smith, R., Bradford, R., & Levin, S. R. (1981). Effects of peer pressure on preschool children's television viewing behavior. *Developmental Psychology, 17*, 446–453.

Austin, B. A., & Gordon, T. F. (1987). Movie genres: Toward a conceptualized model and standardized definition. In B. A. Austin (Ed.), *Current research in film: Audiences, Economics and the Law (Vol. 3).* Norwood, NJ: Ablex.

Auty, S., & Lewis, C. (2004). Exploring children's choice: The reminder effect of product placement. *Psychology & Marketing, 21*, 697–713.

Aveno, A. (1987). A survey of leisure activities engaged in by adults who are severely retarded living in different residence and community types. *Education and Training in Mental Retardation, 22*, 121–127.

Bandura, A., & Huston, A. C. (1961). Identification as a process of incidental learning. *Journal of Abnormal and Social Psychology, 63*, 311–318.

Bandura, A., Ross, D., & Ross, S. A. (1961). Transmission of aggression through imitation of aggressive models. *Journal of Abnormal and Social Psychology, 63*, 575–582.

Bandura, A., Ross, D., & Ross, S. A. (1963). Imitation of film-mediated aggressive models. *Journal of Abnormal and Social Psychology, 66*, 3–11.

Bartlett, F. C. (1932). *Remembering: A study in experimental and social psychology*. New York: Macmillan.
Bauman, J. (July 31, 1998). VA sets up hotline to deal with movie. *Desert News*.
Berenbaum, H., & Williams, M. (1995). Personality and emotional reactivity. *Journal of Research in Personality, 29*, 24–34.
Berry, M., Gray, T., & Donnerstein, E. (1999). Cutting film violence: Effects on perceptions, enjoyment, and arousal. *Journal of Social Psychology, 139*, 567–582.
Bischoff, R. J., & Reiter, A. D. (1999). The role of gender in the presentation of mental health clinicians in the movies: Implications for clinical practice. *Psychotherapy: Theory, Research, Practice, Training, 36*, 180–189.
Blumberg, F. C., & Bierwirth, & Schwartz, A. J. (2008). Does cartoon violence beget aggressive behavior in real life? An opposing view. *Early Childhood Education Journal, 36*, 101–104.
Boksem, M. A. S., & Smidts, A. Brain responses to movie trailers predict individual preference for movies and their population-wide commercial success. *Journal of Marketing Research, 52*, 482–492.
Boltz, M. (2001). Musical soundtracks as a schematic influence on the cognitive processing of filmed events. *Music Perception, 18*, 427–454.
Boltz, M., Schulkind, M., & Kantra, S. (1991). Effects of background music on the remembering of filmed events. *Memory & Cognition, 19*, 593–606.
Bondanella, P. (1991). *Italian cinema: From neorealism to the present*. New York: Continuum.
Bonds-Raacke, J. M. (2004). *Husband-wife decision-making in selecting movies and restaurants*. Ph.D. Dissertation: Kansas State University.
Bozzuto, J. C. (1975). Cinematic neurosis following "The Exorcist": Report of four cases. *Journal of Nervous and Mental Disease, 16*, 43–48.
Brown, C. L., Matherne, C. E., Bulik, C. M., Howard, J. B., Ravanbakht, S. N., Skinner, A. C., Wood, C. T., Bardone-Cone, A. M., Brown, J. D., Perrin, A. J., Levine, C., Steiner, M. J., & Perrin, E. M. (2017). Influence of product placement in children's movies on children's snack choices. *Appetite, 114*, 118–124.
Brown, G. E., Dixon, P. A., & Hudson, D. J. (1982). Effect or peer pressure on imitation of humor responses in college students. *Psychological Reports, 51*, 1111–1117.
Brown, J. D., & Bobkowski, P. S. (2011). Older and newer media: Patterns of use and effects on adolescents' health and well-being. *Journal of Research on Adolescence, 21*, 95–113.
Brown, J. D., Halpern, C. T., & L'Engle, K. L. (2005). Mass media as a sexual super peer for early maturing girls. *Journal of Adolescent Health, 36*, 420–427.
Bruner, J. (1983). *Child's talk: Learning to use language*. New York: W. W. Norton.
Bucksch, J., Sigmundova, D., Hamrik, Z., Troped, P. J., Melkevik, O., Ahluwalia, N., Borraccino, A., Tynjala, J., Kalman, M, & Inchley, J. (2016). International trends in adolescent screen-time behaviors from 2002 to 2010. *Journal of Adolescent Health, 58*, 417–425.
Buswell, G. (1935). *How people look at pictures*. Chicago: University of Chicago Press.
Canby, V. (January 18, 1980). The sorrow of affluence. *New York Times*.
Chapman, J. (2008). *Licensed to thrill: A cultural history of the James Bond films* (2nd ed.). London: I. B. Tauris.
Cheetham, M., Hanggi, J., & Jancke, L. (2014). Identifying with fictive characters: Structural brain correlates of the personality trait "fantasy." *Social Cognitive and Affective Neuroscience, 9*, 1836–1844.
Chethik, N. (July 10, 1994). Disney's "Lion King": Same old sexist jungle out there. *The Seattle Times*.
Clarke-Stewart, K. A., & Beck, R. J. (1999). Maternal scaffolding and children's narrative retelling of a movie story. *Early Childhood Research Quarterly, 14*, 409–434.
Cohen, A. J. (1990). Understanding musical soundtracks. *Empirical Studies of the Arts, 8*, 111–124.
Cousins, N. (1976). Anatomy of an illness (as perceived by the patient). *New England Journal of Medicine, 295*, 1458–1463.
Cowan, P. S. (1984). Film and text: Order effects in recall and social inference. *Educational Communication and Technology, 32*, 131–144.
Cowan, P. S. (1988). Manipulating montage: Effects on film comprehension, person perception, and aesthetic responses. *Empirical Studies of the Arts, 6*, 97–115.

Cox, M. J., Gabrielli, J., Janssen, T., & Jackson, K. M. (May 2, 2018). Parental restriction of movie viewing prospectively predicts adolescent alcohol and marijuana initiation: Implications for media literacy programs. *Prevention Science*. No pagination.
Cuperfain, R., & Clarke, T. K. (1985). A new perspective of subliminal perception. *Journal of Advertising, 14*, 36–41.
Dalton, M. A., Sargent, J. D., Beach, M., Titus-Ernstoff, L., Gibson, J. J., Ahrens, M. B., Tickle, J. J., & Hetherton, T. F. (2003). Effect of viewing smoking in movies on adolescent smoking initiation: A cohort study. *The Lancet, 362*, 281–285.
Darwin, C. (1872). *The expression of the emotions in man and animals*. London: John Murray.
Davis, M. H. (1996). *Empathy: A social psychological approach*. Boulder, CO: Westview Press.
Davis, M. H., Hull, J. G., Young, R. D., & Warren, G. G. (1987). Emotional reactions to dramatic film stimuli: The influence of cognitive and emotional empathy. *Journal of Personality and Social Psychology, 52*, 126–133.
Del Palacio-Gonzalez, A., & Clark, D. A. (2014). Cognitive specificity in fear and sad affect: An investigation of emotional reactivity and recovery from experimental mood induction. *Cognitive Therapy and Research, 38*, 270–279.
DeLorne, D. E., & Reid, L. N. (1999). Moviegoers' experiences and interpretations of brands in films revisited. *Journal of Advertising, 28*, 71–95.
Desai, K. K., & Basuroy, S. (2005). Interactive influence of genre familiarity, star power, and critics' reviews in the cultural goods industry: The case of motion pictures. *Psychology and Marketing, 22*, 203–223.
Devlin, M. B., Chambers, L. T., & Callison, C. (2011). Targeting mood: Using comedy or serious movie trailers. *Journal of Broadcasting and Electronic Media, 55*, 581–595.
Distefan, J. M., Gilpin, E. A., Sargent, J. D., & Pierce, J. P. (1999). Do movie stars encourage adolescents to start smoking? Evidence from California. *Preventive Medicine, 28*, 1–11.
Drabman, R. S., & Thomas, M. H. (1974a). Does media violence increase children's toleration of real life aggression? *Developmental Psychology, 10*, 418–421.
Drabman, R. S., & Thomas, M. H. (1974b). Exposure to filmed violence and children's toleration of real life aggression. *Personality and Social Psychology Bulletin, 1*, 198–199.
Drabman, R. S., & Thomas, H. H. (1976). Does watching violence on television cause apathy? *Pediatrics, 57*, 329–331.
Ebert, R. (September 15, 1996). *Casablanca (1942)*. Chicago-Sun Times.
Elberese, A., & Bharat. (2007). The effectiveness of pre-release advertising for motion pictures: An empirical investigation using a simulated market. *Information Economics and Policy, 19*, 319–343.
Eliashberg, J., & Shugan, S. M. (1997). Film critics: Influencers or predictors? *Journal of Marketing, 61*, 68–78.
Ellis, R. J., & Simons, R. F. (2005). The impact of music on subjective and physiological indices of emotion while viewing films. *Psychomusicology, 19*, 15–40.
Elnour, A. S., & Harrison, J. (2008). Lethality of suicide methods. *Injury Prevention, 14*, 39–45.
Engle, Y., & Kasser, T. (2005). Why do adolescent girls idolize male celebrities? *Journal of Adolescent Research, 20*, 263–283.
Eno, C. A., & Ewoldsen, D. R. (2010). The influence of explicitly and implicityly measured prejudice on interpretations of and reactions to Black film. *Media Psychology, 13*, 1–30.
Eron, L. D. (2001). Seeing is believing: How viewing violence attitudes and aggressive behavior. In A. C. Bohart & D. J. Stipek (Eds.), *Constructive and destructive behavior: Implications for family, school, and society* (pp. 49–60). Washington, D.C.: American Psychological Association.
Eysenck, H. J., & Eysenck, M. W. (1985). *Personality and individual differences: A natural science approach*. New York: Plenum.
Eysenck, H. J., & Eysenck, S. B. G. (1975). *Manual of the Eysenck Personality Questionnaire*. London: Hodder & Stoughton.
Field, D. E., & Anderson, D. R. (1985). Instruction and modality effects on children's television attention and comprehension. *Journal of Educational Psychology, 77*, 91–100.
Finn, S. (1997). Origins of media exposure: Linking personality traits to TV, radio, print, and film use. *Communication Research, 24*, 507–529.

Flavell, J. H., Flavell, E. R., Green, F. L., & Korfmacher, J. E. (1990). Do young children think of television images as pictures or real objects? *Journal of Broadcasting and Electronic Media, 34*, 399–419.

Forgas, J. P., & Moylan, S. (1987). After the movies: Transient mood and social judgments. *Personality and Social Psychology Bulletin, 13*, 467–477.

Forsdale, J., & Forsdale, L. (1966). Film literacy. *Teacher's College Record, 67*, 608–617.

Freud, S. (1900/1911). *On the interpretation of dreams*. New York: Macmillan.

Fuller, K. H. (1996). *At the picture show: Small-town audiences and the creation of movie fan culture*. Washington, D.C.: Smithsonian Institution.

Funk, J. B., Baldacci, H. B., Pasold, T., & Baumgardner, J. (2004). Violence exposure in real-life, video games, television, movies, and the internet: Is there desensitization? *Journal of Adolescence, 27*, 23–39.

Gazley, A., Clark, G., & Sinha, A. (2011). Understanding preferences for motion pictures. *Journal of Business Research, 64*, 854–861.

Gelkopf, M., Gonen, B., Kurs, R., Melamed, Y., & Bleich, A. (2004). The effect of humorous movies on inpatients with chronic schizophrenia. *Journal of Nervous and Mental Disease, 194*, 880–883.

Gelkopf, M., Sigal, M., & Kramer, R. (1994). Therapeutic use of humor to improve social support in an institutionalized schizophrenic inpatient community. *Journal of Social Psychology, 134*, 175–182.

Gibson, J. J. (1947). *Motion picture testing and research*. AAF Aviation Psychology Research Report No. 7. Washington, D.C.: Government Printing Office.

Gordon, P. (1994). The celluloid couch: Representations of psychotherapy in recent cinema. *British Journal of Psychotherapy, 11*, 142–145.

Gould, S. J., Gupta, P. B., & Grabner-Krauter, S. (2000). Product placements in movies: A cross-cultural analysis of Austrian, French, and American consumers' attitudes toward this emerging international promotion medium. *Journal of Advertising, 29*, 41–58.

Greenblatt, S. (2004). *Will in the world: How Shakespeare became Shakespeare*. New York: W. W. Norton.

Greenwood, D. N., & Long, C. R. (2009). Mood specific media use and emotional regulation: Patterns and individual differences. *Personality and Individual Differences, 46*, 616–621.

Grieve, R., & Williamson, K. (1977). Aspects of auditory and visual attention to narrative material in normal and mentally handicapped children. *Journal of Child Psychology and Psychiatry, 18*, 251–262.

Gross, J. J. (2014). *Handbook of emotion regulation*. New York: The Guilford Press.

Gross, J. J., & Levenson, R. W. (1995). Emotional elicitation using films. *Cognition and Emotions, 9*, 87–108

Gunter, B. (1985). *Dimensions of television violence*. Aldershot, England: Gower Press.

Hall, A. (2005). Audience personality and the selection of media and media genres. *Media Psychology, 7*, 377–398.

Hall, A. & Bracken, C. C. (2011). "I really liked that movie": Testing the relationship between trait empathy, transportation, perceived realism, and movie enjoyment. *Journal of Media Psychology, 23*, 90–99.

Harmetz, A. (1992). *Round up the usual suspects: The making of Casablanca—Bogart, Bergman, and World War II*. New York: Hyperion.

Harris, R. J., Hoekstra, S. J., Scott, C. L., Sanborn, F. W., Karafa, J. A., & Brandenburg, J. D. (2000). Young men's and women's different autobiographical memories of seeing frightening movies on a date. *Media Psychology, 1*, 117–140.

Harris, R. J., Hoekstra, S. J., Scott, C. L., Sanborn, F. W., Dodds, L. A., & Brandenburg, J. D. (2004). Autobiographical memories for seeing romantic movies on a date: Romance is not just for women. *Media Psychology, 6*, 257–284.

Havardi, J. (2014). *Projecting Britain at war: The national character in British World War II film*. Jefferson, NC: McFarland.

Hennig-Thurau, T., Marchand, A., & Marx, P. (2012). Can automated group recommender systems help consumers make better choices? *Journal of Marketing, 76*, 89–109.

Hickey, E. W. (2006). *Serial murderers and their victims (4th ed)*. Belmont, CA: Thompson.

Hittner, J. B. (2005). How robust is the Werther effect? A re-examination of the suggestion-imitation model of suicide. *Mortality, 10*, 193-200.

Hoekstra, S. J., Harris, R. J., & Helmick, A. L. (1999). Autobiographical memories about the experience of seeing frightening movies in childhood. *Media Psychology, 1*, 117-140.

Hovland, C. I. (1957). *The order of presentation in persuasion.* New Haven: Yale University.

Howells, G. N., Flanagan, K. A., & Hagan, V. (1995). Does viewing a televised execution affect attitudes toward capital punishment? *Criminal Justice and Behavior, 22*, 411-424.

Hur, Y-M., McGue, M., & Iacono, W. G. (1996). Genetic and shared environmental influences on leisure-time interests in male adolescents. *Personality and Individual Differences, 21*, 791-801.

Huston, A. C., Wright, J. C., Rice, M. L., Kerkman, D., & St. Peters, M. Development of television viewing patterns in early childhood: A longitudinal investigation. *Developmental Psychology, 26*, 409-420.

Hyler, S. E. (1988). DSM-III at the cinema: Madness at the movies. *Comprehensive Psychiatry, 29*, 195-206.

Hyler, S. E., Gabbard, G. O., & Schneider, I. (1991). Homicidal maniacs and narcissistic parasites: Stigmatization of mentally ill persons in the movies. *Hospital and Community Psychiatry, 42*, 1044-1048.

Jaffe, E. (2007). Reel to real: Psychology goes to the movies. *Observer, 20*, 22-27.

Jakab, I. (2004). [Review of J. R. Brandell (Ed). *Celluloid couches, cinematic clients: Psychoanalysis and psychotherapy in the movies.*] *Bulletin of the Menninger Clinic, 68*, 357-358.

Jansma, L. L., Linz, D. G., Mulac, A., & Imrich, D. J. (1997). Men's interactions with women after viewing sexually explicit films: Does degradation matter. *Communication Monographs, 64*, 1-24.

Johansson, G. (1973). Visual perception of biological motion and a model for its analysis. *Perception and Psychophysics, 14*, 201-211.

Johansson, G. (June, 1975). Visual motion perception. *Scientific American, 232*, 76-89.

Johnson, B. R. (1980) General occurrence of stressful reactions to commercial motion pictures and elements in films subjectively identified as stressors. *Psychological Reports, 47*, 775-784.

Johnston. D. D. (1995). Adolescent's motivations for viewing graphic horror. *Human Communications Research, 21*, 522-552.

Junco, R. & Cotten, S. R. (2012). No A 4 U: The relationship between multitasking and academic performance. *Computers & Education, 59*, 505-514.

Karpov. B. A., Luria, A. R., & Yarbus, A. L. (1968). Disturbances of the structure of active perception in lesions of the posterior and anterior regions of the brain. *Neuropsychology, 6*, 157-168.

Karrh, J. A., McKee, K. B., & Pardun, C. J. (2003). Practitioner's evolving views on product placement effectiveness. *Journal of Advertising Research, 43*, 138-149.

Kim, H., & Richardson, S. L. (2003). Motion picture impacts on destination images. *Annals of Tourism Research, 30*, 216-237.

Kleespies, P. M., Van Orden, K. A., Bongar, B., Bridgeman, D., Bufka, L. F., Galper, D. I., Hillbrand, M., & Yufit, R. I. (2011). Psychologist suicide: Incidence, impact, and suggestions for prevention, intervention, and postvention. *Professional Psychology: Research and Practice, 42*, 244-251.

Knobloch, S. (2003). Mood adjustment via mass communication. *Journal of Communication, 52*, 233-250.

Knobloch, S., & Zillmann, D. (2002). Mood management via the digital jukebox. *Journal of Communication, 52*, 351-366.

Knobloch-Westerwick, S. (2006). Mood management: theory, evidence, and advancements. In J. Bryant and P. Vorderer (Eds.), *Psychology of Entertainment* (pp. 239-254). Mahwah, NJ: Erlbaum.

Kraft, R. N. (1981). *The psychological reality of cinematographic principles: Camera angle and cutting.* Dissertation, University of Minnesota.

Krcmar, M., & Kean, L. G. 2005). Uses and gratification of media violence: Personality correlates of viewing and liking violent genres. *Media Psychology, 7*, 399-420.

Kubey, R., & Czikszentmihalyi, M. (1990). Television as escape: Subjective experience before an evening of heavy viewing. *Communication Reports, 3*, 92–100.

Lee, C. J., Andrade, E. B., & Palmer, S. E. (2013). Interpersonal relationships and preferences for mood-congruency in aesthetic experiences. *Journal of Consumer Research, 40*, 382–391.

Levin, D. T., & Simons, D. J. (1997). Failure to detect changes to attended objects in motion pictures. *Psychonomic Bulletin and Review, 4*, 501–506.

Levin, D. T., & Simons, D. J. (2000). Perceiving stability in a changing world: Combining shots and integrating views in motion pictures and the real world. *Media Psychology, 2*, 357–380.

Litman, B. R. (1983). Predicting success of theatrical movies: An empirical study. *Journal of Popular Culture, 16*, 159–175.

Mackworth, J. F., & Mackworth, N. H. (1958). Eye fixations recorded on changing visual scenes by the television eye-marker. *Journal of the Optical Society of America, 48*, 439–445.

Mackworth, N. H., & Bruner, J. S. (1970). How adults and children search and recognize pictures. *Human Development, 13*, 149–177.

Maltz, M., & Shinar, D. (1999). Eye movements of younger and older drivers. *Human Factors, 41*, 15–25.

Matzkin, R. G. (1999). Take me out to a movie! In L. L. Schwartz (Ed.), *Psychology and the media: A second look* (pp. 85–123). Washington, D.C.: American Psychological Association.

Mazur, M. A. & Emmers-Sommer, T. M. (2002). The effect of movie portrayals on audience attitudes about nontraditional families and sexual orientation. *Journal of Homosexuality, 44*, 157–179.

McCrae, R. R., & Costa, P. T. (1987). Validation of the five-factor model of personality across instruments and observers, *Journal of Personality and Social Psychology, 52*, 81–90.

McElhaney, L. J. (1992). Dating and courtship in the later years: A neglected topic of research. *Generations, The Journal of the Western Gerontological Society, 16*, 21–23.

Meischke, H. (1995). Implicit sexual portrayals in the movies: Interpretations of young women. *The Journal of Sex Research, 32*, 29–36.

Miller, G. A. (1956). The magical number seven, plus or minus two: Some limits on our capacity for processing information. *Psychological Review, 63*, 81–97.

Miller, J. (2004). Monster? Portraits of a female "serial killer." *PsycCRITIQUES, 49*, np.

Milton, J. L. (1952). Analysis of pilots' eye movements in flight. *Journal of Aviation Medicine, 23*, 67–76.

Mogg, K., Bradley, B. P., Field, M., & De Houwer, J. (2003). Eye movements to smoking-related pictures in smokers: Relationship between attentional biases and implicit and explicit measures of stimulus valence. *Addiction, 98*, 825–836.

Molitor, F., & Hirsch, K. W. (1994). Children's toleration of real-life aggression after exposure to media violence: A replication of the Drabman and Thomas studies. *Child Study Journal, 24*, 191–206.

Moller, K., & Karppinen, P. (1983). Role of motives and attributes in consumer motion picture choice. *Journal of Economic Psychology, 4*, 239–262.

Motion Picture Association of America (MPAA). (1997). *Incidence of motion picture attendance among the adult and teenage public: Highlights of findings*. Princeton, NJ: Opinion Research Corporation International.

MPAA. (March 21, 2016). Motion Picture Association of American website at MPAA.org.

Mundorf, N., Weaver, J., & Zillman, D. (1989). Effects of gender roles and self-perceptions on affective reactions to horror films. *Sex Roles, 20*, 655–673.

Niederkrotenthaler, T., et al. (2010). Role of media reports in completed and prevented suicide: Werther v. Papageno effect. *The British Journal of Psychiatry: The Journal of Mental Science, 197*, 234–243.

Nunio, A. & Bruner, J. (1978). The achievement and antecedents of labelling. *Journal of Child Language, 5*, 1–15.

Oliver, M. B. (1993). Exploring the paradox of the enjoyment of sad films. *Human Communications Research, 19*, 315–342.

Pardun, C. J., L'Engle, K. L., & Brown, J. D. (2005) Linking exposure to outcomes: Early adolescents' consumption of sexual content in six media. *Mass Communication & Society, 8*, 75–91.

Parkes, A., Wight, D., Hunt, K., Henderson, M., & Sargent, J. (2013). Are sexual media exposure, parental restrictions on media use and co-viewing TV and DVDs with parents and friends associate with teenagers' early sexual behavior? *Journal of Adolescence, 36*, 1121–1133.

Patil, R., & Shiva Kumar, C. (1987). Cinema—A basic psychological need of the day. *Indian Psychological Review, 32*, 14–17.

Pehrs, C., Deserno, L., Bakels, J. H., Schlochtermeier, L. H., Kappelhoff, H., Jacobs, A. M., Fritz, T. H., Koelsch, S., & Kuchinke, L. (2014). How music alters a kiss: Superior temporal gyrus control fusiform-amygdalar effective connectivity. *SCAN, 9*, 1770–1778.

Pennell, A. E. & Browne, K, D (1999). Film violence and young offenders. *Aggression and Violent Behavior, 4*, 13–28.

Peters, K. M., & Blumberg, F. C. (2002). Cartoon violence: Is it as detrimental to preschoolers as we think? *Early Childhood Education Journal, 29*, 143–148.

Pezdek, K., & Stevens, E. (1984). Children's memory for auditory and visual information on television. *Developmental Psychology, 20*, 212–218.

Piaget, j. (1928). *Judgment and reasoning in the child.* London: Routledge & Keegan Paul.

Purcell, C. E., & Arrigo, B. A. (2006). *The psychology of lust murder: Paraphilia, sexual killing, and serial homicide.* Amserdan, Nethlerlands: Elsevier.

Redker, C., Gibson, B., & Zimmerman, I. (2013). Liking of movie genre alters the effectiveness of background product placements. *Basic and Applied Social Psychology, 35*, 249–255.

Roberts, D. F., Foehr, U., & Rideout, V. (2004) *Kids and media in America.* New York: Cambridge University Press.

Rogers, S. (2005). Through Alice's glass: The creation and perception of other worlds in movies, pictures and virtual reality. In J. D. Anderson & B. F. Anderson (Eds.), *Moving image theory: Ecological considerations.* Carbondale, IL: Southern Illinois University Press.

Ross, L. E., & Davis, A. C. (1996) Black-white college student attitudes and expectations in paying for dates. *Sex Roles, 35*, 43–56.

Sackett, S. (1996). *The Hollywood Reporter book of box office hits, revised and enlarged edition.* New York: Billboard Books.

Salame,' P., & Baddeley, A. (1989). Effects of background music on phonological short- term memory. *Quarterly Journal of Experimental Psychology, Section A—Human Experimental Psychology, 41*, 107–122.

Sapolsky, B. S., & Molitor, F. (1996). Content trends in contemporary horror films. In J. B. Weaver & R. Tamborini (Eds.), *Horror films: Current research on audience preferences and reactions.* New York: Routledge.

Sargant, J. D., Wills, T. A., Stoolmiller, M., Gibson, J., & Gibbons, F. X. (2006). Alcohol use in motion picture and its relation with early-onset teen drinking. *Journal of Studies on Alcohol, 67*, 54–66.

Sharabi, L., & Caughlin, J. P. (2017). What predicts first date success? A longitudinal study of modality switching in online dating. *Personal Relationships, 24*, 370–391.

Sharif, I., & Sargent, J. D. (2006). Association between television, movie, and video game exposure and school performance. *Pediatrics, 118*, 1061–1070.

Sharif, I., Wills, T. A., & Sargent, J. D. (2010). Effect of visual media use on school performance: A prospective study. *Journal of Adolescent Health, 46*, 52–61.

Sharp, E. B., & Joslyn, M. (2001). Individual and contextual effects on attributions about pornography. *Journal of Politics, 63*, 501–520.

Sheppes, G., Scheibe, S., Suri, G., & Gross, J. J. (2011). Emotional-regulation choice. *Psychological Science, 22*, 1391–1396.

Shoval, G., Zalzman, G., Polakevitch, J., Shtein, N., Sommerfield, E., Berger, E., & Apter, A. (2005). Effect of the broadcast of a television documentary about a teenager's suicide in Israel on suicidal behavior and methods. *Crisis: The Journal of Crisis Intervention and Suicide Prevention, 26*, 20–24.

Silverstein, M., Reid, S., DePeau, K., Lamberto, J., & Beardslee, W. (2010). Functional interpretations of sadness, stress, and demoralization among an urban population of low-income mothers. *Maternal and Child Health Journal, 14*, 245–253,

Slater, M. D. (2003). Alienation, aggression, and sensation seeking as predictors of adolescent use of violent film, computer, and website content. *Journal of Communication, 53,* 105–121.

Smith, M (February, 2015). NCJJ report shows juvenile crime keeps falling, but reason elusive. *Juvenile Justice Information Exchange.*

Smith, R., Anderson, D. R., & Fischer, C. (1985). Young children's comprehension of montage. *Child Development, 56,* 962–971.

Stack, 2. (2005). Suicide and the media: A quantitative review of studies based on nonfictional stories. *Suicide and Life Threatening Behavior, 35,* 121–133.

Straube, T., Preissler, S., Lipka, J., Hewig, J., Mentzel, H-J., & Miltner, W. H. R. (2010). Neural representation of anxiety and personality during exposure to anxiety- provoking and neutral scenes from scary movies. *Human Brain Mapping, 31,* 36–47.

Strizhakova, Y., & Krcmar, M. (2007). Mood management and video rental choices. *Media Psychology, 10,* 91–112.

Sullivan, J., & Sheehan, V. (2916). What motivates sexual abusers of children? A qualitative examination of the Spiral of Sexual Abuse. *Aggression and Violent Behavior, 30,* 76–87.

Tamborini, R. (1991). Responding to horror: Determinants of exposure and appeal. In J. Bryant & D. Zillmann (Eds.), *Response to the screen: Reception and reaction processes.* Hillsdale, NJ: Lawrence Erlbaum.

Tamborini, R., Stiff, J. & Heidel, C. (1990). Reacting to graphic horror: A model of empathy and emotional behavior. *Communication Research, 17,* 616–640.

Tamborini, R., Stiff, J., & Zillman, D. (1987). Preferences for graphic horror featuring male versus female victimization: Personality and past viewing experiences. *Human Communications Research, 13,* 529–552.

Tannenbaum, Ph. H., Gaer, E. P. (1965). Mood change as a function of stress of protagonist and degree of identification in a film viewing situation, *Journal of Personality and Social Psychology, 2,* 612–616.

Tarvainen, J., Westman, S., & Oittinen, P. (2015). The way films feel: Aesthetic features and mood in film. *Psychology of Aesthetics, Creativity, and the Arts, 9,* 254–265.

Tesser, A., Millar, K., & Wu, C. H. (1988). On the perceived functions of movies. *Journal of Psychology, 122,* 441–449.

Thomas, M. H., & Drabman, R. S. (1975). Toleration of real-life aggression as a function of exposure to televised violence and age of subject. *Merrill-Palmer Quarterly, 21,* 227–232.

Thompson, W. C., Cowan, C. L., & Rosenhan, D. L. (1980). Focus of attention mediates the impact of negative affect on altruism. *Journal of Personality and Social Psychology, 38,* 291–300.

Till, B., & Vitouch, P. (2012). Capital punishment in films: The impact of death penalty portrayals on viewers' mood and attitude toward capital punishment. *International Journal of Public Opinion Research, 24,* 387–399.

Till, B., Tran, U. S., Voracek, M., Sonneck, G., & Niederkrotenthaler, T. (2014). Associations between film preferences and risk factors for suicide: An online survey. *PLOS ONE, 9,* 1–8.

Time Magazine. (June 27, 1960). [Review of *Psycho*], 75, #26.

Trice, A. D. (2010). Sensation-seeking and video choice in second grade children. *Personality and Individual Differences, 49,* 1007–1010.

Trice, A. D., & Holland, S. A. (2001). *Heroes, antiheroes, and dolts: Portrayals of masculinity in American popular films, 1921–1999.* Jefferson, NC: McFarland.

Troseth, G. L., & DeLoache, J. S. (1998). The medium can obscure the message: Young children's understanding of video. *Child Development, 69,* 950–965.

Truffaut, F. (1983). *Hitchcock.* (Revised ed.). New York: Touchstone.

Turan, K. (December 19, 1997). "Titanic" sinks again. *Los Angeles Times.*

Turner, R. J., & Wagonfield, M. O. (1967). Occupational mobility and schizophrenia. *American Sociological Review, 32,* 104–113.

Udry, J. R. (1971). *The social context of marriage.* Philadelphia, PA: Lippincott.

Underwood, B., Berenson, J. F., Berenson, R. J., Cheng, K. K., Wilson, D., Kulik, J., Moore, B. S., & Wenzel, G. (1977). Attention, negative affect, and altruism: An ecological validation. *Personality and Social Psychology Bulletin, 3,* 54–58.

Underwood, B., Gutleben, D., Berenson, R. J., Cheng, K. K., Berenson, J. R., Kulik, J., & Wenzel, G. (1974). Mood, attention, and generosity. *Personality and Social Psychology Bulletin, 1,* 402–403.

Underwood, B., Moore, B. S., & Rosenhan, D. L. (1972). Effect of mood on children's giving. *Proceedings of the 80th annual convention, American Psychological Association.* 243.

Valentine, D. P., & Freeman, M. (2002). Film portrayals of social workers doing children welfare work. *Child and Adolescent Social Work Journal, 19,* 455–471.

Vincenzo, J., Hendrick, C., & Murray, E. J. (1976). The relationship between religious beliefs and attending the fear-provoking religiously oriented movie: "The Exorcist." *Omega: Journal of Death and Dying, 7,* 137–143.

Wahl, O., Wood, A., Zaveri, P., Drapalski, A., & Mann, B. (2003). Mental illness depiction in children's films. *Journal of Community Psychology, 31,* 553–560.

Wakshlag, J., Reitz, R., & Zillman, D. (1982). Selective exposure to and acquisition of information for educational television programs as a function of appeal and tempo of background music. *Journal of Educational Psychology, 74,* 666–667.

Wallace, W. T., Seigerman, A., & Holbrook, M. B. (1993). The role of actors and actresses in the success of films: How much is a movie star worth? *Journal of Cultural Economics, 17,* 1–27.

Walter, G., McDonald, A., Rey, J. M., & Rosen A. (2002) Medical student knowledge and attitudes regarding ECT prior to and after viewing ECT scenes from movies. *Journal of ECT, 18,* 43–46.

Wanner, M., Richard, A., Martin, B., Faeh, D., & Rohrmann, S. (2016). Associations between self-reported and objectively measured physical activitiy, sedentary behavior and overweight/obesity in NHANES 2003–2006. *International Journal of Obesity, 41,* 186–193.

Weaver, J. B. (1991). Exploring the links between personality and media preferences. *Personality and Individual Differences, 12,* 1293–1299.

Weaver, J. B., Brosius, H., & Mundorf, N. (1993). Personality and movie preferences: A comparison of American and German audiences. *Personality and Individual Differences, 14,* 307–315.

Wedding, D., & Boyd, M. A. (1999). *Movies and mental illness: Using films to understand psychopathology.* Boston: McGraw-Hill.

Wedding, D., & Niemiec, R. M. (2014). *Movies and mental illness: Using films to understand psychopathology (4th ed).* San Francisco: Hogrefe.

Weibel, D., Wissmath, B., & Stricker, D. (2011). The influence on neuroticism on spatial presence and enjoyment of films. *Personality and Individual Differences, 51,* 866–869.

Wierzbicki, J. (2008). *Film music: A history.* New York: Routledge.

Wood, D., Bruner, J., & Ross, G. (1976). The role of tutoring in problem solving. *Journal of Child Psychology and Psychiatry, 17,* 89–100.

Wyatt, R. O., & Badger, D. P. (1984). How reviews affect interest in and evaluations of films. *Journalism Quarterly, 61,* 874–878.

Wyatt, R. O., & Badger, D. P. (1987). To toast, pan, or waffle: How film reviews affect readers interest and credibility perceptions, *Newspaper Research Journal, 8,* 19–30.

Wyatt, R. O., & Badger, D. P. (1990). Effects of information and evaluation in film criticism. *Journalism Quarterly, 67,* 359–368.

Xie, G., & Lee, M. J. (2008). Anticipated violence, arousal, and enjoyment of movies: Viewers' reactions to violent previews based on arousal-seeking tendency. *Journal of Social Psychology, 148,* 277–293.

Yeap, J. A. L., Ignatius, J., & Ramayah, T. (2014). Determining consumers' most preferred eWOM platform for movie reviews: A fuzzy analytical hierarchy process approach. *Computers in Human Behavior, 31,* 250–258.

Zajonc, R. B. (1968). Attitudinal effects of mere exposure. *Journal of Personality and Social Psychology, 9,* 1–27.

Zillman, D., & Weaver, J. B. (1996). Gender-socialization theory of reactions to horror. In J. B. Weaver & R. Tamborini (Eds.), *Horor films: Current research on audience preferences and reactions* (pp. 81–101). Mahwah, NJ: Lawrence Erlbaum Associates.

Zillmann, D., Weaver, J. B., Mundof, N., & Aust, C. F. (1986). Effects of an opposite gender companion's affect to horror on distress, delight, and emotion. *Journal of Personality and Social Psychology, 51,* 586–594.

Zillmann, D. Mood management through communication choices. (1988). *American Behavioral Scientist, 31*, 327–340.

Zuckerman, M., & Litle, P. (1986). Personality and curiosity about morbid and sexual events. *Personality and Individual Differences, 7*, 49–56.

Zuckermann, M. (1979). *Sensation seeking: Beyond the optimal level of arousal.* Hillsdale, NJ: Lawrence Erlbaum.

Zuckermann, M., Bone, R. N., Neary, R., Mangelsdorff, D., & Brustman, B. (1972). What is the sensation-seeker? Personality trait and experience correlates of the Sensation-Seeking Scales. *Journal of Consulting and Clinical Psychology, 39*, 308–321.

Zufryden, F. S. (1996). Linking advertising to box office performance of new film releases—A marketing planning model. *Journal of Advertising Research, 36*, 29–41.

Index

academic achievement 19–22
adolescents 17–18, 56–58; sexuality 142–144
attention 72–80
attitudes 156–159
Aristotle 44, 101, 162

Bandura, Albert 147
The Best Years of Our Lives 159–160
Big Five Theory of Personality 24–25
Bobo Doll experiment 147–150
boredom 43
bottom line research 47–52

Casablanca 3, 5–6, 13, 27–28, 117
catharsis 44
change blindness 92
Citizen Kane 108
classical conditioning 97–102
college students 58–60
computer animation 90
continuity 91–92

Darwin's theory of emotion 32–34
depression 163–165, 181–183
desensitization to violence 146, 150–153
discrepancy 78
dishabituation 77
dual relationships 173–178

8½ 112–115, 121–122, 127–129
ellipsis 119
emotion 31–32
Emotional Regulation 41–43
empathy 10–14
extinction (learning) 98
extraversion 10, 22–23, 25
eye fixations 80–91
Eysenck's theory of personality 22–24

factor analysis 52–54
feature detectors 89–91
filters (relationship) 58

foreshadowing 76
Freud, Sigmund 44, 163, 169, 178–179

gender 8–9
genre 7, 27

habituation 77
Harry Potter franchise 48

imitation (distinguished from observational learning) 105
instrumental learning 102–104
intellectual disability 75

James-Lange theory of emotion 33–34
Jaws 96–99

Life Is Beautiful 30, 43, 105

M (film) 125, 165–166
married couples 47, 60–61
mindfulness 110
Moderate Discrepancy Hypothesis 79
montage 91, 118–126
mood 32
mood induction 35–37
Mood Management Theory 38–41
music 98–99, 101, 107–111

neuroticism 23, 25

Ordinary People 181–183

Papageno Effect 145
personality 9–13
Piaget, Jean 115
point-of-view (POV) shot 96–99, 119
pornography 52, 154–156
positive psychology 153
prejudice 157–159
primacy effect 126–128
Psycho 46–50, 64–65, 68, 87, 105, 108, 169
psychoticism 23–24

R-ratings 20–21
Rear Window 69–70, 87, 93, 108
recommenders 56

scaffolding 116–118
Schema Theory 112–115
Scream 18, 63
sensation-seeking 14–18
simultaneity 119
Snuggle Theory 62–64
sound 73–74

subliminal perception 71–72
symbols 92–93

therapists 172–178

La Vita è Bella see *Life Is Beautiful*
Vygotsky, Lev 115

Wagner, Richard 101
Werther Effect 144

www.ingramcontent.com/pod-product-compliance
Ingram Content Group UK Ltd.
Pitfield, Milton Keynes, MK11 3LW, UK
UKHW042004140426
5217IPUK00015B/980